BLACK CHILDREN/
WHITE CHILDREN

BLACK CHILDREN/ WHITE CHILDREN
Competence, Socialization, and Social Structure

ZENA SMITH BLAU

THE FREE PRESS
A Division of Macmillan Publishing Co., Inc.
NEW YORK

Collier Macmillan Publishers
LONDON

The Free Press
A Division of Macmillan Publishing Co., Inc.
866 Third Avenue, New York, N.Y. 10022

Collier Macmillan Canada, Ltd.

Library of Congress Catalog Card Number: 80-1643

Printed in the United States of America

printing number

1 2 3 4 5 6 7 8 9 10

Library of Congress Cataloging in Publication Data

Blau, Zena Smith
    Black children/white children.

    Bibliography: p.
    Includes index.
        1. Intelligence levels—Afro-Americans.
2. Intelligence levels—United States. 3. Intellect—Social aspects. I. Title.
BF432.N5B56   155.8'2   80-1643
ISBN 0-02-903640-2

For Pamela,
my daughter and proudest legacy,
with love

Contents

List of Tables

Appendix

Acknowledgments

My research was made possible by grants from the Social and Rehabilitation Service and Social Security Administration, U.S. Department of Health, Education and Welfare, and support from the Institute for Juvenile Research, State of Illinois, Department of Mental Health. I am grateful in particular to James Cowhig, chief grant officer of SRS at the time I was awarded research funds, to the late Noël Jenkin, former research director of IJR, and to Betty Wharton, executive secretary of IJR, for their cooperation and support in handling the many administrative tasks associated with my research project.

I am grateful, too, for the invaluable assistance of the following members of my research staff during the various phases of data collection and analysis: Richard Appelbaum, Leland Barringer, Linda Freeman, Margaret Taber Gordon, Logan Green, William Gronfein, Michael Kaye, Donna Lamb, Richard Logan, Kathleen McCourt, Starling Pullam, Helen Rosenberg, Batia Sharon, and Michael Stryzk.

For secretarial assistance in typing research reports and the numerous drafts of my manuscript I am indebted to Joann Brown, Carmel Grandall, Nancy Isserman, Sandra Lang, Nancy Morris, Linda Papp, Arlene Thomas, and Catherine Williams.

I am indebted to Gladys Topkis for editing my manuscript with skill and care.

Last, although not least, I am deeply grateful to Ethel Smith, my housekeeper and good friend, who graciously consented to be interviewed during the pretest phase of the study.

Introduction

The basic object of this book is to identify the social processes that influence the development of intellectual competence in black children and white children in order to account for their differences in measured ability in the early years of schooling. The results of my study provide strong evidence that the sources of these differences are social, *not* genetic, in origin.

Longitudinal evidence collected by others shows that intellectual competence in later childhood is strongly associated with scholastic interest and achievements in youth and adulthood (Kagan and Moss, 1962). Scholastic achievement is a strong predictor of educational aspirations and plans in high school and of educationsl attainment beyond high school (Sewell, Hauser, Featherman, 1976). Educational attainment, in turn, has repeatedly been shown to be the strongest direct predictor of occupational attainment (Blau and Duncan, 1967; Sewell and Hauser, 1972; Featherman and Hauser, 1978). It seemed eminently worthwhile, therefore, to pursue further the connections between stratification processes and socialization processes as they influence school performance in this stage of life.

The two measures of school performance chosen as dependent variables for the study were the most recent IQ scores and the achievement scores of black and white fifth- and sixth-graders. Initially, my plan was to concentrate on variations in achievement scores, using IQ scores as one of the control variables in the analysis. The publication of Jensen's article (1969) prompted me to extend my analysis to the social determinants of variations in IQ scores as well as achievement scores. Since I had a far more extensive array of environmental measures (approximately 500 items obtained from interviews with mothers) than the crude measure of socioeconomic status employed by Jensen in his analysis, I was in a position to test and to challenge his assumption that a single crude measure was adequate to encompass the myriad differences in the environments of black and white children.

Anyone familiar with the controversial history of IQ scores and their interpretation knows that at least two schools of thought on the subject have existed for a long time. Jensen's conclusion that IQ score differences reflect inherent intellectual differences between blacks and whites is merely one of the more recent instances of the genetic fallacy.[1] Opposed to the hereditarians, who tend also to be political conservatives in their general outlook, are the proponents of the environmental hypothesis, which simply stated is that *group* differences in performance on school tests reflect differences in the social and cultural environments that characterize different groups. Environmentalists also tend to be more liberal politically than hereditarians (Harwood, 1976, 1977). That is, they advocate reforms and changes aimed at eradicating the social inequalities that they see as producing differences in school performance between differently situated social groups.

A year before Jensen's article appeared, two black psychiatrists (Grier and Cobb, 1968) published a book that powerfully depicted the grievous effects of racism on the psyches of black Americans. One passage in particular is germane to the present discussion:

> In the United States at this time the essential competition between men is an intellectual one. The essential judgment of one's usefulness rests on one's intellectual capability, and if one fails in *fair* competition, it is an intellectual failure. Second only to making certain that Black people have a fair chance is the necessity that they be free of corrosive attitudes about their intellectual inferiority. . . . The conviction that Charlie is shrewder saps a black man's drive. It is a discouraging task to compete against a superman even if "super" only in one's mind. Humans being what they are, it provides an opportunity to opt out of the struggle altogether and develops an attitude of what's the use? Why fight it? . . . [p. 193]

The doubts and fears about their capacity to measure up intellectually to whites are the most insidious effect of racism on black self-esteem. In this context, the rage that Jensen's article provoked and the subsequent assaults on the uses and misuses of IQ tests in schools are understandable. But the abolition of IQ tests has not so far and will not in the future cause differences in school competence between black and white children to disappear.

IQ tests are designed to predict scholastic performance, and all available evidence shows that they are indeed predictive of the scholastic achievement and educational attainment of children as the schools are presently constituted.

Jensen and others of his persuasion share some common ground with the militants who oppose the use of IQ tests in schools in that they confound symptoms with causes. Jensen opined that IQ tests measure inherent group differences. Militants in retaliation attack the tests as culturally biased but have no satisfactory explanation for why many black children score as high as white children and some even higher.[2] Children know very well by the first or second grade how they measure up to their classmates in their scholastic performance and so do their teachers, even in the absence of IQ tests. It could be argued that intelligence tests administered early in their school career are useful diagnostic devices for identifying children who are at risk of having learning difficulties and who are in need of further *individualized* diagnosis to identify the specific deficits in language skills and experience that may later create problems in assimilating ever more difficult learning tasks. However, that is not the way schools have generally used IQ tests. Instead they have used them to label and to isolate low-scoring children.[3] This only confounds the learning problems of children who enter school without the knowledge or experiential base that white middle-class children, as a rule, possess.

The important issue is not tests or their abolition but rather the identification of the properties of social structures and the social processes that promote differential intellectual and scholastic competence among children being reared in families that are very differently situated in American society. That is the principal issue addressed in this book.

The Data

Interviews conducted in 1968 with 579 black and 523 white mothers of fifth- and sixth-graders in three communities in the Chicago metropolitan area[4] and the IQ and achievement scores of their children provided the data for this study.

In the two largest communities information was obtained from the records of all fifth- and sixth-graders in nine selected schools. In the third community, which had recently integrated its schools (resulting in a 3:1 ratio of white to black children), the same procedure was followed in three schools; in thirteen other schools, samples containing equal numbers of black and white children matched by sex were drawn from all fifth-grade classrooms.[5]

Four of the schools in the two larger communities were located in working-class neighborhoods composed of all or mostly all black children; two other schools were located in black neighborhoods which contained middle- and working-class households; and three schools had a white or mostly white student body from working- and middle-class families. In the largest community, it was also possible to gain access to two racially integrated schools which contained both working- and middle-class children. Although the schools were integrated, black children constituted a majority (about 60 percent and 70 percent, respectively) in each school.

The information obtained from school records included the most recent IQ test scores of each child (usually on tests administered in the second grade), the latest achievement test scores for fifth-graders (obtained at the end of the fourth grade), and achievement scores for sixth-graders (obtained at the end of the fifth grade).

Letters explaining the nature of the study and inviting their cooperation were sent out initially to all mothers and followed up by phone calls or visits to set up appointments for interviews. In the largest community the completion rate was 75 percent; in the other two communities it was 81 percent and 73 percent.[6] Black interviewers were assigned to black mothers and whites were assigned to interview white mothers.

A massive amount of data was obtained and a massive amount of analysis was performed employing a variety of methods: correlations, contingency tables, factor and principal component analysis, analyses of variance and covariance and multiple regression. By a process of successive approximations, variables were combined to yield reliable and theoretically meaningful measures of parental background and present status, family structure, mother's beliefs and practices, and mother's reports of selected child-rearing practices of their husbands.

This book reports the final results of my own analysis of the data, for which I take sole responsibility. The data also served as the basis for the dissertations of four doctoral candidates who, while serving as members of my research staff, designed and carried out their own independent studies (Richard Appelbaum, 1971; Leland Barringer, 1972; Margaret Gordon, 1972; Richard Logan, 1970). Their studies contributed significantly to advancing my understanding of the data and helped me in designing the final analysis reported in this book.

Notes

1. For example, observed differences between white children with fathers in higher- and lower-status occupations were in earlier decades interpreted as stemming from inherent differences in intelligence. The superior performance of soldiers in World War I from urban areas compared with those from rural areas was taken as evidence of the selective migration of the more intelligent to cities. The poorer performance of children of Jewish immigrants from Eastern Europe relative to native British children was interpreted as a sign of Jewish intellectual inferiority. Similarly, lower scores of children with Eastern and Southern

European immigrant backgrounds in the United States were taken as evidence of the intellectual superiority of native Americans and the Northern European stock from which they stemmed (Kamin, 1977).

2. The same controversy over IQ tests raged twenty years earlier with reference to the interpretation of score differences between children from middle- and working-class backgrounds and inspired two psychologists, A. Davis and K. Eels, to develop an "unbiased" test that turned out to be unsuccessful because it provided no meaningful behavioral criteria against which it could be validated. Moreover, middle-class children, were found to score higher, as a rule, even on those tests. See I. Lorge (1993) and W. W. Charters, Jr. (1913).

3. In his most recent book, *Bias in Mental Testing (1980)*, Arthur Jensen avoids taking an explicit position on the sources of black-white IQ differences and instead carefully examines the grounds on which IQ tests have been attacked. He makes a distinction similar to mine between the use of IQ tests to diagnose and assess the nature and extent of cognitive deficits and their use for purposes of selection and placement. It is the latter use of IQ tests, which affects black and Hispanic children disproportionately, that he asserts has engendered charges of "stigma, unequal opportunity, and biased placement procedures, including biased tests" (p. 46). What he fails to mention, however, is that it was his premature conclusion in his widely circulated article (1969) that score differences reflect *inherent* racial differences in intelligence that largely precipitated opposition to IQ testing in schools.

4. The interviews elicited approximately 500 items of information covering the backgrounds and current status of mothers and fathers of the children, including questions about the composition and characteristics of their families of origin, characteristics of mother's neighborhood and closest friends, and their beliefs, and rearing practices during their child's preschool years as well as currently. The interviews, composed mainly of structured questions, averaged about an hour and a half each and were conducted by black and white interviewers under the auspices of the National Opinion Research Center of the University of Chicago.

5. The elementary school system there extended from kindergarten through grade five. Sixth-graders were part of the junior high school system and therefore were not included in the study.

6. Interviews completed amounted to 339 cases in the largest community, 396 in the second, and 369 in the third. The final sample when data processing was completed amounted to 1,102 cases.

CHAPTER 1

Racism, Social Mobility, and Education

To understand how and why the observed differences in measured school competence between black and white children develop it is necessary first to trace the sociohistorical differences between the races as these relate to socialization processes.

The most fundamental division in American society historically has been along racial lines. As slaves, blacks were excluded from the American stratification system altogether. Following the abolition of slavery, laws and social practices operated to maintain them in a subordinate status group, largely undifferentiated by class. The large majority of black people remained in the South as poor, rural dwellers removed from any sort of egalitarian relationship with white people, poor or rich. Even though both races were largely Protestant, mostly Baptists or Methodists, they were as segregated in religion as in every other aspect of social life.

During the entire period that the United States was becoming an industrial urban nation, black Americans were largely excluded from that process. There exists no *precise* analogy between the position of American blacks and any groups in European nations. The position of the peasantry following the abolition of serfdom in the eighteenth and nineteenth centuries is in some ways analogous to that of black Americans but is not the same. Peasants were of the same race and shared the religion of the landowners. They participated together in worship and in religious festivals and often shared the same priest, who on occasion would sponsor and direct talented sons of peasants into the seminary. Members of the peasantry who migrated to the towns and cities and who succeeded in entering the industrial sector could at least join the ranks of the working class and either individually or through collective action with fellow workers improve their economic and social status. Because opportunities in industry were far less for them in their native lands than in the rapidly growing American industrial sector, many members of the peasantry migrated to the United States to find work in the mills and factories.

By and large the opportunities that had long been open to white immigrants were not open to black Americans until World War II. In industry, they were usually hired to perform the lowest-paid, most menial work, as sweepers, porters, and the like. Mostly, however, they were confined to the agricultural sector and to menial service jobs marginal to the industrial-business sector of the economy; thus they were excluded from work experiences that promote modernization of attitudes and behavior.[1] Moreover, whatever economic advancement black Americans achieved did not alter their social standing vis à vis the larger white society. The achievement of middle-class status, rare as it was, did not open up to blacks the same opportunities afforded other minority ethnic groups to observe and to assimilate the attitudes and behavior of the mainstream culture. The small black middle class was largely separate from the white middle class, occupationally, residentially, and socially.

Thus, there developed in the United States not a single stratification system but rather two quite distinct systems, one constituted by the white majority, the other by the black minority. The shape of the two systems differed markedly and so did (and still does) the economic, occupational, and religious composition of the strata within each system.[2]

The marked and persistent differences in socioeconomic position, occupational experiences, and access to other resources have resulted in differences between the races in family structure and in modes of socializing children. Black Americans were not merely deprived of economic resources and therefore usually poor. They had been first enslaved and then kept in a subordinate and separate status in the South by a complex array of social and political mechanisms, not the least of which were separate and grossly unequal educational systems. Gross inequalities in their status as citizens persisted whehter they resided in rural areas, as most did, or migrated to southern citites. Survival required adaptation to poverty *and* to subordination, continuously backed up by actual and threatened violence against any black who did not "keep his place."

The mode of socializing black children that evolved under slavery was also adaptive for survival in a caste situation. Obedience to arbitrary authority was the keystone to survival and hence became a central tenet in the socialization of black children, particularly males, over the long endurance contest that marks the history of black people in American society. Being still largely poor, rural folk during the period when whites were migrating to urban areas, black Americans have maintained longer the tradition of large families that is characteristic in agricultural economies the world over. Poverty coupled with high birth rates sharply circumscribes the amount of material and nonmaterial resources that parents can allocate to each child in a family.

The family characteristics enumerated above are not unique to black Americans but were also characteristic of white ethnics with a rural heritage who emigrated to the United States from predominantly Catholic nations in Europe during the late nineteenth and early twentieth centuries.[3]

An important difference exists, however, in the opportunity structure that confronted white European immigrants in earlier eras and that which has confronted the large waves of black and Hispanic migrants to the cities since the 1940s. There was a greater demand for unskilled and semiskilled manual workers in earlier eras, and while the remuneration for such occupations was low, it was a considerable improvement over the wages paid in the immigrants' native lands. Most white immigrants were eager for their children to complete the minimal required years of schooling so that they could become self-supporting and assume some of the burden of supporting their characteristically large families. With the exception of the Jews, most European immigrants did not have high educational aspirations for their children and therefore were not greatly concerned that the children's school performance was not on a par with that of white children from native American families.

Black and Hispanic Americans face a vastly different structure of opportunities. Technological advances have reduced the demand for unskilled and semiskilled workers in the corporate industrial sector and have increased the demand for clerical, technical, and professional workers. Discrimination that formerly largely barred blacks from such higher-level occupations has substantially abated owing to the civil rights legislation enacted during the 1950s and 1960s, and affirmative action pressure from the federal government in the 1970s.

Education and Social Mobility

As opportunities for higher educational and occupational attainments have been extended to black Americans, their ambitions for their children have soared. Like the Jewish immigrant parents of an earlier era, many working- and middle-class black parents view education as the major route to upward mobility for their children, and indeed the disparity in educational and occupational achievements between the races has been materially reduced in the past decade and a half. Since World War II, the size of the black middle class has been substantially augmented by the influx of blacks who succeeded in raising their educational attainment and thereby their occupational attainment far above those of the working-class families in which they were born and reared. Thus, the percentage of black males in low-paying service, unskilled labor, and farming declined from about 80 percent in 1940 to 36 percent in 1970 (Wilson, 1978).

However, a new impediment has arisen to the economic and social advancement of poor minorities. The rise in the supply of nonmanual jobs relative to manual occupations has led increasing numbers of people to extend their years of schooling. Among each successive age cohort of whites and blacks since World War II, educational attainment has risen. Concomitantly educational requirements for a wide array of occupations have also increased. Thus, the higher the educational credentials, the greater is the competitive advantage of job candidates, other things being equal, for nonmanual occupations. As the proportion of college graduates increases, the value of a high school diploma has been deflated. Currently, the failure to attain a high school diploma often bars job aspirants from consideration for employment not merely in nonmanual but also in manual and technical occupations. Critics of these inflationary trends argue that for many jobs educational attainment does not predict successful performance (Berg, 1970); that educational credentials are required by employers because they denote valued traits of character rather than the possession of cognitive skills (Persell, 1977; Bowles and Gintis, 1976); and that credentials are part of the arsenal of cultural weapons used by the propertyless working and middle classes to carve out "professional and technical monopolies over lucrative services and vulnerable organizational sectors" (Collins, 1976, p. 251). Whatever, latent functions are served by the inflationary tendencies of educational expansion, the fact remains that educational attainment has become an increasingly important mechanism by which the white and black middle and upper classes maintain and transmit their advantages to their children. Even though children from white middle-class families score higher on school tests, a good deal of variability is found in their intellectual competence and motivation. Whatever level of competence they exhibit, however, such children are more likely to attain higher education than those from lower-class backgrounds, for several reasons. Their parents have and generally use the resources to encourage and support them, because they understand that the transmission of their middle-class status to their children could be jeopardized without the content and credentials that higher education confers. Thus, Randall Collins (1976) makes an astute observation that the "dominant classes claim education for *themselves* even more than they impose it on others.... Education is important for elites, and even for

privileged specialists in mid-level positions, because it gives them the sol-
idarity of an esoteric in-group culture, which pays off rather nicely in struggles for organizational privilege and income" (p. 250). By the same token,
higher educational attainment has assumed ever increasing importance as a
means of attaining upward social mobility, and there is no basis for expecting
any major reversal in the importance of educational achievement in American society in the foreseeable future.[4]

Systematic research on stratification processes in the tradition established by Peter Blau and Otis Dudley Duncan (1967), which initially was
confined to the explanation of variation in the occupational attainments of
white males, has recently been extended to include black males and white
and black females (Duncan, Featherman, Duncan, 1972; Lieberson and
Wilkinson, 1976; Lieberson, 1978; Sewell and Hauser, 1975; Sewell,
Hauser, Featherman, 1976; Treiman and Terrell, 1975). Consistently, it has
been demonstrated that educational attainment is the strongest predictor of
occupational attainment. To be sure, class origins influence educational attainment. It has also been demonstrated, however, that increasing proportions of people from working-class backgrounds have entered the ranks of
college graduates, and that those who have done so as a rule have substantially improved their occupational and social status. Upward mobility, however, has not been confined to college graduates. People from poor and
working-class families who graduate from high school also tend to increase
their occupational options, although not as much as those with more years of
schooling. Thus, there is overwhelming evidence that, despite the advantages that children born to white middle-class parents enjoy, the process of
occupational attainment is much the same for blacks as for whites and for
females as for males with continuous labor force participation. In all these
groups, educational attainment is the strongest, although not the sole, predictor of occupational outcomes.

Stratification research that has focused on the role of education as the
route to upward mobility has been labeled by neo-Marxists as "functionalist"
and criticized as serving to perpetuate the "structure of dominance" of the
white upper and middle classes. The neo-Marxists, in contrast, have focused
their theory and research on the ways in which educational systems serve to
perpetuate existing economic and social inequalities.

Provocative work from this perspective that has appeared in recent years
analyzes in some detail the processes that operate in schools to perpetuate
the structure of dominance of the upper and middle classes over lower-status
groups in the larger society rather than to foster greater social equality
(Bowles and Gintis, 1976; Persell, 1977; Bourdieu, 1973; Bourdieu and Saint
Martin, 1974; Bourdieu and Passeron, 1977; Collins, 1977). The manifest
function of universal compulsory education has traditionally been represented as affording children born into low-status families the same opportunity to acquire the knowledge and skills necessary for economic and social

advancement as is provided to the offspring of higher social classes. Thus, school competence is purported to operate as a selective criterion across the entire stratification system: the more competent children from lower-status groups would move upward in the occupational system; the less competent students from higher-status groups would move downward in the system.

The contributions of this conflict perspective cannot be gainsaid, but it also has some serious limitations. Writers sharing this perspective acknowledge that a considerable degree of class mobility has been and continues to be a significant feature of American society, but they minimize its importance, sometimes by distorting empirical evidence. A passage in Persell's otherwise excellent analysis exemplifies this strategy:

> Blau and Duncan emphasize mobility within this occupational structure, thereby implying that it is a major feature of the system. But stability rather than mobility is the predominnat characteristic of the American social structure. In the United States, 42 percent of the men with fathers in the top fifth of the occupational hierarchy end up there themselves (Jencks et al., 1972:179). Moreover, where mobility does occur, it is most likely to take place within a narrow range. These findings do not deny the existence of social mobility in America but do suggest that large numbers of people either do not change their occupational status from one generation to another or change it by only a small amount. . . . [1977, p. 155]

So intent is Persell on emphasizing the stable aspects of the stratification system that she distorts the very point that Jencks and his colleagues (1972) convey, namely that status mobility is actually more prevalent than status inheritance. Thus, they write:

> The role of a father's family background in determining his son's status is surprisingly small, at least compared to most preconceptions. The correlation between a father's occupational status and his son's status is less than 0.50. If two fathers' statuses differ by, say, 20 points, their sons' statuses will differ by an average of 10 points. Fathers thus pass on half their occupational advantage or disadvantage to their sons. Stating it another way, 42 percent of men whose fathers are in the top fifth of the occupational hierarchy end up there themselves.
>
> If we extended this analysis over several generations, the relationship between a man's status and his ancestors' statuses grows progressively weaker. . . . If we look at a single generation, we will find a lot of "short distance" mobility, but relatively little mobility from the very bottom to the very top, or from the very top to the very bottom. If we look at changes over two generations, we will find many more rags-to-riches and riches-to-rags stories. [p. 179].

Persell *is* correct, however, in observing that the existence of social mobility in a society helps to maintain and legitimate the structure of dominance. Social mobility is much more salient to those who experience it than is the knowledge that social inequality exists. However, to those who do not achieve economic and social advancement, particularly in a context where it becomes more common, the sense of relative deprivation often is greater than when opportunities for mobility are more limited (Stouffer et al., 1949;

Merton and Lazarsfeld, 1950). The operation of this principle is currently evident in the situation of black Americans.

The work of Bowles and Gintis (1973 and 1976) and more recently of Persell (1977) is important because it goes beyond rhetoric to carefully document the ideologies, the forms, and the processes by which public schools serve to reward and encourage white middle-class children to succeed in school and by the same means to discourage and alienate some poor and minority-group children. Thus, often schools have operated as an integral part of "the structure of dominance" serving to perpetuate economic and social inequality in society.[5]

The other side of the coin, however, is that public schools and higher education have also served more than any other social mechanism to promote mobility from the working class into the middle class. Since World War II, the size of the black middle class has increased very substantially and higher educational attainment has been the major mechanism for effecting this upward economic and social mobility.[6]

Owing to the expansion of salaried white-collar positions and to the pressures of affirmative action programs in the private and public corporate sectors of the economy, the occupational opportunities for *educated* blacks has grown at an unprecedented rate over the past twenty years and today are at least comparable to those open to whites with the same qualifications, according to the black sociologist William J. Wilson (1978). But these changes in the economy have resulted in vastly different mobility opportunities for different segments of the black population. In contrast to the opportunities now enjoyed by educated black men and women, the job prospects of poorly educated black, Hispanic, and white Americans increasingly are restricted to the shrinking unskilled, low-wage sector of the economy. The unemployment rates of poorly educated yough have risen precipitously (Wilson, 1978) as have those of poorly educated female heads of household (Blau, Rogers, Oser and Stephens, 1978), and rising numbers in both groups are reduced to depend on welfare for their survival. Low educational attainment, not merely sexism or racism, is the key to the present plight of these groups. And the relative deprivation and alienation of these groups can be expected to increase. To the extent that their better-educated ethnic and sex peers succeed in raising their occupational attainments it will become increasingly difficult to ignore the fact that low educational attainment places in jeopardy all individuals, regardless of sex or race, not merely during their years of labor force participation but for the entire span of life.

Consequences of Educational Attainment

Evidence from a recent analysis of predictors of economic, physical, and emotional well-being of people aged fifty-five and beyond reveals that low educational attainment is the strongest predictor of poverty in later life, stronger than race and ethnicity and stronger than age, marital status, or work status among both sexes (Blau, Rogers, Oser, Stephens, 1978).

No less important is the accumulating body of evidence that educational attainment not only extends the occupational options of individuals in the labor force and their earnings, whatever their race and socioeconomic origins (Jencks, 1979). A review of a large body of research shows that college graduates differ in many other significant ways from less educated Americans; there is a widening gap between young people who graduate from college and those who do not, and students from low socioeconomic backgrounds who raise their educational attainment change in the same areas and in the same direction as those from more privileged homes (Withey et al., 1971).[7]

Moreover, educational attainment is a significant predictor of virtually all measures of social and communal activity and involvements, and of the physical and mental health of aging men and women even when race and ethnicity, work status, marital status and age are adjusted for (Blau, Rogers, Oser, Stephens, 1978; Blau, Oser, Stephens, 1979).

These far-reaching effects of educational attainment over the life cycle are probably a result not simply of years of schooling alone but of the cumulative occupational options and experiences that are more accessible to the college-educated. For example, a recent longitudinal study of college students ten years after graduation reveals that about 96 percent of the sample are in professional, managerial, or technical occupations (Mortimer and Lorence, 1979). Other recent longitudinal studies have shown that the substantive complexity of jobs promotes intellectual flexibility, and that intellectual flexibility is a significant factor in the selection of more complex jobs that afford people greater work autonomy (Kohn and Schooler, 1978). The lack of a college education is a barrier to entry into high-level occupations that entail cognitive complexity and afford more work autonomy. Thus, less well educated people have fewer opportunities for psychological growth in adulthood that such jobs afford incumbents.[8]

In sum, educational attainment is a critical variable not merely in the level and nature of occupational achievement; it also significantly influences a wide range of other attributes of individuals over their entire life span.

Status inheritance and status mobility are each a major feature of the American stratification system, and educational institutions are a mechanism of considerable importance in both social processes. For some individuals born into poor families, and for some groups both disadvantaged economically and victims of discrimination, schooling has served and continues to serve as a mechanism for economic and social mobility. For example, successful performance in public schools materially enhanced the chances and the motivation of immigrant Jewish, Chinese, and Japanese children to pursue higher education. The attainment of higher education enabled many members of these minorities to achieve middle-class status in a single generation. Since World War II, ever-increasing numbers of black Americans have achieved middle-class status via the same educational route.

Socialization and Test Performance

Performance on written IQ and achievement tests primarily, although not solely, determines the degree of success or failure of children in elementary school. Moreover, since written tests are a recurrent feature of school life, early success or failure may well exert influence on future test performance. If initially children display competence, their self-esteem and motivation to learn are strengthened (Coopersmith, 1967; Rosenberg, 1965; Rosenberg and Simmons, 1971). Poor performance, in contrast, engenders feelings of inferiority and anxiety that if carried over to subsequent test situations become independent impediments to learning and test performance; some children may not even be able to reproduce what they know, much less figure out answers to questions about which they are in doubt. It does not take many trials of this nature to establish a patterned avoidance to tests and to learning generally if support, reassurance, and help are not forthcoming from a teacher, a parent, an older sibling, or a peer to counteract the cumulative effects of failure. Such positive forms of intervention are more often available to children in middle-class homes. Thus, even initially less competent middle-class children often are able to improve their school performance as they progress through school and eventually obtain a college education, whereas working-class and minority children's scores often decline over the same time span (Douglas, 1964).

A careful delineation of patterns of school behavior and performance observed among school children in Central Harlem (Silverstein and Krate, 1975) strongly suggests, however, that even among poor black ghetto children there is a good deal of variability in school performance and motivation, stemming to a significant degree from variations in parental modes of socialization from the preschool years through the years of elementary schooling. Silverstein and Krate write, for example:

> We cannot be sure what was responsible for the differentiation of Central Harlem children into the types we have described. The socialization factors that we believe were very important influences include the degree and extent of adult attention and emotional support the children had received before and during their school years . . . the extent to which children had faced restrictions on autonomous strivings for mastery and effective coping with objects and people in their environment and the nature and extent of punishment the children experienced in their preschool and school years [p. 196].

The present study, based on interviews with mothers, provides systematic evidence in support of the impressions of Silverstein and Krate gained from observing and interacting with children in the classroom and from observing mothers interacting with their children at school and at home.[9]

This evidence that public schools as they are presently organized and constituted do not have as much impact on children's abilities as the family in which they are born and reared should not be interpreted as confirmation of the genetic hypothesis.

The belief shared by Jensen and others of his persuasion, that group differences in black and white children's IQ test performance are genetically determined is not amenable to direct proof since genetic endowment cannot be measured directly without the confounding factor of knowledge of the standard written language that IQ tests employ (Becker, 1977). Further, the four studies from which Jensen's estimates of the relative contribution of genetic and environmental factors are derived all measure individual variations within white samples; none of those studies reflects the magnitude of variations in the environments of black and white children (Scarr-Salapatek, 1976).[10] The gravest flaw in the *logic* of Jensen's argument, however, has been stated trenchantly by Richard Lewontin (1976), an eminent biologist whose field of study is genetic variation in natural populations:

> The fundamental error of Jensen's argument is to confuse heritability of character within a population with heritability of the difference between two populations. Indeed, between two populations, the concept of heritability of their differences is meaningless. This is because a variance based upon two measurements has only one degree of freedom and so cannot be partitioned into genetic and environmental components. The genetic basis of the differences between two populations bears no logical or empirical relation to the heritability within populations and cannot be inferred from it. . . . In addition, the notion that eliminating what appear a priori to be major environmental variables will serve to eliminate a large part of the environmentally caused difference between the populations is biologically naive. In the context of IQ testing, it assumes that educational psychologists know what the major sources of environmental difference between black and white performance are. [p. 89]

The limitations of Jensen's knowledge even of the components of socioeconomic status, not to mention other differences that differentiate the environments of black and white children, will become evident in the chapters that follow. Perhaps the evidence from the present study and from Mayeske's work (1973, 1975) will help put to rest the fallacy that it is possible simply by controlling "gross socioeconomic factors" (Jensen's phrase) to equate the social environments of black and white Americans.

To propose that parental values, attitudes, and behavior are significant intervening variables between the stratification system of a society and performance in the student role in later childhood (the most significant determinant of later educational attainment) should not be construed as a case of "blaming the victim."[11]

To seek understanding of the processes by which some poor black and white parents have been able to help their children escape their lower-class destiny despite the shortcomings of schools is not to blame those martyred by the system but rather to fortify the courage of those not yet demoralized by their situation. I believe that the findings of my study can give hope and lend understanding to black and white parents who view education as a means to a better life, who are genuinely concerned about their children's school performance and want to know what modes of behavior have proven effective for others in their situation who shared similar ambitions.

The Theoretical Model

While one object of my study is to identify those aspects of family structure and socialization processes that make for class and color differences in the development of intellectual competence and scholastic aptitude in childhood, this represents only part of a broader theoretical model that I set out to develop and test.

My point of departure in Chapter 2 is a comparison of the association between various components of socioeconomic origin and the current status of black and white parents in order to determine whether differences in stratification structures make for differences in the test-score predictors of children in the two races.

Religious and denominational affiliation and religiosity of mothers, the second set of variables in my model, are discussed and their effects on children's test scores are assessed in Chapter 3.

In Chapter 4 selected aspects of family structure, extrafamilial roles of mothers, and sex of the study child are added to the other social structural variables in the model to determine what contribution such variables taken together make to the explanation of test score differences within each race and between the two races.

The remaining part of the book is concerned with maternal socialization processes and a comparison of their effects on black and white children's IQ and achievement test performance. Chapter 5 identifies two dimensions of socialization—mothers' valuation of education and investment of time and other resources in the child—and analyzes the relationship between them. In Chapter 6, a third dimension of socialization—mothers' belief in and use of aversive descipline—is introduced; the modal socialization strategies of black and white mothers are then identified and their effects on children's test scores are discussed. The chapter concludes with a comparison of the explanatory power of the social structural and socialization models.

Chapter 7 compares the social sources of variation in the socialization strategies of black and white mothers.

Chapter 8 describes variations in the manner in which mothers socialize boys and girls among different socioeconomic and religious subgroups in the two races.

In Chapter 9 the social structural and the socialization models are combined to form the full theoretical model and variables are identified that constitute sources of variation in children's test scores within each race. The analysis then identifies those religious groups in which the full model entirely accounts for race differences in children's IQ scores and those where such differences, though attenuated, persist. The chapter concludes with a comparison of the social sources of race differences in the test scores of boys and girls and of the predictors of test scores of black and white boys and girls.

Chapter 10 summarizes my major substantive findings, discusses their theoretical implications and concludes with a brief discussion of some of their social policy implications.

Notes

1. There is evidence that physical labor of a nonmechanical nature coupled with little or no formal schooling impedes the development of cognitive and intellectual skills. Inkeles and Smith (1974) report significant differences between factory workers and workers engaged in traditional agriculture in six developing nations in feelings of personal efficiency, openness to new experience and to unfamiliar people and places, and orientation to time and punctuality. Kohn (1977; Kohn and Schooler, 1978) provide evidence that the differences in the work experiences of blue- and white-collar occupations make for observed differences in child-rearing values of parents. Bernstein (1961) calls attention to observed differences in the language that working- and middle-class parents employ in communicating with their children and how that influences the differences in verbal ability that repeatedly have been found between children of working- and middle-class backgrounds.

2. Recent work in the field of social stratification processes takes a similar view of the American stratification system (Lieberson, 1973, 1978; Lieberson and Wilkinson, 1976; Hogan and Featherman, 1977). The latter report that in 1962 black and white male processes of stratification were markedly different but that by 1973 northern-born black males exhibit similarities to whites in the degree to which they attain occupations commensurate with their educational attainment. However, for southern-born males, particularly those still residing in the South, the consistency between educational attainment and occupational achievement was no greater than it had been for northern black males a decade earlier. These findings indicate that internal differentiation and socioeconomic inequality is growing *within* the black American population (Wilson, 1978).

3. Mexican-Americans' move from the agricultural to industrial sector is even more recent. Their fertility rates are consequently higher than those of blacks, and their educational attainment is lower.

4. On the contrary, there are already indications that the value of a high school diploma has become deflated, because high schools have failed to teach students basic cognitive skills but have nevertheless promoted and awarded credentials merely for attendance. Proposals are afloat for instituting nationwide, statewide, or communitywide proficiency examinations. New York City, for example, has

modified open enrollment in the city colleges by requiring students to pass examinations demonstrating verbal and numerical proficiency at at least the eighth-grade level, and schools all over the country are reinstituting emphasis on the mastery of cognitive skills, the traditional three R's, and this movement appears to have wide support among both white and minority-group parents.

5. A similar conclusion is voiced by Wesley Becker (1977) on the basis of his own empirical work: "Probably the most important implication to arise from our nine years of work in teaching more than 25,000 disadvantaged students is that schools are designed to teach middle class children and need to be redesigned for teaching all students. . . . schools systematically fail to provide instruction in the building blocks crucial to intelligent functioning, namely, words and their referents. Children from homes where there is stong adult support for refining the use of language are more likely to succeed in school than those from homes with less adult-child contact and adults with less education." (pp. 518–543).

6. Outstanding athletic skill and musical talent also serve as vehicles of mobility for blacks as they have for white native and ethnic groups. The most successful of these attain visibility and serve as culture heroes but they constitute a much smaller fraction relative to those who achieve mobility through higher educational attainment. According to recent census data, the number of blacks attending college rose from 282,000 in 1966 to 1,062,000 in 1976. The number of black women in college rose more than fourfold, while the number of black men in college tripled. Black women in college now exceed black men by 84,000. Data in the present study can help account for these differences.

7. College graduates, for example, are better informed on a whole range of national and international events and issues. They use the printed media—newspapers, magazines, books—more. They have more job opportunities, better working conditions, more security, fewer job changes. They use various resources and societal services more. They belong to more organizations, and more often hold positions of leadership. They are more introspective, have a greater sense of social efficacy, and are more optimistic. They have fewer children, exercise more control over fertility, more often hold developmental, long-range views concerning their children. Many of the above differences persist when income is held constant.

8. These characteristics of the occupations of middle-class parents explain why they more often value self-direction and autonomy in the realm of child rearing than working-class parents (Melvin Kohn, 1969, 1977).

9. My findings are also in substantial agreement with the results of a secondary analysis of data (Mayeske, et al., 1973; Mayeske and Beaton, 1975) from the well-known *Equality of Opportunity Study* (Coleman, et al., 1966), which remains the most comprehensive nationwide comparative analysis of white and minority children's school achievement. Mayeske et al. (1973, p. 15) sum up the state of current knowledge authoritatively: "By the time a child enters school he has already accumulated a store of learning experiences. Many if not most of these experiences are from his relationships with parents, siblings, and playmates. Such early socializing agents may play a critical role in the development of his abilities. Not only may they stimulate him to learn; they may offer learning experiences that will be of use in the mastering of later learning situa-

tions (Hebb, 1949; Hunt, 1961, 1969). A number of large scale studies have further documented the effects of early socialization on later student achievement and motivation (Flanagan et al., 1964; Coleman et al., 1966; Shaycroft, 1967; Husen, 1967; Plowden, 1972)."

10. Moreover, data from one set of studies carried out by British psychologist Cyril Burt, recently reviewed in its entirety by an eminent psychologist, are under suspicion of having been fabricated (Kamin, 1976a,b).

11. Let me remind those ready to invoke this cliché that the same conditions *never* have perfectly uniform effects. For example, even under the most extreme conditions of deprivation and degradation, such as those suffered by black people in slavery, or by inmates of German concentration camps during the Holocaust, or by political prisoners in the Russian Gulag, some of the victims survived to bear witness (De Pres, 1976). Such accounts extend our understanding of the sources of strength and resilience whereby some individuals throughout recorded history have managed to beat even the most oppressive systems.

CHAPTER 2

Race, Social Status, and Social Milieu

To report that scholastic competence, as measured by IQ and achievement tests, is influenced independently by the race of children and by the social class of their families is simply to confirm the findings of other studies (Coleman et al., 1966).

In my sample, as Table 2-1 shows, white middle-class children on the average score highest and black working-class children lowest on both tests, as might be expected. More interesting is that the mean IQ score of black middle-class children and white working-class children are identical and that their mean achievement scores are also very similar, though white working-class children average slightly higher scores than black middle-class children.

In this chapter we begin the intricate process of identifying the social sources of these observed patterns of differences.

At the beginning it is essential to address the basic question of whether for comparative purposes a single measure of social status suffices to equalize the social environments of black and white children from families classified as middle class or working class. If the occupational status score of the father, or the highest-ranking parent, is the same—for example, 40 or 50, or 60 on

T A B L E 2 - 1 . Mean IQ and Achievement Scores by Race and Class

	Middle Class Scores			Working Class Scores		
	N	*IQ*	*Achievement**	*IQ*	*Achievement*	*N*
Black	266	100	4.9	94	3.9	120
White	403	109	6.7	100	5.4	313

*Achievement scores are in stanines (grade levels).

Duncan's Socio-Economic Index—does this signify that material and other resources of black and white families labeled "middle class" are the same? If not, in what ways and how much do they differ? Furthermore, if they differ, which differences are significant sources of observed disparities in children's intellectual and scholastic competence in the two races?

Table 2-2 provides evidence that on five measures of socioeconomic status a similar pattern of differences exists between black and white parents labeled middle class and those labeled working class. White middle-class families have the highest scores; black middle-class families have lower scores than their white counterparts but higher scores than the white working class. The scores of black working-class families are the lowest in the whole sample.

The differences between the two middle classes, as a rule, are considerably smaller than those between the middle and working classes in each race. However, on some variables, such as child's father's educational attainment, middle-class exposure, and average education of mother's three closest

T A B L E 2 - 2 . Five Components of SES by Race and Class*

	Means			
	Middle Class		Working Class	
	WHITE	BLACK	WHITE	BLACK
Occupational status (parent with highest SEI score)	71.1	62.6	24.8	19.7
Mother's education	6.2	5.6	4.4	4.2
Father's education	6.7	5.6	4.3	4.1
Middle-class exposure score	2.2	1.7	1.2	1.1
Average education of mother's friends	3.4	2.7	2.1	1.3
N	403	266	120	313
Total N = 1102				

*Respondents with scores of 0–39 on Duncan's Socio-Economic Index (Reiss *et al.*, 1961) are designated as "working class," and those with scores of 40 or higher are designated as "middle class" in both races. The same pattern of results is found when higher cutting points are employed to differentiate the two strata. See Appelbaum (1971) and Margaret Gordon (1972).

friends, the differences between black and white middle-class parents are as pronounced as those between the black middle class and the white working class.

Thus, the average occupational status of the family, the educational attainment of parents, and the social milieu of black middle-class mothers are lower than that of their white counterparts. And because the social characteristics of mothers' friends and neighbors influence their child-rearing beliefs and practices, black and white middle-class women differ in important ways with respect to their child-rearing orientations and practices (Appelbaum, 1971; Margaret Gordon, 1972). These make for differences in the intellectual and scholastic aptitudes of their children.

The differences in social status and social milieu between black and white working-class families are less pronounced than those between middle-class families in the two races, with one exception: white working-class mothers have, on the average, better-educated friends than black working-class mothers do.

In sum, on every indicator of social status, black families who seeming to be similarly located relative to white families in fact possess fewer resources than white families with which they are usually compared.

Gains in educational and occupational attainment have the effect of enhancing the sheer amount of resources that parents in both races are capable of allocating to child rearing. But deprivations imposed on blacks through discrimination and segregation continue to constitute significant impediments to their translating a gain in occupational status or educational attainment into comparable access to role models and informed advice about modern modes of child rearing (Zena Blau, 1964, 1965). This difference in social milieu is an important source of the differences in black and white children's intellectual and scholastic competence. Evidence of this proposition is provided in the balance of this book.

Occupational status and education, the most commonly used indicators of social class position, are at best crude measures when employed on white samples. But in comparisons of white and black samples, it is a mistake to assume that the use of these indices alone or in combination suffices to equalize the social environments of black and white respondents with the same scores. Each measure, of course, is related to the characteristics of parents' and children's friends and neighbors, which constitute the social context in which parents socialize their children. But social milieu is an analytically distinct dimension of social status which generally is not taken into account or measured either in stratification research or in comparative research on the two races. It turns out to be a variable of great importance in understanding observed differences in black and white children's test scores. The nature of the social milieu surrounding the family influences parental values and goals and the modes through which parents seek to implement their objectives.

The proportion of close neighbors in white-collar occupations, of college-educated neighbors, and of neighbors with a child who has gone to college is a component of the middle class exposure score. A separate measure was constructed based on the mean education of mother's three closest friends. These two measures combined constitute the index of social milieu which was added to the traditional measures of socioeconomic status in the present analysis. Though associated with occupational status and education of parents, it is analytically distinct from each of them.

It is particularly important to take this distinction into account in making racial comparisons of test scores, for the associations between social milieu and other components of socioeconomic status are markedly lower in the case of blacks, and social milieu proves to be the strongest predictor of black children's scores. The correlation between occupational status and mother's middle-class exposure score is .6 among whites and only .3 among blacks. Similarly, the correlation between occupational status and average educational attainment of mother's three closest friends is .7 among whites and .5 among blacks. The correlations between mother's and father's educational attainment and family occupational status is higher among whites (.6 and .7) than for each parent among blacks (.5). Even the mothers' and fathers' education is more strongly correlated among whites (.7) than among blacks (.5). In sum, greater consistency is found among the components of social status in the case of white than of black families. A gain in educational attainment is translated more readily into a gain in occupational status, and each in turn is translated more readily into greater access to mainstream middle-class influences and role models in the case of white than of black parents. Consequently, the use of occupational status and/or educational attainment does not truly serve to equalize the social environments in which children in the two races are reared.

There is still another important social-structural difference that needs to be taken into account in comparisons between the races. For blacks, whatever their social-class position, the opportunities of exposure to white society and all that signifies constitute a variable of some importance, whereas for whites no such independent variable exists.

The diffusion of scientific knowledge and theories of child development is accomplished not merely through formal channels such as the writings of child-rearing experts, but also informally through processes of social exchange and influence among social equals—friends, relatives, co-workers, and neighbors.

Variations in styles of life are, to be sure, matters of taste, and tastes are cultivated, not inborn. In a society in which mass advertising is institutionalized it takes no time at all to cultivate a taste for material goods, such as luxury automobiles. A taste for serious books and magazines, in contrast, takes considerably longer to cultivate. It is more likely to become established in the course of growing up in a home in which parents themselves possessed and were able to transmit such a taste to their offspring. Formal schooling, particularly higher education, also promotes the taste for reading and increases the likelihood of exposure generally to products of past and contemporary high cultures. But by now it is all too evident that exposure to cultural products does not automatically inculcate a taste for them, particularly when they are taught by the average elementary school teacher. By and large, the educational attainment of parents and the milieu within the home and among friends and neighbors constitute stronger and more enduring influences on the nature and extent of exposure to the constantly evolving knowledge, ideas, and other cultural products in modern society which become disseminated first among intellectuals and the well-educated, established members of the middle class. Somewhat later, newer arrivals to the middle class, through formal education and informal association with longer-tenured members of their stratum, gradually acquire the more subtle nonmaterial tastes and modes of behavior that, as a rule, distinguish more recent from longer-tenured members of the middle class.

Despite the considerable political, economic, and educational gains that black Americans have made since World War II and the significant increase in the size of the black middle class, formidable barriers persist to free, unfettered association between blacks and whites, even between members of the two races with the same formal educational and occupational attainment. Informal social relations, in school, work, religious worship, residence, or voluntary associations, remain largely separate. Consequently, it is misleading at the present time to equate either the economic or social position and opportunities of the white and black middle classes. Structurally they continue to be quite separate entities, and different in important respects. The diffusion of the mainstream, literate culture proceeds at a slower rate among black than among white social classes. Advances in scientific knowledge, still very largely the products of a small segment of the white upper middle class, become diffused through formal *and* informal channels by stages from more- to less-educated strata in the society.

To propose that, all other things being equal, black parents who have white friends and/or co-workers will thereby become exposed sooner to the products and artifacts of the mainstream culture and will incorporate them sooner into their modes of rearing children is not at all to arrogate to whites any innate social superiority. Rather, it merely draws attention to important *social* processes that operate in white society which barriers of social segregation deny to black Americans to the extent that they remain isolated from more or less equalitarian relationships with whites.

In sum, variations in exposure to whites[1] constitute an analytically distinct component of the social milieu of black families which must be taken into account in comparative research on the two races. To understand further why and how the social segregation of blacks and whites impedes the diffusion of what Fred Strodtbeck (1964) terms the "hidden curriculum" of

the white middle-class home among black middle-class families, it is necessary to compare the *composition* of the two strata, not merely with respect to
present status attributes of parents but also with respect to their social and
demographic *origins*. By composition is meant the proportions of members
of each class who were reared in middle-class homes relative to those reared
in working-class homes and whose ascent to middle-class status is more
recent. In an earlier study dealing with the social processes by which information about modern child-rearing theory and methods is disseminated, I
provided evidence (Blau, 1964, 1965) that the social class *origins* of mothers
independently of their current socioeconomic level influence the extent of
exposure to child-rearing experts and the readiness to adopt their recommendations. Markedly greater exposure to child-rearing experts and greater
proneness toward change was found among white compared with black upwardly mobile mothers in the two middle classes. These findings suggested
the more general proposition that the diffusion of modern theories and practices pertaining to the socialization of children is likely to occur more slowly
in a largely *new* middle class than in one containing a more substantial
proportion of parents who grew up and were socialized in middle-class
families.

The present study, based on a much larger sample and more extensive
data, provides further confirmation of the significance of structural differences between the middle classes of the two races, not only for maternal
behavior but also for children's scholastic competence. Table 2-3 shows that
an overwhelmingly large proportion of the black middle-class mothers sampled (82 percent) have working-class origins, as compared with only 32 percent in the white middle-class sample.[2] In the two working classes, the

TABLE 2-3. **Class by Class Origins of Black and White Mothers
and of Wives of Men in a National Sample**

	White		Black		National Sample*	
	N	%	N	%	White	Black
Middle Class						
Stable	272	68	49	18	44	19
Upward mobile	131	32	217	82	56	81
	403	100	266	100	100	100
Working Class						
Downward mobile	22	18	19	6	13	6
Stable	98	82	294	94	87	94
	120	100	313	100	100	100

*These figures are from a representative sample of 20,000 American men between ages 20 and
64 (Blau and Duncan, 1967). The national figures shown are for married men with wives from
age twenty-two to forty-one. I am indebted to O. D. Duncan for providing raw data from which
to calculate the percentages shown.

TABLE 2-4. Mean Class Origin, Size of Origin Community, and Size of Origin Families of Children's Parents, by Race and Class

	Means			
	Working Class		Middle Class	
VARIABLE	BLACK	WHITE	BLACK	WHITE
Mothers SES origin	15.2	26.2	23.7	51.7
Size town where mother grew up	4.0	4.6	4.9	4.8
Number of mother's siblings	5.3	3.9	3.8	2.2
Husband's SES origin	14.0	24.3	24.6	47.5
Size town where husband grew up	3.8	4.2	4.8	4.9
Number of husband's siblings	5.7	4.7	3.8	2.4
N	313	120	266	403
Total N = 1102				

proportions of mothers reared in middle-class homes are 18 percent and 6 percent in the white and black strata respectively.

The black and white samples differ in constituency in a number of other ways. Forty-seven percent of the black mothers were born and reared in the South, compared with only 9 percent of the whites. Although the black middle class has considerably fewer mothers with southern origins than the black working class (31 percent versus 60 percent), southerners are substantially more prevalent in this subsample than in either white group.

Table 2-4 summarizes the differences in origin characteristics of parents in the two races. It shows that the origins of black middle-class parents closely resemble those of white working-class parents, *not* those of white middle-class parents, with a single exception—namely, the size of communities in which they grew up. Thus, the mean social-class origin of black middle-class fathers is virtually identical to that of white working-class fathers, and that of black middle-class mothers is slightly lower than that of white working-class mothers. The size of origin families is virtually the same for black middle-class and white working-class mothers (an average of four siblings as compared with only two in the origin families of white middle-class mothers). On the average, black middle-class fathers had one fewer sibling than white working-class fathers but two siblings more than white middle-class fathers. Black working-class parents, as might be expected, grew up in the largest families.

In sum, although black middle-class parents have higher educational and occupational achievements than those in the white working class, the level of their social origins is much the same, just as are the IQ and achievement test scores of their children. These findings suggest that not merely the present achievements of parents but also past resources invested in them and the social milieu in which they grew up may have a bearing on the performance of their children.

Were there free and equal association between members of the two races with similar educational and occupational attainment, then the class origins of black parents might show as little association with their children's test scores as is found in the case of whites, for then the processes of acculturation would proceed at the same rate among upwardly mobile blacks as among their white counterparts. Unfortunately, however, segregation in informal social relations remains the rule rather than the exception, and as long as this persists, it is more accurate to conceive of the American stratification system as a dual system in which seemingly parallel strata actually have markedly different properties. These differences make for differences in the rate of diffusion of modern child-rearing beliefs and practices, in the magnitude of association between the components of social status, and in the variables that predict test scores of children in the two races.

Correlations of Components of Socioeconomic Status with Children's Test Scores: A Comparison of Black and Whites

The correlations between children's measured intelligence and scholastic achievement, on the one hand, and parents' current status and origin status characteristics, on the other, exhibit some noteworthy differences between the two races.

Mother's and father's educational attainment scores were combined into a single variable, hereafter referred to as parents' education.[3] Occupational status continues to be that of the parent with the higher SEI score. Mother's middle-class exposure score and the average education of mother's three closest friends[4] were combined to form a measure of social milieu. Mother's and father's origin SEI scores were combined to form the measure hereafter referred to as origin SES.[5]

Parents' demographic origins is a composite score based on four measures: (1) mother's and father's region of origin score,[6] i.e., location of the community in which each parent grew up, and (2) the size of that home community, (3) origin family size, a composite measure of the number of siblings in mother's and father's origin family, hereafter referred to as origin family size;[7] and (4) mother's exposure to whites, described earlier. Needless to say, this last measure constitutes a variable only with respect to black people.

A comparison of the magnitude of correlation between children's IQ scores and the six measures of family status (Table 2-5) reveals several noteworthy differences between the two races. First, the association of occupational status and parents' education with children's IQ and achievement is somewhat stronger among whites, but social milieu is less strongly related to their children's test scores. Indeed, social milieu is the strongest correlate of both IQ and achievement among blacks (.34 and .41, respectively),

TABLE 2-5. Correlations of Family SES Components with Children's Test Scores by Race

Blacks

Parents'	IQ	Achievement	1	2	3	4	5	6
1. Occupational status	.246	.327						
2. Education	.287	.392	.574					
3. Milieu	.338	.412	.516	.595				
4. Origin SES	.254	.275	.403	.462	.427			
5. Demographic origins	.140	.192	.305	.403	.340	.315		
6. Origin family size	-.124	-.145	-.203	-.192	-.189	-.208	-.233	
7. Mother's exposure to whites	.211	.186	.256	.315	.339	.204	.176	-.125

Whites

Parents'	IQ	Achievement	1	2	3	4	5
1. Occupational status	.278	.367					
2. Education	.312	.418	.709				
3. Milieu	.276	.391	.653	.775			
4. Origin SES	.187	.231	.568	.598	.600		
5. Demographic origins	.198	.103	.229	.262	.228	.304	
6. Origin family size	-.232	-.228	-.463	-.535	-.476	-.454	-.342

whereas among whites, parents' education is the strongest correlate of both IQ and achievement (.31 and .42, respectively). Among blacks, occupational status of the higher-ranking parent is less associated with children's test scores than either education or social milieu, whereas among whites its correlation with IQ is virtually identical to that between social milieu and IQ. In both races, social milieu is a stronger correlate of achievement scores than is occupational status.

The second important finding is that the three measures of family status under discussion are decidedly more strongly intercorrelated among whites than among blacks. In sum, status consistency is higher among whites than among black families, as already noted, and therefore the use of any single index of socioeconomic status is more likely to reflect the social environment of white children than of black children. Moreover, the convention of using fathers' occupational status as *the* measure of family socioeconomic status does not appear to be warranted in research dealing with black and white children's test scores since it is the weakest correlate of black children's scores among the three measures under consideration.

Measures of parents' family and demographic origins, as might be expected, are not as strongly correlated with children's test scores as are measures of parents' current status, with one exception. Among blacks, parents' social-class origins are as strongly related to children's IQ scores (.25) as is the occupational status of the higher-scoring parent, whereas among whites, parents' origin status is a weaker correlate (.19) of children's test scores than any of the measures of current family status. But demographic origins and origin family size are somewhat stronger correlates of white than of black children's IQ scores.

Black mothers' exposure to whites is less strongly correlated with their children's test scores than any current status measure or even parents' class origins, but it is a stronger correlate than either demographic origins or origin family size. The extent of exposure to whites varies more with social milieu and with parents' education than with occupational status or origin variables.

Predictors of Children's IQ Test Scores

It is evident that there are interrelationships among all status measures in the analysis, particularly among measures of current status, and also that the magnitude of association is generally different in the two races. It is reasonable to expect, therefore, that the variables that significantly predict children's test scores will also be different in the two races. That expectation is borne out by the results of the multivariate analysis that ascertains the contribution of each component of family status to the explanation of variations in scores within each race, independently of the effects of other variables in the equation.

When black and white children's IQ scores are regressed on the previously discussed measures of family status, it becomes evident that the
variables that predict white children's scores are not significant predictors of
the scores of black children (see Table A-1, page 231). For whites, parents'
education exerts the strongest net effect (beta = .21) on IQ scores, followed
by parents' demographic origins (beta = .12). Occupational status enters the
equation (beta = .10), but it adds less than one percent to the variance
explained in white children's IQ once the effects of the first two variables are
taken into account. All together these three variables explain 12 percent of
the variation in white children's IQ scores.

An additional 2 percent of the variance in black children's IQ (14 percent)
is accounted for by four variables, three of which are not the same as the
predictors of white scores. Mother's social milieu exerts the largest effect
(beta = .21), followed by parents' origin social class (beta = .11) and extent of
mother's exposure to white friends and co-workers (beta = .09). Parents'
education enters the equation (beta = .08) but does not significantly increase
the amount of variance in black children's scores explained by the first three
variables.

The results of the analysis indicate that the use of either occupational
status or parents' education (or even both these variables) as controls does
not achieve the intended purpose of equalizing the social environment of
families in the two races. The social milieu of white families is more consistent with the status achievements of white upwardly mobile parents than of
black ones. Consequently, social milieu supercedes any other component of
social status as a predictor of black children's IQ scores. And independent of
the immediate social milieus of the mothers, the extent of their equalitarian
association with whites makes a modest but significant contribution to the IQ
scores of their children. How that happens will be discussed later in the
analysis.

Socioeconomic Status and the Black-White IQ Gap

How much of the observed IQ difference between black and white children is attributable to the six components of socioeconomic status? By com-
bining blacks and whites and entering race as a variable in the equation, we
can derive an estimate, as shown in Table 2-6.

Five variables account for about 23 percent of the variance in IQ scores in
the sample. The largest net effect on IQ is exerted by race (beta = .21)
followed by mother's social milieu (beta = .16) and parents' educational
attainment (beta = .13). The independent effect of occupational status is
small (beta = .07) and by itself adds less than one percent to the variance
explained in IQ scores after the first three variables enter the equation. The
mean size of parents' family of origin exerts the smallest effect (beta = −.05).

Although race exerts the largest effect relative to other variables in the

TABLE 2-6. Whole Sample: Regression of IQ Scores on SES Components and Parents' Origins

Variable	Raw Regression Coefficient	Standardized Coefficient	Standard Error	F-Value
Education	1.250	.132	.415	9.10*
Race[a]	5.943	.206	.857	48.11*
Milieu	1.859	.159	.475	15.34*
Occupational status	0.039	.073	.021	3.50
Origin family size	−0.101	−.049	.060	2.77
Intercept	78.54007	R^2 = .226	N = 1102	

*Significant at .05 level or higher.
[a] Blacks and whites are coded 0 and 1 respectively. Exposure to whites is omitted from combined sample analyses.

equation, the inclusion of other variables reduces the difference in mean IQ between black and white children from 10 to 5.9 points.

Jensen's conclusion (1969) that the 15-point difference observed between the mean IQ scores of black and white children was evidence for the genetic hypothesis was, to say the least, premature and, as noted earlier, has been challenged by many social scientists and statisticians. Light and Smith (1971), for example, developed a statistical model with hypothetical environmental measures which reduced the 15-point difference by 9 points, leaving a residual difference of 6 points between the mean scores of black and white children—just about the residual differences shown at this early point in my analysis.

In my sample the mean difference in IQ scores between black and white children is 10 points without introducing any controls.[8] The *net* contribution of race to the difference in IQ scores is materially reduced merely by introducing several components of family socioeconomic status which, if not taken into account in comparative research on blacks and whites, lead to incorrect conclusions. The fact that this result can be achieved with a relatively small number of variables, which by no means exhaust the range of social opportunities and handicaps that are differentially distributed in white and black populations, substantially strengthens the case for the explanation of observed race differences in measured intelligence in *social* as opposed to genetic terms.

While the variables considered thus far serve to reduce considerably the variance in IQ and achievement scores attributed to race, they are not comprehensive enough to eliminate that difference entirely. To label the residual remaining effect a "race effect" is not, strictly speaking, correct. A more precise definition of "race effect" is the unexplained variance produced by correlates of race not yet taken into account in the first stage of the theoretical model being developed in this book.

Predictors of Black and White Children's Achievement Test Scores

Three variables—parents' social milieu (beta = .25), education (beta = .19), and occupational status (beta = .09)—explain 21 percent of the variance in black children's achievement scores. The same three variables account for 20 percent of the variance in white children's achievement scores: parents' education (beta = .23), mother's milieu (beta = .14) and occupational status (beta = .11). Thus, social milieu is the strongest predictor of black children's achievement and IQ scores whereas for whites, parents' education is the strongest predictor of performance on both tests.

When children's IQ scores are entered as a variable in the equation, the variance explained in achievement scores is substantially increased—39 percent in the case of whites and 42 percent in the case of blacks (see Table A-2, page 232). There is virtually no difference in the contribution IQ makes to the prediction of achievement test performance in the two races (beta = .49 and .48 for black and whites respectively). Among blacks, parents' education (beta = .14) and social milieu (beta = .13) make virtually the same contribution, but occupational status (beta = .06) does not significantly increase the variance explained. Among whites, parents' education has a slightly stronger independent effect (beta = .18) than social milieu (beta = .14), and occupational status does not enter the equation. Interestingly, with the effects of these variables removed, the zero-order positive effects on white children's achievement of having parents of native birth who grew up in larger northern communities are reversed (beta = −.07). I take this to mean that no *direct* advantage accrues to white children's scholastic ability from having parents who were reared in northern and larger communities. Such parents are likely to have higher educational attainment (Blau and Duncan, 1967), and it is through this effect that children benefit academically from parents of higher demographic origins. But it appears that once parents' education is controlled, such children score slightly lower on achievement test than children of foreign-born or southern-born parents.

In sum, it is evident that the antecedents of early intellectual development are in important respects different for the two races. The properties of mothers' social milieu is the component of socioeconomic status that exerts the strongest effect on black children's IQ. Furthermore, parents' origin social class exerts a small but significant effect on the IQ test performance of black children, but not of white children. The extent of mother's exposure to white friends and co-workers also exerts a small but significant effect on the variance in black children's IQ. After these variables are taken into account, parents' educational attainment no longer adds significantly to the explanation of variance in IQ scores of black children. But mother's social milieu *and* parents' education are the components of SES that account most for the variance in black children's achievement scores. Occupational status is the weakest predictor of black children's achievement, and it is not a significant predictor of their IQ scores.

In the case of White children, parents' education is the strongest predictor and occupational status is the weakest predictor of both IQ and achievement test performance. With respect to IQ, parents' demographic origins and mother's social milieu each have a stronger effect than occupational status. Thus, in both races, the variable most frequently used as a control when comparing the abilities of children in the two races turns out to be the weakest predictor among the components of socioeconomic status considered in the present study.

The mean difference in achievement scores between black and white children in my sample is 2.04 stanines. That is, black children's test performance is about two grades lower on the average than that of white children. But this difference is cut in half when differences in the family status of children in the two races are taken into account.

Four variables account for 40 percent of the variance in achievement scores of children in the sample with the races combined (Table 2-7, top). Race continues to exert the strongest net effect (beta = .33); white children still average 1.3 stanines higher than black children. Parents' education and mother's social milieu exert somewhat smaller but equal independent effects (beta = .20), and occupational status exerts the smallest, albeit a still significant, effect (beta = .09).

When IQ score is included in the equation (Table 2-7, bottom), it proves, not surprisingly, to be a stronger predictor of achievement test performance than any of the family status measures, including race. However, even after IQ scores are taken into account, these variables continue to exert significant, although reduced, effects. Thus, race (beta = .23) remains a stronger predictor than other variables. At the same time, with IQ controlled, the disparity between black and white achievement scores declines from 1.3 points to slightly less than one stanine (.94). Parents' education (beta = .13) and mother's social milieu (beta = .12) exert approximately equal effects, and parents' occupational status continues to exert a weak effect (.06) but does not add significantly to the variance explained. With IQ in the equation, the percentage of variance in achievement explained in the total sample rises from 40 to 55 percent. The substantial increment in the variance explained is further confirmation of the predictive power of IQ tests administered early in children's school careers.

The results of the foregoing analyses also clearly indicate that race and social status, particularly parents' education and mother's social milieu, not only influence the scholastic ability of children through their effects on IQ test performance early in the child's school career, but persist in their effects and continue to influence children's scholastic ability *directly*, independently of the children's early level of intellectual proficiency.

Achievement test scores are more strongly correlated than IQ scores with

TABLE 2-7. Whole Sample: Regression of Achievement Scores on SES Components and Parents' Origins

Variable	Raw Regression Coefficient	Standardized Coefficient	Standard Error	F-Value
Education	0.253	.189	.053	24.32*
Race	1.325	.325	.106	157.60*
Milieu	0.315	.191	.059	28.65*
Occupational status	0.007	.092	.003	7.19*
Intercept	0.58009	R² = 40%	N = 1102	

Whole Sample: Regression of Achievement Scores on SES Components, Parents' Origins, and Children's IQ Scores

Variable	Raw Regression Coefficient	Standardized Coefficient	Standard Error	F-Value
IQ	0.063	.443	0.003	373.89*
Race	0.941	.231	0.093	101.58*
Education	0.171	.127	0.045	14.67*
Milieu	0.195	.118	0.051	14.50*
Occupational status	0.004	.056	0.002	3.65
Intercept	−4.23035	R² = 55%	N = 1102	

every measure of family status (see Table 2-5). The correlation of achievement scores with race is also stronger (.50) than with IQ scores (.36). Thus, the lag in the development of verbal skills and abilities found disproportionately among working-class and black children, as revealed by IQ tests in the early years of schooling, becomes compounded as they advance from one grade to the next. As the curriculum content children are expected to master becomes more difficult, deficiencies in basic skills become an ever greater impediment to learning.[9] Children's sense of efficacy is thereby undermined, and discouragement and alienation follow. A longitudinal study (Douglas, 1964) of a large sample of British children from birth to adulthood provides evidence that in contrast to the test scores of middle-class children, which exhibit steady score gains, those of working-class children decline between the ages of eight and eleven. An analysis (Gordon, 1972) based on data from my study provides evidence that underachievement is far more prevalent among black than among white children. By the time they reach the fifth grade, many more black children have lower achievement scores than their second-grade IQ scores would predict. These results strongly suggest that their underachievement stems not from an inherent lack of competence but rather from the joint failure of parents and teachers to provide effective instruction, encouragement, and support as children are required to master progressively more complex concepts and skills.

Summary

In this chapter I began the process of identifying the social sources of observed differences in black and white children's IQ and achievement scores. The first major finding was that four components of family socioeconomic status—parents' education, occupational status of higher-ranking parent, mother's social milieu, and parents' socioeconomic origin—are more highly correlated among whites than among blacks, which signifies that among whites, gains in educational and occupational attainment are more readily translated into access to a middle-class social milieu in which mainstream cultural and social influences prevail. Because status consistency is higher among whites, the use of any single index of socioeconomic status is more likely to reflect the social environment of white than of black children.

A second important finding is that the socioeconomic predictors of black and white children's IQ scores are different. The strongest predictor of black children's scores is mother's social milieu followed by parents' social class origins and mother's exposure to whites. These variables account for 14 percent of the variance in black children's IQ scores. In contrast, parents' education and parents' demographic origins are significant predictors of white children's scores. Parents' occupational status enters the white equation, but does not significantly increase the variance explained, which amounts to 12 percent.

Race, social milieu, and parents' education are significant predictors of children's IQ scores with the races combined. Occupational status of higher-ranking parent and parents' origin family size enter the equation for the combined sample, but each alone does not increase significantly the variance explained, which amounts to 23 percent. When the above variables are controlled, the zero order mean IQ difference between black and white children of 10 points is reduced to 5.9 points. Thus, a substantial portion of the disparity in IQ test scores of black and white children is the result of differences in parents' educational attainment and access to a comparable middle-class social milieu.

In the next chapter, the religious and denominational composition of the two races is compared and found to be different in important ways. These differences prove to have significant implications for the development of intellectual competence of black and white children.

Notes

1. My white-exposure score is based on three measures: whether or not a mother had any white friends while growing up; whether she has any white friends currently; and whether she has any white co-workers. A score of 3 denotes high exposure; a score of 0 denotes no exposure to whites of an equalitarian nature. The

correlations between the two friendship measures is .22; between current friends and co-workers, .23; and between earlier friends and current co-workers, 16.

2. A comparison with the figures based on a national probability sample shown in Table 2-3 reveals that our black sample distribution is virtually identical to the national one, but in the white sample the proportion of upward mobiles is underrepresented, and to a lesser degree, the proportion of downward mobiles is overrepresented. However, since parents' social-class origins are expected to exert some independent effects and are therefore taken into account in the analysis, this discrepancy does not pose the problems it might otherwise.

3. Mother's and father's educational attainment scores were added and divided by two to yield the measure of parents' education.

4. The average educational attainment of mother's three closest friends was added to her score on middle-class exposure multiplied by two and divided by two.

5. Mother's score and father's score were added and divided by two to form the origin SES index.

6. Native-born respondents were scored 2 and foreign-born respondents were assigned a score of 1. Regions of the country were ordered according to the mean SEI score of respondents' home region: eastern-born (68) = 4; western-born (62) = 3; midwestern-born (53) = 2; southern-born (36) = 1. Size of parents' home region was ordered along a continuum ranging from farm/open country = 1 to suburbs to cities with a million or more inhabitants = 6. The location of home communities scores of fathers and mothers were summed and divided by 2. The same procedure was followed with respect to size of each parent's home community. The two scores combined constitute parents' demographic origin score.

7. The sum of these scores divided by two constitutes the index of origin family size.

8. One can only speculate about the reasons why I found a lesser difference between the mean IQ's of black and white children than Jensen did. My sample is not a probability sample. It has an overrepresentation of both black and white middle-class children. It is drawn from a northern urban population of fifth- and sixth-graders in 1968, whereas the sample used by Jensen (Kennedy, Van de Riet, and White, 1963) was a probability sample of elementary school children drawn from the black population in the southeastern United States in 1960. Southeastern black children average lower IQ scores than those in other regions of the United States (Westinghouse Learning Corporation and Ohio University, 1969).

9. Wesley Becker (1977), on the basis of ten years of experimental research on teaching reading and language to children from low-income families, reports "a progressive loss on percentiles from the end of grade one to the end of grade three on MAT Reading Tests, which is paralleled by a progressive change in the tests toward an adult vocabulary by the end of third grade" (p. 535). He attributes this loss to the failure of schools to systematically teach vocabulary-concept knowledge. "Current programs are structured to teach middle class children or children who, to a large extent, are taught oral-language comprehension at home . . . children from homes with weak support for language development fall progressively behind on current reading tests" (p. 536).

CHAPTER 3

Race, Religion, and Denominational Membership

Viewed in historical perspective, sociological work on the significance of religion in social life peaked with the work of Weber and Durkheim. Thereafter, with certain notable exceptions, interest in the subject waned. Noting the secularizing tendencies brought about by urbanization and industrialization, sociologists shifted their attention increasingly to the study of the secular determinants and consequences of stratification systems and of social-class membership.

This is not to say that continuing differences associated with religious affiliation were not reported from time to time in various substantive areas. In the political arena, for example, religious affiliation has been shown to be a significant factor in election outcomes and in voters' choices (Lipset, 1964; Lazarsfeld et al., 1948; Berelson et al., 1960; Ringer and Glock, 1954–55, and others). Religion as a factor in proneness to alcoholism (Pittman and Snyder, 1968) and mental disorder (Srole and Langner et al., 1962) and the continuing significance of religion in the selection of marital partners (Hollingshead, 1950) have been studied and reported on. But aside from such isolated and occasional attention, the use of religion as a variable in sociological analysis has been rare, particularly when contrasted with the empirical investigation of the role of socioeconomic status in social life.

The appearance of Gerhardt Lenski's *The Religious Factor* in 1961, in which he demonstrated that even when socioeconomic status is taken into account, religious affiliation has an independent effect on educational attainment, orientation to work, occupational achievement, and income, served to revive sociological interest in the study of religious effects in stratification processes. Also notable is the fact that Lenski's analyses included comparisons of blacks and whites in the effects of religious affiliation.

A shortcoming of Lenski's otherwise excellent study was his adherence to the traditional practice among sociologists of ignoring the denominational character of American Protestantism. Results from studies in other communities in some cases contradicted Lenski's results (Burchinal et al., 1962), and he has since been faulted for not taking into account the differences in ethnic background of Detroit Catholics compared with Catholics nationwide (Babbie, 1965). Finally, it has been shown that Lenski's Detroit sample overrepresented "high" Protestant denominations, such as Episcopalians and Presbyterians, and underrepresented Methodists and Baptists, compared with the national distribution of Protestant denominational membership (Warren, 1970).

Lenski's book represents an important landmark because of its excellence *and* its shortcomings, for it inspired new interest in the study of religious effects utilizing multivariate approaches that make it possible to begin to disentangle the effects of differences in the socioeconomic composition of ethnic and religious groups from the effects of membership in these groups. Recent work utilizing sophisticated methodologies has confirmed and refined Lenski's findings. For example, Gockel (1969) reports significantly higher average income among Episcopalians and Jews compared with other religious and denominational groups, even when such variables as education, occupation, size of community, and race are controlled. Warren (1970) confirms these results with respect to Jews, Episcopalians, and Presbyterians but finds that Methodists and Catholics fall near the mean on socioeconomic status, while Baptists are below the mean, even after social origins and early achievements are controlled.

Other work examining the effects of religion on parents' educational expectations for their children (Morgan, 1962) and on need achievement (Veroff et al., 1962) indicates that while religion is confounded with socioeconomic differences, it exerts some significant independent effects. After reviewing a number of such recent studies, Warren (1970) concludes that "verifying and determining how religious preferences influence educational achievement appears to be a very fertile area for research.... Assuming that all of the correlations between early religious preference and education cannot be accounted for by the correlations between religious preference and father's education, father's occupation and number of siblings, research needs to be undertaken to determine in what other ways religion may influence education" (1970, p. 141).

Race and Religion

Blacks were largely brought to this nation as slaves, and their diverse indigenous cultures, including their non-Christian heritage, were destroyed over the period of their enslavement in the South. Protestantism was the dominant religion of the white South with the exception of Louisiana, and when black people were missionized it was done by Protestant masters and Protestant ministers. As a result, the overwhelming majority of American blacks have traditionally been and still are Protestant, and for various historical reasons they are concentrated in the Baptist and Methodist denominations. Although originally integrated, these denominations became racially segregated after the Civil War and have remained so by and large (Niebuhr, 1929).

The religious structure of whites in America is less homogeneous. The white founders and early settlers in the East and South were predominantly Protestant-Anglican, mostly Congregationalist or Presbyterian. During the nineteenth century, Baptism and Methodism spread rapidly in the Midwest, West, and South. Immigration from Germany and Scandinavia promoted the growth of Lutheranism. The immigration of Irish and Germans in the mid-nineteenth century started the flow of large numbers of Catholics into the United States, which was substantially augmented by immigration from Southern and Eastern Europe in the latter part of the nineteenth century and the first quarter of the twentieth century. Indeed, the white immigrants of that period were predominantly Roman Catholic, including significant numbers who were affiliated with the Eastern branches of Catholicism.

Jews, the third major religious grouping in white America, currently constitute about 3 percent of the American population but make up a far larger proportion of the population of the largest urban metropolitan areas, particularly on the eastern seaboard, as is also true of Catholics of European origin. Both groups tend to concentrate in large cities in the East and Middle West.[1]

These differences in religious homogeneity between the two races are reflected in my sample. Protestants constitute 91 percent of the black sample of mothers, compared with 47 percent among whites; the proportion of Catholics is only 6 percent among blacks but 19 percent among whites. There are no Jews in the black sample, but 21 percent of the white sample is Jewish.[2] Finally, the proportion with no denominational or religious affiliation constitutes only 3 percent of black respondents, compared with 13 percent among the white sample.

When white and black Protestants are classified according to denominational membership, one finds further confirmation that religious stratification is far less marked among blacks, at least among the generation of women represented in my sample. The most pronounced difference is observed with respect to Baptist and other fundamentalist denominational affiliations; 64

percent of the black sample but only 12 percent of the white sample is Baptist or other fundamentalist. The incidence of Methodists and Lutherans, combined, is very similar for the two groups: 19 percent among the blacks and 17 percent among the whites. But the incidence of "high Protestants" (i.e., Episcopalian, Presbyterian, and Congregationalist) is considerably higher among whites (18 percent) than among blacks (7 percent).

In an important comparative study of church membership (Stark and Glock, 1968) an interesting distinction is made between churches characterized as moral communities and those whose members function primarily as religious audiences. Operationally, Stark and Glock use two criteria to characterize denominations: the extent to which the friendships of members are confined to others of their own denomination, and the extent to which member's organizational activities tend to center within their denomination. Stark and Glock report that Southern Baptists and members of other fundamentalist sects, theologically the most orthodox among Protestants, function more as primary groups composed of persons who restrict their friendships and organizational participation to their own denomination. The more liberal denominational members (e.g., Congregationalists, Episcopalians) do not typically select their friends and organizational affiliations along denominational lines.

Other terms have been used by sociologists to distinguish normatively and associationally "dense or loose" groups, e.g., Gemeinschaft and Gesellschaft (Tonnies, 1957); primary and secondary groups (Cooley, 1909). Durkheim (1951) saw Catholicism as possessing a more unified normative and social structure owing to its hierarchical organization and elaborate sacraments. The church could exert more pervasive control over the behavior and beliefs of its members than could Protestantism, which has become increasingly differentiated in structure and doctrine since the Reformation.

A considerable body of literature exists which traces and analyzes the historical development of differences in doctrine, organizational structure, and social characteristics of the ministry and memberships of the various denominations of white Protestantism (Niebuhr, 1929; Mead, 1962; Hofstadter, 1963), but the development and significance of denominationalism among black Protestants is discussed only briefly or not at all by these writers. Sociologists, by and large, have also confined their work mainly to white denominationalism, except for occasional references to social differences in the membership or pastorates of different black denominations (Wilson, 1960; Drake and Cayton, 1945). Lenski included black Protestants in some of his analyses (1961), but, as mentioned earlier, he did not break down Protestants according to denominational affiliation.

Sociologists have largely neglected the study of the effects of religion, and more specifically the effects of denominationalism within Protestantism, on socialization processes and the development of intellectual competence in childhood. Nor has any research been carried out on the small but growing proportion of Americans who either are nonreligious altogether or belong to groups that stress ethical principles shared by Judaism and Christianity, such as the Unitarians and the Ethical Culture Society, as opposed to the theological doctrines that set the two religions apart.

Owing to the dearth of research on these groups, a necessary preliminary to the discussion of religious effects on the development of intellectual and scholastic competence is a comparison of the social origins and current social status of black and white respondents and of the test scores of children from various religious and denominational backgrounds. Such a comparison, shown in Table 3-1, indicates that religion is indeed significantly associated with variations in social origins within each race and between races.

It is evident that in every instance the average class origin of whites is considerably higher than that of blacks with the same religious affiliation. Indeed, using a score of 40 on the Duncan scale as the lower limit of middle-class social origin, it is clear that in *all* black denominations, members are typically of working-class origin; fundamentalists have the lowest scores, Methodists and Catholics rank second, nonreligious rank third, and high Protestants on the average have the highest scores. Among whites, only fundamentalists and Catholics typically originated in working-class families. Methodists and Lutherans have considerably higher social-class origins on the average than these groups, but they are lower than Jews, high Protestants, and the nonreligious, who average the highest social-class-origin scores.

The pattern with respect to the social origins of respondents' husbands differs in several respects from that of the wives. Although, in all the black denominations, husbands typically originated in working-class families, with fundamentalists again scoring lowest, the husbands of nonreligious black women have the highest social origins, on the average, while those of Methodists, high Protestants, and Catholics are intermediate. Among whites, the husbands of fundamentalist and Catholic women are typically of working-class origin. The average social-class origin of husbands is somewhat higher among Methodist and Lutheran women, still higher among the nonreligious and high Protestants, and highest among the husbands of Jewish respondents.

With respect to size of origin community, in both races fundamentalist women and their husbands typically grew up in smaller communities than those of other denominations, and Jewish women and their husbands, on the average, grew up in the largest communities, as did also nonreligious black women and their husbands, nonreligious white women, black and white Catholic women, and the husbands of black Catholics. Methodists and high Protestants in both races, the husbands of black Catholics, and nonreligious white women on the average grew up in communities intermediate in size.

In both races, fundamentalist women and their spouses grew up in the largest-sized families, but in each instance black fundamentalists' origin

TABLE 3-1. Mother's Religion by Race and Social Origins of Mother and Father (Means)

	Baptist and Other Fundamentalists		Methodist		High Protestant		Catholic		Jewish		Non-denominational	
	Black	*White*	*Black*	*White*	*Black*	*White*	*Black*	*White*	*Black*	*White*	*Black*	*White*
Mother												
Origin SES	16.2	28.8	22.3	42.5	30.4	54.7	22.0	33.2	—	52.7	24.9	58.5
Region of origin community*	1.9	2.5	2.3	3.1	2.4	3.0	2.8	3.2	—	3.0	2.5	2.9
Size of origin community	4.2	3.9	4.7	4.6	4.8	4.3	5.3	5.0	—	5.6	5.5	4.8
Size of origin family	5.0	4.0	3.6	2.4	3.8	2.2	4.0	3.7	—	1.6	3.7	2.1
Father												
Origin SES	16.2	33.0	20.9	39.7	22.3	48.0	24.4	31.0	—	50.8	34.8	45.2
Region of origin community*	1.7	2.5	2.2	3.0	2.3	3.2	2.6	3.3	—	3.1	2.5	2.9
Size of origin community	3.9	3.7	4.7	4.3	4.5	4.5	5.3	4.7	—	5.7	5.3	5.1
Size of origin family	5.6	4.5	3.8	3.1	3.6	2.6	3.0	3.8	—	2.0	3.1	2.0
N	367	64	112	85	42	91	37	95	—	109	17	67
Percentage of sample	63%	12%	19%	16%	7%	17%	6%	18%	—	21%	3%	13%

Total N
Black 579
White 523

*South is coded low and East is high.

families were larger, on the average, than those of white fundamentalists. This same pattern of differences between the races is observed with every subgroup except Catholics. Black and white Catholic women average about the same number of siblings (4), but the husbands of black Catholic women average fewer siblings (3) than white Catholic husbands (4). Jewish women and their husbands and nonreligious white women and their husbands grew up in the smallest families, averaging two siblings. Black Methodists, high Protestant wives and their husbands, and nonreligious women all average about the same number of siblings as black Catholic women (4), but among whites the average number of siblings is two for women in these denominations and three for their husbands.

Perhaps the most important conclusion that can be drawn from these comparisons is that in both races members of fundamentalist denominations have the lowest class origins, come from the smallest communities, and grew up in the largest families, all factors that are negatively associated with educational and occupational achievement. But even among fundamentalists there are marked differences between the races on all origin variables considered except size of community, and on all except the latter, blacks are the more disadvantaged. That is to say, the characteristics associated with upward social mobility are less prevalent among black fundamentalists than among white ones.

The same pattern of differences found between black and white co-religionists in their social origins is also found on all measures of current socioeconomic status. Table 3-2 shows, for example, that black Baptist and other fundamentalist women, their husbands, and their closest friends average the lowest educational attainment in the sample; their occupational attainment, exposure to middle-class influences, and exposure to whites are also lower than those of any other black or white group. Relative to black Baptists, white Baptists and Catholics average higher scores on all measures of socioeconomic status. Black Catholics are the only black group with higher scores on all measures of current socioeconomic status than their white co-religionists. They are also the only group in the black sample in which husbands average more years of schooling than their wives, a pattern found among whites in all religious groups.

From the standpoint of status characteristics, black Catholic families closely resemble black Methodist families. High Protestants average higher status than either of them, and nondenominational black families rank highest on all current status measures among blacks just as they do among whites. Jewish families average higher socioeconomic status scores than white Protestants but lower ones than nondenominational white families. It is interesting, in particular, to compare the status characteristics of white Jewish and black nondenominational families, for the IQ and achievement scores of their children bear the closest resemblance. While Jewish fathers have more education than nondenominational black fathers, this is not true

TABLE 3-2. Components of SES by Mother's Religion and Race (Means)

	Baptist and Other Fundamentalists		Methodist		High Protestant		Catholic		Jewish		Non-denominational	
	Black	White	Black	White	Black	White	Black	White	Black	White	Black	White
Respondent's education	4.4	4.8	5.4	5.5	5.9	6.2	5.1	5.0	—	6.4	6.5	6.7
Husband's education	4.3	5.0	5.4	5.9	5.8	6.5	5.3	5.0	—	6.8	6.1	7.0
Occupational status	32.0	46.3	49.5	54.4	56.7	65.8	51.4	46.0	—	72.2	61.5	73.8
Middle-class exposure	1.2	1.4	1.6	1.9	1.8	2.2	1.7	1.4	—	2.3	2.0	2.5
Average education of friends	3.1	3.3	3.8	3.7	4.1	4.2	3.7	3.2	—	4.4	4.5	4.6
Exposure to whites	4.6	—	5.1	—	5.4	—	5.2	—	—	—	5.3	—
Organizational memberships	1.3	1.6	2.0	1.9	2.6	2.1	1.7	1.5	—	2.5	1.6	1.7
N	367	64	112	85	42	91	37	95	—	109	17	67

Total N
Black 579
White 523

TABLE 3-3. Social Class, Race, and Mother's Religion*
(Percentages)

Religion and Denomination	Black		White	
	Middle Class	Working Class	Middle Class	Working Class
Protestant	83	97	44	58
	(219)	(302)	(171)	(69)
Baptist/other fundamentalist	54	82	19	46
	(117)	(250)	(32)	(32)
Methodist/Lutheran	32	14	34	38
	(71)	(41)	(59)	(26)
High Protestant	14	4	47	16
	(31)	(11)	(80)	(11)
Catholic	11	3	14	35
	(29)	(8)	(53)	(42)
Jewish	—	—	26	4
			(104)	(5)
Nondenominational/nonreligious	6	0	16	3
	(16)	(1)	(63)	(4)
N	100	100	100	100
	(264)	(311)	(391)	(120)

*Sixteen cases were left out of the analysis: 2 cases are missing from the black middle class; 2 from the black working class, and 12 from the white middle class. Categories omitted from the analysis are Christian Scientists, Quakers, and unclassified Protestants.

of Jewish mothers or of their closest friends relative to black nondenominational mothers and their friends.

Fundamentalists constitute nearly two-thirds of the black sample[3] but only 12 percent of the white sample. When class is controlled, it is evident (see Table 3-3) that an overwhelming majority of the black working-class Protestants are Baptist or other fundamentalist (82 percent). A smaller proportion, although still a majority, of the black middle-class Protestants in my sample (54 percent) are members of Baptist and other fundamentalist denominations. In the white sample, fundamentalists constitute only about a fifth of middle-class Protestants, a proportion only slightly larger than that of nondenominational and nonreligious respondents in the white middle class. Fundamentalists constitute 46 percent of the white working-class Protestant sample, but even among the latter, they are less preponderant than in the black middle class. Indeed, once again, as noted with respect to variables discussed in the previous chapter, there are very pronounced differences between the white and black middle classes. The latter more closely resembles the white working class, which is markedly less homogeneous in religious composition than the black working class.

When Protestantism is treated as a unitary phenomenon, its denominational character is obscured, and this in turn obscures very important differences between the two races in the social contexts in,which women and men learn and practice their parental roles. These contexts have significant implications for the development of intellectual abilities among children within each race as well as between the races.

Race, Religion, and IQ Differences in Four Class-Color Groups

Religious affiliation of mothers clearly varies independently with both race and social class, and each of these three variables is associated with variations in children's intellectual competence, as measured by both IQ and achievement tests.

Table 3-4 shows that even when occupational status is covaried, religious affiliation continues to exert a significant effect on children's IQ and achievement scores within each race, particularly among blacks. Further findings of interest emerge when instead of covarying occupational status statistically, the black and white samples are actually divided according to working- and middle-class occupational status (see Table 3-5).

Among blacks, children of fundamentalist mothers exhibit the lowest

TABLE 3-4. Children's IQ and Achievement Scores by Race and Mother's Religion Uncontrolled and Controlled by Social Class (Means)

Religion	IQ		Difference Between Races	Achievement Score		Difference Between Races	N	
	Black	White		Black	White		Black	White
Baptist/other fundamentalist	94	102	8	4.0	5.8	1.8	367	64
Methodist	100	105	5	4.7	6.1	1.4	112	85
High Protestant	103	109	6	5.4	6.6	1.2	42	91
Catholic	101	103	2	4.8	5.7	0.9	37	95
Jewish	—	110		—	6.6		—	109
Nonreligious	109	112	3	6.4	7.4	1.0	17	67
F^P (uncontrolled)								
Black	14.71***			18.92***				
White			7.25***			9.26***		
F^P (controlled by social class)								
Black	8.36***			9.53***				
White			2.40*			2.88**		

* = $p < .05$
** = $p < .01$
*** = $p < .001$

TABLE 3-5. Mean IQ by Race, Social Class, and Religion

Religion and Denomination	Black		White	
	Middle Class	Working Class	Middle Class	Working Class
Baptist/other fundamentalist	97	93	105	99
	(117)	(250)	(32)	(32)
Methodist/Lutheran	103	95	107	100
	(71)	(41)	(59)	(26)
High Protestant	105	98	110	98
	(31)	(11)	(80)	(11)
Catholic	100	103	104	101
	(29)	(8)	(53)	(42)
Jewish	—	—	110	110
			(104)	(5)
Nondenominational/nonreligious	109	0	112	110
	(16)	(1)	(63)	(4)
F =	7.43***	2.08	3.00*	1.21

mean scores in both the middle and working classes, although the latter average lower scores. Indeed, working-class children of fundamentalist mothers, who constitute fully 64 percent of the black sample, average the lowest scores in the entire sample. In the working class, children of Methodist and high Protestant mothers average somewhat higher IQ scores, and those of Catholic mothers have the highest scores, although the number of such cases is small and therefore possibly not reliable. In the black middle class, which is more heterogeneous in religious affiliation, Catholic children score somewhat higher than those of fundamentalists, but they score lower than the children of Methodist and High Protestant mothers. The highest scores, on the average, are exhibited by children of nondenominational and nonreligious mothers in the black middle class. (There is one such mother in the black working class whose child's IQ is 108, virtually the same as the mean score of black middle-class nondenominational children.)

A similar pattern of differences is found in the white middle class, except that the average IQ of Catholic children is virtually the same as that of the children of fundamentalist mothers; children of Methodists and Lutherans score somewhat higher, the children of high Protestants and Jewish mothers still higher, and children of nondenominational mothers highest, just as in the black middle class. In the white working class very little difference is observed between children of the various Protestant denominational and Catholic mothers. Although there are too few cases of Jewish and non-denominational children in the white working class to make any firm generalizations, they average the highest scores and differ very little from the nondenominational children in the black and white middle classes. A comparison of the average social-origin score of the working-class Jewish and nondenominational mothers shows, as might be anticipated, that they are downward mobiles: that is, they originated in middle-class families and married men in working-class occupations. Nine percent of white nondenominational mothers report their mothers as Jewish.

While differences in children's test scores among the various religious groups within each of the four class-color groups are of considerable magnitude, only the differences between the two middle classes are statistically significant, probably because of the very small number of nondenominational and Jewish women in the two working classes.[4]

When religious and denominational affiliation is taken into account along with social class, it is seen (Table 3-5) that the most pronounced differences by race *and* by social class occur among Protestants of various denominations, whereas the differences among non-Protestants are small. Thus, the average IQ scores of children of nondenominational mothers in the black middle class and in both white strata, and those of Jews in both classes and of high Protestants in the white middle class, are very similar, ranging from 109 to 112. Among high Protestants, working-class white and black children have identical mean IQ scores; among the middle classes, the mean score of white high Protestants exceeds that of blacks by five points. Among the Methodist and Lutheran groups, the class differences within each race are somewhat larger than the differences between races, with class held constant. Only among fundamentalists do white children's mean scores markedly exceed those of black children; the highest scores are in the white middle class, the lowest scores in the black working class, while the mean scores of black middle class and white working class children are intermediate, the same pattern of test score differences between the four class color groups reported in Chapter 2.

Taking religion into account helps to explicate this pattern of findings. In the black middle class, fundamentalists constitute 44 percent and Catholics 11 percent, a total of 55 percent. In the white working class, fundamentalists constitute a considerably smaller proportion (27 percent) but Catholics a higher proportion (35 percent); together they constitute 62 percent. There is very little difference in children's mean IQ scores among these four groups; middle-class black Baptists' average score is 97, compared with 99 among white working-class Baptists; black middle-class Catholic children's average score is 100, compared with the virtually identical mean score of 101 of white working-class Catholic children. In short, these strata are similar insofar as they are composed of two religious groups whose children on the average exhibit lower performance on IQ tests. A further similarity between the black middle class and white working class is the low representation within them of those religious subgroups whose children tend to score higher on IQ tests, i.e., high Protestants, Jews, and the nondenominational/nonreligious, who are characteristically middle class in socioeconomic status and of high educational attainment.[5]

Race, SES, Religion, and Scholastic Achievement

Mother's religious affiliation has no significant effects on the achievement test performance of either black or white working-class children (see A-3, page 232). By the time they reach fifth or sixth grade, white working-class children's test performance, as a rule, is on a par with national norms for their grade level, regardless of their religious background, except for the children of nondenominational mothers, who average two stanines higher than their race and social-class peers. It would hardly be worth mentioning the latter finding because of the very small case base were it not for the consistently high performance of such children in both the black and white middle classes.

There is no visible effect of mother's religious affiliation on the achievement test performance of black working-class children. By the time they are in fifth grade they test, on the average, a year below their grade level, regardless of religious background.

In the black and white middle classes, however, achievement test performance does vary with religious background, and indeed, more markedly in the black than in the white middle class. Black middle-class children with fundamentalist backgrounds, on the average, do not score significantly higher than black working-class children, in contrast to their social class peers from other religious backgrounds. The deficit of this group is important since they constitute over two-fifths of the black middle class sample. Black middle-class Methodist and Catholic children on the average are higher achievers, performing at grade level, while the children with high Protestant backgrounds average a stanine higher.

In the white middle class, children of Catholic and Baptist mothers on the average have lower achievement scores than Jewish children and those of other Protestant backgrounds. The highest achievement scores, however, are exhibited by children of nondenominational or nonreligious mothers, the same group that exhibits the highest achievement scores in the black middle class. Indeed, the latter is the one group of children in the black middle class whose achievement level is on a par with that of high Protestant and Jewish children in the white middle class. Although such children constitute a very small proportion of the black sample, they represent an identifiable group which merits further exploration to determine the social characteristics, beliefs, and socialization practices that account for their markedly greater intellectual proficiency relative to other middle-class black children.

The foregoing discussion has provided evidence to suggest that variations in the religious and denominational background of children, although confounded with race and socioeconomic status, also may exert independent effects on the early development of intellectual ability of children in both races, as measured by IQ tests in the early years of school, and later on, as reflected in differences in scholastic ability. To ignore the pronounced differences in denominational affiliation of black and white Protestants obscures an important source of differences in the scholastic ability of black and white children, even those whose families occupy seemingly parallel positions in the stratification system.

The findings reported to this point suggest that within each race and class group religious denominations constitute distinctive subgroups. Within each social stratum they represent bases for community. A class is a social aggregate of individuals who share, more or less, some common characteristics— of occupational rank and income, and some aspects of work functions. For example, within the working class, blue-collar workers predominate. They participate in the production of objects or the provision of services that require relatively little formal learning and skill. In the middle classes, the range of occupational functions is more extended, from clerical work to the most complex professional and executive tasks. People do, of course, form social bonds based on occupational association; they have occupational identities as welders, truckers, physicians; their work provides opportunities for contact and their common run of experience constitutes a basis for association. But occupation constitutes only one basis of community.

Within each race and within the range of occupations represented in each social stratum, religion and denominations constitute subcommunities within which, more often than not, people marry and rear children, who, in turn, typically inherit the identification of their parents. That this is the case with respect to Catholics and Jews is readily apparent. Within Protestantism the various denominations constitute boundaries for the associational life of individuals as well. Not merely doctrinal differences but also differences in style of worship and in values, status characteristics, and style of life distinguish members of the different Protestant denominations within each race. In addition, and even more pervasive, is the longstanding historical division between the races within Protestant denominationalism. Thus, Richard Niebuhr, decades ago, commented:

> The existence of the racial schism in America is one of the clearest facts in the whole mixed pattern of American denominationalism. . . . Nearly ninety per cent of all Negro Christians . . . are members of churches which are restricted to their race. Furthermore, most of the Negroes who are members of denominations in which the white race predominates are separated into special conferences or districts while almost all of them are segregated into racial local churches. Only in a negligible number of instances are Negroes members of churches with a mixed racial constituency. [1929, pp. 239–40]

Niebuhr goes on to observe that the racial schism, at least during the time in which he wrote, was growing steadily more acute. The subordination of blacks by whites was as characteristic within the church as it was in the general social life of the country. It was this threat to their autonomy that often led blacks to secede from predominantly white churches in which they had originally held memberships.

Another factor that Niebuhr identifies as responsible for the continuing racial division within American Protestantism is the need of blacks, as of other disinherited groups, for an "emotional, empirical reigion." He observes, however, that emotionalism is not merely a reaction against the drudgery and bleakness of the life of blacks in a repressive social order but also a result of the denial to blacks of the educational opportunities which were gradually opened to poor immigrant and native lower-class whites. The lay minister, no more educated or sophisticated in doctrinal matters than his parishioners, leads through charisma rather than through knowledge and thereby operates to reinforce the traditionalism and emotionalism of his flock. With the expansion of economic and educational opportunities for black Americans, the cultural isolation of black fundamentalism is waning, as it has waned among white fundamentalists. The lay ministry is slowly giving way to a professional clergy with broader general educational and theological preparation that can utilize their ministerial role to educate and guide their parishioners in worldly issues and activities as well as offer them spiritual guidance and emotional release.

Black Americans have been identified with Baptist and other Pentacostal sects since at least the early part of the nineteenth century. The Baptists, struggling to develop a following against the older and established Protestant denominations, such as the Anglicans (Episcopalians), Congregationalists, and Presbyterians, carried their evangelical efforts to new frontiers in the South and West, directing their appeal very successfully to the segments of the population, both white and black, which had little education and little in the way of worldly possessions. This population, spread over vast expanses of territory, responded readily to the itinerant Baptist and Methodist ministers, who stressed the emotional and expressive aspects of Christianity. In contrast, the educated ministry of the older established denominations, most of them products of the eastern colleges and seminaries, offered a more complex, more intellectual approach. The emphasis on religious experience as a release and an escape from daily worldly activities has had enormous appeal for lower-class blacks and whites not merely in rural areas but also in the cities to which they in time migrated.

Hofstadter (1963) has described at length the anti-intellectual stance of the evangelical, fundamentalist denominations, their resistance to science and modern knowledge, and their general resistance to the secularizing tendencies brought about by industrialization and urbanization. They view such influences as antithetical to the teaching of the Bible, which they regard as the repository of all truth, past, present, and future. Such a doctrinal orientation denigrates the importance of educational attainment, intellectual curiosity, and scientific inquiry, perceiving such activities as a threat to the authority of a fundamentalist world view. To doubt, to question, to discover new knowledge is to open the Pandora's box of antireligious forces and to undermine the appeal and power of fundamentalism. This position has characterized particularly those denominations that gained their following from among the poorer, less-educated segments of the populace. Hofstadter argues convincingly that this also has been the traditional stance taken by the functionaries of the Catholic church in America, which, like the more fundamentalist Protestant denominations, had a predominantly working-class membership. He calls attention to the similarity in political viewpoint (and in working-class origins) that characterized fundamentalist Protestantism and American Catholicism, particularly the anti-intellectualism shared by both groups.[6]

Race, Religion, and Socioeconomic Status as Predictors of Children's IQ Scores: A Multivariate Analysis

In view of the myriad differences in social origins and current status found among various religious and denominational groups within each race and between the two races, it becomes important to determine whether mothers' religious and denominational affiliations have effects on children's intellectual development independent of social origin and current status differences associated with religious group membership.

A preliminary inspection of zero order correlations reveals fairly strong and consistent negative correlations between children's test scores only with a Baptist/fundamentalist background among blacks, −.27 with IQ and −.29 with achievement test scores. A weaker positive association is found between black children's test scores and other religious affiliations, the strongest being with a nondenominational background (.17 with IQ score; .21 with achievement test score). A similar pattern of correlations is found between white children's test scores and mother's religious affiliation. However, the magnitude of negative association between test scores and a Baptist/fundamentalist background is weaker among whites (−.12 with IQ and with achievement test scores) than among blacks. But the positive association between test scores and a nondenominational background is virtually of the same magnitude among whites (.14 with IQ and .21 with achievement test scores) as among blacks.

The same pattern of differences is observed in correlations between religious background and origin and current status measures among blacks. Negative correlations of about .4 are found between Baptist/fundamentalist religious affiliation and occupational status, educational attainment, and social milieu, whereas positive correlations, albeit of a weaker magnitude, are found between current socioeconomic status measures and all other religious group memberships. Baptist/fundamentalist mothers are also the only groups of black mothers in which a negative correlation is found with exposure to whites (−.28).

A pattern of correlations that is similar but of lesser magnitude is found among whites. Baptist/fundamentalist mothers are less advantaged in their social origins and current status relative to all other whites except Catholics but not nearly to the same degree as their black counterparts.[7]

Religion exerts significant and independent effects on black children's IQ scores but not on those of white children (see Table A-4, page 233). Five variables account for 16 percent of the variance in black children's IQ scores. Mother's social milieu exerts the strongest net effect (beta = .20), followed by fundamentalism (beta = −.12) and parents' social-class origin (beta = .11). A weak net effect in the opposite direction from fundamentalism is exerted by a nonreligious background (beta = .08) and mother's exposure to whites (beta = .08). The last variable, however, no longer adds significantly to the variance accounted for by the other variables in the equation.

Adding religious variables to the analysis increases by 2 percent the variance explained in black children's IQ scores compared with the model in the previous chapter, which employed only socioeconomic variables in the equation. Black children of fundamentalist mothers average about three points lower on IQ and children of nonreligious mothers score about 6 points higher even after the marked differences between the two groups of mothers in origin and current status are taken into account. With religious variables in the equation, the partial correlation between parents' education and black children's IQ and that between occupational status and IQ are virtually eliminated (.04 and .03, respectively). This is an important finding when one remembers that Baptists and other fundamentalists constitute nearly two-thirds of the black sample.

In contrast to blacks, the addition of religious variables to the equation does not increase the amount of variance explained in IQ scores of white children. While a Baptist/fundamentalist as well as Catholic affiliation is negatively associated with the components of SES among whites, the magnitude of these zero order correlations is considerably lower than among blacks. And indeed, when IQ scores of white children are regressed on socioeconomic and religious variables, neither a Baptist nor a Catholic background exerts any independent effects (see A-1, page 231). Parents' education has the strongest effect on IQ (beta = .19), and parents' demographic origins have a weaker but still significant effect (beta = .12).[8] Occupational status (beta = .10) and a nondenominational/nonreligious affiliation also have weak positive effects on IQ, but neither variable alone significantly increases the amount of variance explained. These four variables explain 12 percent of the variance in white children's IQ scores, the same amount explained in the model that did not include religion (see Chapter 2).

Thus, it is evident that in the case of whites, mother's religious affiliation, with the possible exception of nondenominationalism, does not exert independent effects on the development of children's intellectual competence and that the zero order variations among religious groups in mean IQ scores of children can be explained by the differences in parents' educational attainment and demographic origins that characterize these groups.

That fundamentalism exerts an independent negative effect on the development of intellectual competence among black children but not among white children raises a further question about the possible confounding effects of religion and mother's religiosity, which is measured by answers to the question asked of all mothers in the sample: "How important is your religion to you personally—extremely important, fairly important, not very important, or not at all important?"

An association of $-.24$ is found between religiosity and race. That is, black mothers tend to be more religious than white ones. While Baptist/fundamentalist mothers in both races are as a rule more religious than other women, as Table 3-6 shows, black Baptists are the most religious of all. In all groups except Catholics, black women have higher mean religiosity scores than their white counterparts. Mother's religiosity is negatively associated with children's IQ ($r = -.19$) and achievement scores ($r = -.25$). The question is whether religiosity has effects on the development of children's intellectual competence independent of mother's religious affiliation.

The addition of mother's religion and religiosity to a composite measure of socioeconomic status[9] with race included in the equation increases the variance explained in the IQ scores of children in the sample, but it also serves to reduce considerably the net effect of race as a predictor of IQ scores. In the early model, containing discrete measures of SES and race, the standardized beta weight of race was .21 and white children average 5.94 points higher than black children. In the model shown in Table 3-7 the beta weight of race is reduced to .13 and the net advantage of whites averages only 3.87 points. Treating the four components of SES as a unitary variable eliminates the complex problem of interactions between these variables as well as of interactions between each of them and race and religion.

The "race effect" is further reduced by taking into account the very substantial differences in religious affiliation of blacks and whites. Not only is a much higher proportion of the black sample Baptist and other fundamen-

T A B L E 3 - 6 . Mother's Religiosity by Race and Religious Affiliation

Religion	Blacks	Whites
Baptist/other fundamentalist	3.6	3.4
Methodist/Lutheran	3.5	3.2
High Protestant	3.4	3.2
Catholic	3.3	3.3
Jewish	—	2.9
Nondenominational/nonreligious	3.2	2.9
	$F = 3.10$	$F = 5.87*$

TABLE 3-7. Whole Sample: Regression of IQ Scores on SES, Race, Origins, Religion, and Religiosity

	Raw Regression Coefficient	Standardized Coefficient	Standard Error	F-Value
SES	.227	.293	.027	73.31*
Race	3.865	.134	.949	16.58*
Baptist/other funda-mentalist	−2.810	−.095	.993	8.01*
Nondenomination-al/nonreligious	3.273	.060	1.514	4.67*
Mother's religiosity	−0.969	−.046	.584	2.76
Intercept	87.79299	R^2 = 23%	N = 1102	

talist, but also on every measure of socioeconomic status black fundamentalists are more disadvantaged than their white co-religionists. Indeed, as was shown earlier, neither a Baptist nor a Catholic background exerts any independent effect on white children's IQ scores once parents' education, occupational status, and demographic origins are taken into account; this is an indication that the lower socioeconomic status of white Baptists and Catholics "explains" why white children from these groups average lower IQ scores than children from other religious backgrounds. But in the case of blacks, socioeconomic variables do not "explain" the negative effect of a Baptist/fundamentalist religious background on children's IQ, since it exerts a significant effect net of SES variables and increases the variance accounted for in black IQ scores. Thus, there appear to be complex higher-order interactions between race, SES, fundamentalism, and IQ which are beyond my limited powers of statistical analysis to unravel. What seems clear, however, is that black fundamentalism, over and above its many correlates of disadvantaged origin and current socioeconomic status, is a significant source of disparity between black and white children in the development of intellectual competence, in ways that still remain to be analyzed. Furthermore, mother's religiosity as a correlate of race and of fundamentalism is a variable that merits further examination, because along with fundamentalism it evidently registers as a "race effect" in comparisons of black and white children, but it is clearly a variable that is analytically and empirically distinct from race.

The foregoing discussion has concentrated on the effects of fundamentalism because it represents the denominations with the largest proportion of adherents in the black sample. But the reader will remember that children of nondenominational/nonreligious mothers score significantly higher than other children even when the other variables in the equation are taken into account, and this is true for the sample as a whole as well as for each race taken separately. While numerically children from nondenominational homes are a small subgroup in each race, particularly among blacks, they are interesting because they constitute the polar opposite, so to speak, of the fundamentalists, in the case of blacks, and in the case of whites of fundamentalists and Catholics, in all their social characteristics. While the Fundamentalist and the nonreligious mothers each exhibit high-status consistency, the former are consistently lowest on all measures in both races, particularly among blacks, whereas the nondenominational/nonreligious group is consistently the highest in both races. Thus, one can think of black Baptists and other fundamentalists as embodying a cumulative set of disadvantages. In this group are found the poorest, the least educated, the most removed from middle-class influences, and the most isolated from egalitarian contacts with whites. While nonreligious blacks are not as advantaged as their white counterparts, they are the most advantaged relative to other black religious groups on all measures of current socioeconomic status.

In the analysis of the antecedents of IQ for the whole sample and for blacks, the negative effect of fundamentalism is stronger than the positive one of nondenominationalism. But in the analysis of the antecedents of scholastic achievement, to which I now turn, their relative importance as predictors is reversed.

Race, Religion, and Socioeconomic Status as Predictors of Achievement Test Scores

When each race is analyzed separately, using the same components of socioeconomic status as in the previous chapter but with religion added to the equation, the variance accounted for in white children's achievement scores is increased by 1 percent; in black children's scores the variance explained is increased by 2 percent.

Mother's social milieu continues to be the strongest predictor of black children's achievement (beta = .23), followed by parents' education (beta = .17). Independently of these effects and of the weak effect of occupational status (beta = .08), children of nonreligious mothers (beta = .13) and High Protestant mothers (beta = .08) average higher scores than other black children. Taken together, this set of variables accounts for 23 percent of the variance in black children's achievement scores. But when IQ scores are included in the equation (beta = .49), the effects of a High Protestant background on achievement disappear, as Table 3-8 (top) shows, while the benefits of a nonreligious background are sustained (beta = .07) net of the stronger effects of parents' education (beta = .15) and mother's social milieu (beta = .14).

With respect to white children's achievement scores, parents' education remains the strongest predictor (beta = .24) followed by mother's social milieu (beta = .16) and occupational status (beta = .13). Net of these effects, just as in the case of blacks, children of nonreligious mothers average higher scores (beta = .10).[10] Taken together, the above set of variables account for 21 percent of the variance in white children's achievement scores.

Table 3-8 (bottom) shows that even with IQ in the equation (beta = .48), parents' education (beta = .17), mother's social milieu (beta = .12), and a nonreligious background (beta = .07) each continue to exert significant effects on white children's achievement.[11] These variables together account for 39 percent of the variance on white children's achievement, which is slightly less than the 42 percent that is accounted for in the achievement scores of black children's by SES and religious variables. The net effects of IQ and social milieu on achievement scores are only slightly stronger among blacks than among whites. On the other hand, the effect of parents' education is slightly stronger among whites. But the net advantage of a nonreligious background for scholastic achievement is the same for both races.

The addition of mother's religion and religiosity to SES and origin variables does not increase the amount of variance explained in achievement scores of the whole sample, which remains 40 percent, but as in the case of IQ scores it seems to reduce the net effect of race. The strongest predictor of achievement is the composite measure of SES (beta = .37)[12] followed by race (beta = .26). Smaller albeit still significant contributions to raising achieve-

TABLE 3-8. Regression of Black and White Children's Achievement Scores on SES Components, Origins, Religion, Exposure to Whites, and IQ

Variable	Blacks			
	B	Beta	Standard Error	F
IQ	.064	.489	.004	205.94*
Parents' education	.185	.154	.048	14.97*
Social milieu	.219	.141	.063	12.11*
Nondenominational/nonreligious	.707	.073	.317	4.97*
Intercept	−3.43066	R^2 = 42%		N = 579

Variable	Whites			
	B	Beta	Standard Error	F
IQ	.062	.473	.005	168.10*
Parents' education	.229	.174	.072	9.88*
Social milieu	.188	.125	.082	5.25*
Nondenominational/nonreligious	.404	.072	.201	4.05*
Demographic origins	−.080	−.068	.042	3.65
Intercept	−1.93390	R^2 = 39%		N = 523

TABLE 3-9. Whole Sample: Regression of Achievement Scores on SES, Origins, Mother's Religion, Religiosity, and Children's IQ Scores

Variable	Raw Regression Coefficient	Standardized Coefficient	Standard Error	F-Value
IQ Score	.063	.445	.003	373.67*
SES	.028	.255	.003	94.22*
Race	.843	.207	.100	70.82*
Nondenominational/ nonreligious	.416	.054	.168	6.11*
Mother's religiosity	−.110	−.037	.063	3.03
Jewish	−.246	−.036	.155	2.52
Intercept	−3.45044	$R^2 = 55\%$	N = 1102	

ment are made by a nondenominational/nonreligious background (beta = .09), whereas mother's religiosity reduces achievement (beta = −.05). Although fundamentalism enters the equation, it does not increase significantly the variance explained by the preceding four variables.

With the religion variables taken into account, the disparity in achievement scores between white and black children is reduced from 1.3 stanines to about 1 stanine.

The mean difference between the races in achievement is further reduced, to about four-fifths of a stanine, when children's IQ is included in the equation. The effects of the other variables in the equation are also reduced. Thus, as Table 3-9 shows, IQ scores are by far the strongest predictor of achievement (beta = .45). The effect of SES is reduced (beta = .26) along with those of race (beta = .21) and a nondenominational background (beta = .05), and the effect of mother's religiosity, while still negative (beta = −.04), does not significantly increase the variance explained in achievement scores. With IQ scores included as a variable along with the other variables in the equation, Jewish children tend to underachieve relative to non-Jews, although not to a degree sufficient to increase the variance explained in the whole sample.[13]

Summary

The results of the regression analyses reported in the foregoing pages provide support for the hypothesis that not only socioeconomic differences but also differences in the religious composition and religiosity of the two races contribute to the disparity in the development of intellectual and scholastic competence in black and white children. The addition of religious variables to measures of socioeconomic status increases the variance explained in black children's IQ scores from 14 percent to 16 percent but does not increase significantly the variance explained in white children's scores, which remains 12 percent. Thus, the initial observed difference of 10 IQ points between the races is reduced to approximately 6 points by taking into account several components of socioeconomic status and is further reduced to approximately 4 points when differences in the religious composition of the two races are taken into account.

The environmental deficits of children born to and reared by black Baptist and other fundamentalist mothers appear to be of a cumulative nature. As a consequence of their largely southern rural and extremely low socioeconomic origins, they have the lowest educational and occupational attainment, they have been and continue to be the most removed from middle-class social influences within their own race, and they appear to be the farthest removed from the mainstream middle-class culture and from the processes of rapid modernization that have taken place in every realm of economic and social life since World War II. In all these respects black Baptists and other fundamentalist families are more deprived than either white Baptists or Catholics. Although the latter groups as a rule are less advantaged than other whites, they are usually more advantaged on every score (including the fact that they are white) than black families who continue their adherence to a fundamentalist creed and to traditions of child rearing that inhibit the development of intellectual competence in children.

The addition of religious variables to measures of socioeconomic status and IQ does not increase the variance explained in achievement scores of either black or white children, which remains 42 percent and 39 percent, respectively, for each race, and 55 percent for the races combined. But taking religious background into account does reduce the weight of race as a predictor and diminishes slightly the residual difference in mean achievement scores between black and white children from about 1 stanine to about four-fifths of a stanine. A fundamentalist background has a negative effect on black children's IQ scores, but no independent effects on achievement scores are observed once IQ scores are taken into account. A nondenominational background, in contrast, significantly benefits achievement test performance of black and white children independent of its contribution to performance on IQ tests. Just as the cumulative deficits of a black fundamentalist home constitute an impediment to the development of intellectual competence, so the cumulative benefits of high educational and occupational attainment and strong exposure to middle-class, mainstream secular culture seem to promote enduring scholastic motivation and ability of children in both races. A further explication of how and why religious background exerts the above effects will be reserved for later chapters.

The next chapter will identify selected measures of family structure and extrafamilial roles of mothers that further explain the social sources of differences in intellectual competence between black and white children.

Notes

1. The first and last time that the U.S. Census Bureau collected data on religious affiliation, on a national subsample of 25,000 cases, was in 1958. Results, not controlled for race, show that at that time 66 percent of the American population were Protestant, 26 percent Catholic, 3 percent Jewish, 1 percent other non-Christian, and about 3 percent had no religious affiliation. Among Protestants, 20 percent were Baptist, 14 percent Lutheran, 6 percent Presbyterian, and 20 percent Episcopalian, Congregational, or other Protestant.

   For my sample as a *whole*, 70 percent are Protestant, 12 percent Catholic, 10 percent Jewish, and 8 percent nonreligious. Among Protestants, 57 percent are Baptist or other fundamentalist as against 20 percent in the census sample; 26 percent are Methodist or Lutheran, and 17 percent are high Protestant as against 21 percent and 17 percent respectively in the census sample. The very large overrepresentation of Baptists in my sample is, of course, a function of the fact that over half the women sampled are black. Since race and religion are both controlled in my multivariate analyses, however, the significance of these biases can be assessed.

2. The overrepresentation of Jewish respondents occurred by design in order to ensure a sufficient number of cases to test certain hypotheses formulated in an earlier article (Blau, 1967). The underrepresentation of Catholics arises from the fact that the white working-class population is underrepresented in the sample.

3. The proportion of Baptists and other fundamentalists in my sample is very close to 67 percent, which was the proportion of Baptists among blacks in the nation as a whole in 1936. At that time there were only 5.5 million blacks in the United States, but they are reported to have constituted 10 percent of the country's entire church membership (Gaustad, 1962).

4. Evidence that this indeed is the case is that when SES is covaried in an analysis of covariance, which entails also a statistical adjustment for unequal cell sizes, the religious effect is significant in both races (see Table 3-4).

5. Thus, in the black middle class only 12 percent are Episcopalian, Presbyterian, or Congregationalist; and in the white working class these high Protestants constitute 11 percent. Nondenominational women constitute an even smaller fraction of these two strata, amounting to 6 percent of the black middle-class sample and only 3 percent of the white working-class sample; adding the 4 percent of Jews in the latter stratum makes a total of only 7 percent who did not identify themselves as either Protestant or Catholic.

6. The irony, of course, is that traditionally fundamentalist Protestants have been most strongly anti-Catholic.

7. A slightly stronger negative correlation is observed between a Catholic background and white children's IQ and achievement scores ($-.15$ and $-.17$, respectively) than between a Baptist background and children's test scores. The same pattern is observed with respect to origin and current status variables of white Catholics. Thus, among whites but not among blacks, Catholics are less advantaged than Baptist and other fundamentalists. The latter, however, are more apt than Catholic mothers to have grown up in smaller communities in the South.

8. White fundamentalists have markedly more rural demographic origins than white Catholics or mothers from other religious groups.

9. Since it has been determined how the four components of SES influence black and white scores and it was found that the predictive value of each component differs for the two races, a composite variable was formed, hereafter called SES, which is a weighted score based on parents' origin SES scores, occupational status, middle-class exposure scores, and average education of mothers' friends. The resulting weighted sum was then divided by four. This measure will be employed in all subsequent regression analyses based on the whole sample. There is reason to believe, as I shall show later in the analysis, that entering discrete variables that are substantially associated with each other into the regression raises the value of the coefficient for race, whereas when these same variables are combined into a single variable, the coefficient for race is substantially reduced.

10. With the above variables taken into account, the residual effect of parents' demographic origins is reversed but does not significantly increase the variance explained in white scores.

11. With the above variables taken into account, parents' demographic origins can be seen to create no advantage to white children's achievement.

12. In the previous chapter, it will be recalled that parents' education and mother's social milieu had the same net effect (beta = .19) and occupational status had a weaker but still significant effect (beta = .09) on achievement scores.

13. The white working class in my sample contains five Jewish children. While their mean IQ score is identical to that of middle-class Jewish children (110), their mean achievement score (4.7) is lower than that of children from other religious groups in the white sample. On the basis of so few cases it would be idle to attempt to do more than to make note of this finding.

CHAPTER 4

Family Structure and Mother's Extrafamilial Roles

This chapter focuses on four aspects of family structure associated with racial variations in children's intellectual and scholastic competence—mother's marital status, number of children, duration of employment, and organizational memberships. The problem is to determine, first, to what extent variations in intellectual and scholastic competence within each race and between the races are associated with such variables overall; second, to determine whether these relationships are uniform in different religious contexts, independently of social-structural factors with which each is confounded; and, finally, to determine what independent effects family structural variables exert on children's test scores.

For example, the higher incidence of black children reared in fatherless homes was singled out in the Moynihan Report (1967) as a major source of failure and pathology of successive generations of blacks. That conclusion provoked heated controversy and criticism but not much systematic research aimed at testing the validity of Moynihan's pronouncement.[1]

Moreover, the higher rates of father absence is only one of several differences in the modalities observed among black and white families. Black women, for example, have more children, as a rule, than white women, and their rates of maternal employment traditionally have exceeded those of whites. To identify such differences, however, is not sufficient for making causal imputations about any of their effects.

Consequently, the point of departure of the present analysis is an examination of the relationships among family variables and the extent of association of each with children's test scores in each race and among the religious groups that constitute each race.

Family Measures and Children's Test Scores

The first finding of importance is that the relationship between mother's marital status and children's IQ scores is weak relative to other variables considered in the present chapter. In both races, the mean IQ scores of children in homes with father present are slightly but not significantly higher than those of children from father-absent homes: 97 compared with 95 among black children and 107 compared to 104 among white children. However, black children in father-present homes average significantly higher achievement scores than those from father-absent homes (4.5 vs. 4.0). Among whites, in contrast, the average scores of the corresponding two groups are identical (6.4).

The number of children in the family bears a much stronger relationship to children's IQ and achievement scores than does mother's marital status, particularly in the case of blacks. There is a 10-point difference in the mean IQ scores of black children in homes with one or two children compared with those with five or more children (102 vs. 92), a magnitude of difference as large as that found between the two races in my sample. The corresponding difference in scores among whites is 7 points: 109 as compared to 102.[2] A similar pattern of differences in achievement scores is found within and between the races. The mean achievement scores of black children from families with one or two children is 5.1 compared to 3.9 among children from families with five or more children. The corresponding scores for white children are 6.6 and 5.8. Thus, black children's IQ and achievement test scores vary more markedly with family size than white children's scores.[3]

The number of years that mothers were employed outside the home since the study child's birth is differently related to intellectual and scholastic competence in the two races. Black children whose mothers have never worked outside the home during their child's lifetime average lower IQ scores than those whose mothers have worked from one to four years (93 vs. 96), and the latter average a lower score than children of mothers employed five years or longer (99). In contrast, white children whose mothers have not worked since their birth average slightly but not significantly higher IQ scores than children of mothers who had worked from one to four years or five years or longer (109 vs. 106).[4] Virtually no differences are noted with respect to achievement scores, an indication that for white children the initial slight disparity in IQ scores has no lingering effects on scholastic motivation or ability. In the case of black children, the initial advantage in IQ test performance of children of mothers with five or more years in the labor force *is* sustained, and their mean achievement scores are significantly higher (4.6) than those of children whose mothers have been full-time homemakers during all of their child's lifetime (4.0) or for part of it (4.3).

That maternal employment appears to benefit the intellectual development of black children but not of white children may simply be a function of differences in the relationship between socioeconomic status and mother's labor-force participation in the two races. For in the case of black women, there is a significant monotonic increase in socioeconomic status with average length of employment, whereas white women at the middle SES level exhibit longer labor-force participation than mothers of either low or high socioeconomic status.[5]

But is it also possible that the work role enables mothers to become involved in networks of information and influence which bring them into closer touch with the mainstream culture and social institutions and thereby enhances their knowledge about the opportunity structure and modern approaches to socializing children for achievement in an advanced industrial society. Such knowledge is less accessible to mothers who are solely homemakers in a disadvantaged minority group. Deprived of such inputs, the latter could be expected to adhere to modes of socializing children traditional to the poorer strata of the rural South. In short, I am suggesting that the world of gainful employment represents a vehicle of modernization for black women over and above that afforded by formal educational attainment in a society that is still characterized by segregated neighborhoods, segregated schools, segregated churches, and segregated social networks.

Intercorrelations Among Family Measures in the Two Races

A comparison of the intercorrelations among the four variables introduced in this chapter reveals a number of differences between the two races. Table 4-1 shows, for example, that the only variables associated to the same degree in the two races are marital status and mother's organizational affiliations (r = .17). In both races, married mothers are more inclined than those without husbands to belong to voluntary associations, probably primarily because in two-parent families fathers can look after the children when mothers attend meetings, whereas in one-parent families arrangements for the presence of a surrogate adult are more problematic. With respect to other relationships, a number of differences are observed. The negative relationship between marital status and years of employment is

TABLE 4-1. Intercorrelations of Marital Status, Years of Employment, Family Size, and Organization Memberships with Children's Test Scores among Blacks and Whites

		1	2	3	4
1. Marital status*	black	—			
	white	—			
2. Mother's years employed	black	−.11	—		
	white	−.18	—		
3. Number of children in family	black	−.00	−.31	—	
	white	.08	−.07	—	
4. Mother's organizational membership	black	.17	.12	−.13	—
	white	.17	−.01	−.01	—
5. Children's IQ score	black	.06	.20	−.28	.21
	white	.07	−.06	−.13	.13
6. Children's achievement score	black	.11	.14	−.24	.19
	white	−.01	−.10	−.14	.17

*Marital status is coded 1 = not married and 2 = married.

more pronounced among whites (−.18) than among blacks (−.11), a reflection of the higher rates of labor-force participation among married black than among married white mothers in the sample[6] as well as in the population as a whole.[7]

Participation in voluntary associations is another means of broadening the informational and social nexus of influence to which mothers have access, whether they are black or white. In both races, children's mean IQ and achievement scores rise with the extent of mother's organizational affiliations, but the association of children's IQ scores with mother's organizational memberships is somewhat stronger among blacks (r = .21) than among whites (r = .13). The association between mother's organizational memberships and achievement scores is very similar for blacks (r = .19) and for whites (r = .17).

A much more pronounced negative association is observed between mother's years of employment and family size among blacks (−.31) than among whites (−.07), an indication that opportunities for and commitment to gainful employment are stronger deterrents to fertility in the case of black mothers than white ones,[8] or, alternatively, that higher fertility operates as a stronger deterrent to employment in the case of black mothers than in the case of white mothers.

Mother's tenure in the labor force shows a positive although weak association with organizational memberships among blacks (.12), but no such association is found among white women (−.01). A similar association between family size and organizational participation, but in the opposite direction, is observed among black mothers (−.13) but not among white mothers (−.01). Among black mothers, in short, participation in extrafamilial roles, such as employment or voluntary associations, operates to reduce the traditionally higher fertility of black women as compared with whites, the variable of family structure that appears to be the strongest negative correlate of IQ and achievement among black children.[9]

It is worth noting, in the present context, that family size among black mothers is negatively associated with extent of exposure to whites (−.24), and the latter variable is positively associated with years of labor-force participation (.28) and with organizational memberships (.26).[10] This pattern of relationships suggests that gainful employment outside the home often provides black women with some opportunities for interaction with whites and exposure to the mainstream urban pattern of smaller families. These factors serve to counteract the tradition of higher fertility in the black family of the rural South[11] and also serve to promote more enlightened modes of socializing children, as will be shown later in the analysis.

Socioeconomic Status, Family Structure, and Extrafamilial Participation

To be sure, mother's participation in optional roles outside the family and mother's fertility are also influenced by socioeconomic variables in both races, but not always to the same degree. Among blacks, but not among whites, weak positive associations (.1) are observed between marital status and respondents' and husbands' education, middle-class exposure, and average education of mother's friends. The association of family size with SES measures is stronger in both races, but especially among blacks, as Table 4-2 shows. For example, the association between family size and mother's edu-

T A B L E 4 - 2 . Correlations of SES Components with Marital Status, Family Size, Years Employed, and Organization Memberships

Measures of Current Status and Social Milieu	Race	Marital Status	Mother's Years of Employment	Number of Children	Mother's Organization Memberships
Mother's education	black	.09*	.28	−.35	.43
	white	−.04	.07	−.26	.31
Father's education	black	.08*	.20	−.25	.32
	white	−.04	−.03	−.22	.30
Occupational status	black	.00	.23	−.26	.31
	white	−.04	.06	−.23	.32
Middle-class expo-	black	.10*	.22	−.25	.32
sure score	white	−.02	−.03	−.17	.28
Average education	black	.14*	.22	−.32	.42
of mother's friends	white	−.04	.09	−.20	.27

cational attainment is −.35 among blacks compared with −.26 among whites. Similarly, the association of family size with average education of mother's friends is −.32 among blacks and −.20 among whites. The differences between the races in the magnitude of correlations of family size with the other three SES measures are smaller, but in all three cases they are slightly stronger for blacks than for whites. A similar pattern of differences is found between the races with respect to correlations between SES measures and mother's organizational participation. The latter varies with mother's educational attainment and, in particular, average education of friends, but more among blacks (.4) than among whites (.3). In both races, mother's organizational participation varies somewhat more with SES measures than family size does.

The most pronounced difference between the races is in the association of mother's years of labor force participation and SES measures; an association of .3, for example, is found with black mother's educational attainment, compared with .1 among white mothers. Similarly, a .2 correlation occurs between black mother's labor-force tenure and other SES measures compared to .1 or less among white mothers.

Marital status of mothers varies by race but not by social class within each race. Thus, the proportion of white mothers who are married and living with their spouses is 92 percent in the middle class and 93 percent in the working class. These proportions are considerably lower, though still high, in the case of black mothers: 73 percent in the black middle class and 72 percent in the working class.

With respect to family size, variations by race *and* class occur. Black working-class mothers average 5 children; black middle-class and white working-class women average 4 children; and white middle-class women average three children. The only blacks and whites in the sample who exhibit parity in family size are college-educated women.

With respect to mother's employment status at the time of the interview in 1968 (as distinguished from duration of employment), the proportion of working mothers in my sample was highest in the black middle class (73 percent), compared with 42 percent in the black working class, 40 percent in the white middle class, and 23 percent in the white working class.

In both races, children in father-absent families average lower IQ scores than children from father-present homes in all except one religious subgroup, as Table 4-3 shows.

The magnitude of score differences among blacks is very slight in three religious groups—Baptists, Methodists, and Catholics (1 or 2 points). But among High Protestant and nondenominational blacks, scores of children in father-absent homes are considerably lower (6 and 9 points, respectively) than those of children in two-parent families.

Among whites, children in father-absent homes average from 3 to 6 points lower on IQ scores except among Catholics, where the mean score of

TABLE 4-3. Mean IQ Scores by Race, Religion, and Marital Status

Religion	Race	Marital Status: *Not Married*	*N*	*Married*	*N*	Percentage Married
Baptist/other fundamentalist	black	93	(105)	95	(262)	71
	white	97	(4)	103	(60)	94
Methodist/Lutheran	black	99	(29)	100	(83)	74
	white	100	(5)	105	(80)	94
High Protestant	black	99	(11)	105	(31)	74
	white	107	(16)	110	(75)	82
Catholic	black	100	(9)	101	(28)	76
	white	106	(5)	102	(90)	95
Nondenominational	black	100	(5)	109	(12)	71
Nonreligious	white	108	(7)	114	(60)	90
Jewish	black	—	—	—	—	—
	white	107	(4)	110	(105)	96

children in father-absent families is four points higher (106) than in father-present families (102).[12]

A comparison of IQ scores of black children without fathers in the home shows very little variation except for children of black Baptist or other fundamentalist mothers, who average lower scores (93) than other black children in father-absent homes (99–100). Among whites, children of Baptists and Methodists in father-absent homes also average lower IQ scores than white children from other religious backgrounds. As Table 4-3 shows, children in father-absent Baptist homes average 97 compared with 103 in father-present homes. The corresponding scores among Methodists are 100 and 105. But the proportion of Baptist and Methodist white children in father-absent homes is very small (6 percent in each group) compared with that of their black co-reco-religionists (29 percent and 26 percent, respectively). However, the average scores of black Baptist and Methodist children in intact homes are hardly any higher, which suggests that in these two groups, which constitute the largest proportion of the black sample (83 percent), father absence is not a significant factor in the development of intellectual competence. In contrast, as noted, black children from High Protestant and nondenominational backgrounds in father-present homes average 6 and 9 points higher scores, respectively, than those in father-absent homes, an indication that father absence represents a greater deprivation of intellectual stimulation in cases where the father is better educated than where he has had limited schooling. The pattern of differences with respect to the latter two black groups is similar to that found in all white groups except Catholics.

The differences in mean IQ scores by religious background are more pronounced among black children in two-parent families. In this group, children of nondenominational mothers score highest and average virtually the same scores as white High Protestant and Jewish children, whose scores are exceeded only by white nondenominational children.

Black and white Catholic children in father-present families average virtually the same IQ scores, but Catholics represent a considerably larger proportion of the white sample than of the black sample. Conversely, mean IQ differences between the races are most pronounced among married Baptists/fundamentalists, and the latter constitute a much larger proportion of the black than of the white sample.

Comparisons within each religious grouping in the two races, shown in Table 4-4, help to further explicate the finding that black children in two-parent families average higher achievement scores than those from father-absent homes, but no such differences were observed with respect to white children.

Among white Baptists and Methodists, children in two-parent families average higher achievement scores than those in father-absent homes, but the latter amount to a very small number of cases among the white sample, as Table 4-4 shows. In all other white religious groups, there is virtually no difference in the mean achievement scores of children in one- and two-parent families, with the exception of the Jews and Catholics, among whom the children in father-absent homes average higher scores than their co-religionists in two-parent families. However, in both these groups, the proportion of one-parent families is very small. The different directions of the

TABLE 4-4. **Mean Achievement Scores by Race, Religion, and Marital Status**

Religion	Race	Marital Status			
		Not Married	N	Married	N
Baptist/other	black	3.7	(105)	4.1	(262)
fundamentalist	white	4.4	(4)	5.9	(60)
Methodist/	black	4.7	(29)	4.8	(83)
Lutheran	white	5.4	(5)	6.2	(80)
High Protestant	black	4.3	(11)	5.7	(31)
	white	6.7	(16)	6.6	(75)
Catholic	black	5.0	(9)	4.7	(28)
	white	6.1	(5)	5.7	(90)
Nondenominational	black	5.5	(5)	6.7	(12)
Nonreligious	white	7.5	(7)	7.4	(60)
Jewish	black	—	—	—	—
	white	7.3	(4)	6.6	(105)

differences in achievement scores according to marital status among the Jews and Catholics, on the one hand, and the Baptists and Methodists, on the other, serve to cancel out effects of marital status on achievement among whites, at least on the univariate level of analysis currently being discussed.

Among blacks in all groups except Catholics, children in two-parent families tend to average higher achievement scores than those in father-absent homes. Pronounced differences averaging more than one stanine are found in only two groups: High Protestant and nondenominational children, the same two groups in which IQ differences by mother's marital status also are most pronounced. In these two groups the most pronounced difference between the races is found in father-absent families. Among High Protestants in one-parent homes, white children average 2.4 stanines higher than black children, and among children of nondenominational mothers there is a difference of 2.0 stanines between the races. In two-parent homes, the differences between black and white High Protestants and nondenominational children amount to less than one stanine.

Children of nondenominational mothers average higher achievement scores than other black children in one-parent families. They score a stanine higher than black children of High Protestant mothers in the same marital situation and almost two stanines higher than the children of black Baptist mothers without husbands, who average the lowest scores in the entire sample.

Race, Religion, Family Size, and Test Scores

A more pronounced association persists between family size and children's IQ test scores than between any other family variables, especially among blacks in different religious groups.

The proclivity toward large families varies with mother's race and religion, as Table 4-5 shows. Forty-six percent of black Baptist mothers have five or more children; a smaller proportion (30 percent) of their white co-religionists and black Methodists (29 percent) have large families. Fewer black and white Catholics (approximately 25 percent) and still fewer white Methodists and black and white High Protestants (16–17 percent) have large families. Among nondenominational black and white mothers and Jewish mothers, large families are very rare.[13]

Among all black Protestant groups, a monotonic decline in mean IQ scores occurs as the number of children in the family rises (Table 4-5). Among black Catholics there is virtually no variation in IQ scores with family size. Only among nondenominational mothers is the mean score of children from medium-sized families higher (115) than that of children from small families (107). These exceptions to the overall pattern, however, involve a very small proportion of the black sample relative to the very large propor-

T A B L E 4 - 5 . Mean IQ Scores by Race, Religion, and Number of Children

Religion	Race	Number of Children						Percentage Large Families
		1–2	N	3–4	N	5 or More	N	
Baptist/other	black	99	(68)	95	(130)	92	(169)	46
fundamentalist	white	99	(13)	107	(32)	99	(19)	30
Methodist/	black	104	(40)	101	(40)	93	(32)	29
Lutheran	white	103	(25)	107	(46)	102	(14)	16
High Protestant	black	106	(17)	102	(18)	99	(7)	17
	white	111	(23)	108	(53)	111	(15)	16
Catholic	black	100	(8)	101	(21)	100	(8)	22
	white	105	(24)	103	(50)	99	(21)	25
Nondenominational/	black	107	(10)	115	(6)	97	(1)	6
nonreligious	white	113	(24)	113	(37)	104	(6)	9
Jewish	black	—	—	—	—	—	—	—
	white	112	(45)	109	(61)	119	(3)	3

tion that exhibits the dominant pattern, and they occur in the only two black religious groups which are not predominantly of lower SES.

Among whites, for the most part, children from medium-sized families average IQ scores at least as high as those from small families. A monotonic decline in IQ scores occurs with rising family size only among Catholics, the group with the largest proportion of working-class respondents in the white sample.

It is interesting to note that there is no difference in mean IQ scores between black and white Baptist children and virtually none between black and white Methodist children in *small* families. But the difference between the races among Baptists with medium-sized families is very large (12 points), which suggests that even an increment of one or two children in fundamentalist families disadvantages the black child considerably relative to the white child of similar religious background. This is of some significance since a much larger proportion of black than white children have Baptist or other fundamentalist mothers. Among Methodists and High Protestants with medium-sized families, white children's mean IQ score is 6 points higher than that of black children. But there is virtually no racial difference in mean IQ scores among Catholics and children of nondenominational mothers with medium-sized families. Among children in large families, virtually no racial differences in IQ are observed among Catholics. But in all other religious groups, White children's mean IQ scores exceed those of black children by as much as 12 points among High Protestants, 9 points among Methodists, and 7 points among Baptists and nondenominational children.[14]

Mother's Extrafamilial Roles and Children's Test Scores in Various Religious Contexts

Among blacks in all religious groups, with one exception, a monotonic rise in mean IQ scores occurs with mother's years of employment, as Table 4-6 shows.[15]

Among whites no single pattern prevails. There is a slight tendency for IQ scores to decline with an increment of years of mother's employment among Baptist and Catholics, but this pattern is pronounced among High Protestants. Children of High Protestant full-time homemakers have a markedly higher mean IQ score than those whose mothers worked for a shorter or longer period. Among nondenominational and Jewish whites, in contrast, children of mothers with extended labor-force participation average the highest IQ scores in their respective groups.[16]

Children's test scores show no linear relationship to mother's organizational memberships when religion is controlled, except among Baptists and other fundamentalists, as Table 4-7 shows. In both races, there is a monotonic rise in IQ scores of Baptist children as mother's organizational participation rises. The same pattern is observed among children of white High Protestant mothers. In other groups, children of mothers with no organizational ties score about as high as co-religionists whose mothers belong to several organizations. Black nondenominational children whose mothers belong to no organizations average slightly higher scores than children of mothers with organizational ties.

The foregoing discussion suggests that the relationships between chil-

TABLE 4-6. Mean IQ Scores by Race, Religion, and Mother's Years of Employment Since Child's Birth

Religion	Race	None		1–4 Years			5 Years or More		
		IQ	N	Percent	IQ	N	IQ	N	Percent
Baptist/other	black	92	(95)	26	93	(114)	96	(158)	43
fundamentalist	white	103	(31)	48	102	(16)	101	(17)	27
Methodist/	black	94	(19)	17	100	(34)	101	(59)	17
Lutheran	white	105	(38)	45	106	(28)	102	(19)	22
High Protestant	black	93	(3)	7	103	(16)	104	(23)	55
	white	117	(41)	45	104	(29)	101	(21)	23
Catholic	black	96	(6)	16	101	(7)	102	(24)	65
	white	103	(40)	47	102	(39)	101	(16)	19
Nondenominational/	black	107	(2)	12	112	(5)	108	(10)	59
nonreligious	white	112	(24)	36	112	(25)	114	(18)	27
Jewish	black	—	—	—	—	—	—	—	—
	white	110	(58)	53	109	(33)	113	(18)	17

TABLE 4-7. Mean IQ Score by Race, Religion, and Mother's Organizational Participation

Religion	Race	None	N	One Organization	N	Two or More Organizations	N
Baptist/other	black	91	(98)	94	(132)	96	(137)
fundamentalist	white	97	(20)	103	(20)	106	(24)
Methodist/	black	100	(20)	97	(27)	101	(65)
Lutheran	white	102	(13)	99	(24)	109	(48)
High Protestant	black	104	(1)	98	(9)	105	(32)
	white	105	(16)	109	(20)	110	(55)
Catholic	black	102	(5)	100	(14)	101	(18)
	white	102	(25)	102	(29)	103	(41)
Nondenominational/	black	111	(5)	108	(4)	108	(8)
nonreligious	white	114	(16)	108	(18)	114	(33)
Jewish	black	—	—	—	—	—	—
	white	108	(13)	112	(20)	110	(76)

dren's test scores and the four family-structure variables considered are not uniform but vary both with race and religious background.

Black children's test scores, for example, exhibit a stronger relationship to family size than do those of white children except among Catholics. In all black Protestant groups and among white Catholic children, there is a monotonic decline in IQ scores as family size rises, but virtually no score variations were found among black Catholics. Further, in all religious groups—black and white—children in families with five or more children averaged lower IQ scores than their counterparts in smaller families except among Jews, where the average score of the children in large families is higher than the average scores of children in small or medium-sized families.

Father absence, though more frequent in black families, does not appear to exert a significant detrimental effect on the intellectual competence of children in religious groups where father's educational attainment typically is low, such as among black Baptists and Methodists and among white Catholics. But in religious groups where fathers as a rule are well educated, as in the case of black High Protestants and nondenominational families of both races, children in two-parent families seem to average higher IQ scores than those in father-absent homes.

A monotonic rise in IQ scores of black children with mother's years of employment was observed in all religious groups except among children of nondenominational mothers, the best-educated mothers in my black sample. Among whites no single pattern prevails. Decrements in children's IQ scores with years of maternal employment were observed among children of white Baptist, Catholic, and especially High Protestant mothers. In contrast, children of nondenominational and Jewish mothers with extended years of employment exhibit higher scores than other children from the same religious background.[17]

Finally, no linear relationships are found between children's IQ scores and mother's organization memberships except among Baptists and other fundamentalists in both races and among white High Protestants.

Independent Effects of Family and Extrafamilial Variables: A Multivariate Analysis

The extent to which the familial and extrafamilial measures under discussion influence children's test scores independently of social-structural and religious variables can be ascertained only by performing new multivariate analyses in which family variables are added to the social-structural variables presented in previous chapters.

Addition of family measures to the equation increases the variance explained in black children's IQ scores by 2 percent compared with the model based only on SES and religious variables (A=5 , page 000). The two strongest predictors of black children's scores become socioeconomic status (beta = .16) and family size (beta = −.15). A fundamentalist background depresses scores (−.11) and a nondenominational background enhances them (.08). Mother's years of employment and organizational memberships have positive effects of about equal magnitude (beta = .08), while mother's religiosity has a negative effect (beta = −.08).[18] Together these variables account for 18 percent of the variance in black children's IQ scores.

Addition of the family-structure variables and sex of child also increases the variance explained in IQ scores of white children, but there are some interesting differences in the variables that enter the equation and in the direction of the effect of one variable on IQ scores (Table A-5, page 000).

Eight variables, including sex of the child, enter the white equation and account for 15 percent of the variance in white children's IQ scores. SES (beta = .21) has a considerably stronger effect than any other variable. Parents' demographic origin (i.e., being native-born and from a larger-sized community) has a net weight (beta = .13) similar to that of mother's years of employment (beta = −.12). But in contrast to its positive effect on black children's IQ, the latter variable is a negative predictor of white children's scores. Children of nonreligious mothers average higher scores than other white children (beta = .10), just as among blacks. Family size also has a negative but weaker effect on white children's scores (beta = −.09) than on black children's scores (beta = −.15).[19]

In the case of blacks, mother's marital status does not enter the equation, but among whites a two-parent family has a positive but weak effect (beta = .08). Children from a High Protestant background appear to sustain a slight advantage in IQ score net of the other variables (beta = .07). Each of the last three variables by itself does not significantly increase the variance explained, but together they do so.

It becomes increasingly evident that while there are some similarities between the races in the predictors of test performance, there are also differences of a complex nature. For example, SES is a stronger predictor of white children's IQ scores relative to other variables in the equation than of black children's scores. Conversely, family size is a stronger independent predictor of black children's scores, closely matching in strength the effect of SES. Having a Baptist or other fundamentalist background has a stronger zero-order association with IQ among blacks than among whites and a stronger zero-order association with southern rural origins among whites. Furthermore, among blacks the negative association of fundamentalism with IQ scores is considerably stronger than the association of IQ with demographic origins, whereas just the reverse is the case among whites. It is evident that these differences are reflected in the result of the regression analysis. Among blacks the negative effects of a fundamentalist background on children's IQ scores persist even after other variables that are confounded with fundamentalism are taken into account, but in the case of whites, it is not a fundamentalist background per se but the more rural southern background associated with that particular denominational affiliation that exerts a significant effect on white children's IQ.

In short, white fundamentalism has a less socially homogeneous character than black fundamentalism. It is not merely that black Baptists and other fundamentalists, as a rule, are of the lowest SES and have the lowest social-class origins, are more uniformly from the rural South and more religious, have the largest families, the lowest labor-force participation, less communal involvement outside their church, and less exposure to whites; the cumulation of disadvantages serve to isolate them from the mainstream secular urban culture and from the influences that promote socialization practices and forms of stimulation conducive to early intellectual growth. At this juncture of the analysis, merely the link between fundamentalism and IQ has been established and the fact that its negative effects among blacks persists even when SES and family factors are controlled for. The hypothesis that fundamentalism has negative effects on maternal strategies of socializing children still remains to be examined and tested. That task is reserved for the second part of this book.

The opposite effects of maternal employment on children's IQ scores in the two races, already discernible in the analyses presented earlier in the chapter, persist even when possible confounding variables are controlled. Apparently, the differences in the association between SES and length of tenure in the labor force in the two races and the considerably stronger depression of fertility that extended labor-force participation exerts on black compared with white women do not account for the opposite effects of this variable on IQ scores of children in the two races.[20]

One other important difference between the races is that net of the other variables in the structural model, sex of the child is a significant predictor of white but not of black children's IQ scores. Numerous studies which compare the abilities of boys and girls, based mostly on white samples, quite consistently report that girls score higher than boys on IQ tests (Maccoby and Jacklin, 1974), as is the case among whites in my sample. The mean score of white boys is 105 and that of white girls is 109. Among blacks the mean IQs of boys and girls are virtually the same (96 and 97, respectively).

Sex of the study child remains a significant independent predictor of white children's IQ scores (beta = .12) (A-5, page 234). However, the zero-order advantage of 4 points exhibited by white girls compared with boys is reduced to 3.3 points when other social and family structural variables are controlled.[21]

When the IQ scores of all children in the sample are regressed on SES, parents' origins, mother's religious affiliation and religiosity, family structure, and extrafamilial participation with race in the equation, eight variables account for 25 percent of the variance in IQ scores (Table A-5, page 234). SES exerts the strongest net effect (beta = .23), as is the case when the races are analyzed separately. Race and family size are weaker predictors (beta = .12). A fundamentalist background has a weak but significant negative effect (beta = −.08) and a nondenominational background exerts a weak positive one (beta = .07). Mother's religiosity also exerts a weak but significant negative effect (beta = −.06). Neither marital status nor mother's organizational memberships alone exerts significant effects, but together they add about 1 percent to the variance explained.

Addition of family structure measures, expecially family size, to SES and the religious variables increases the variance explained in IQ scores of the whole sample by 2 percent. It also has other interesting effects. For example, it reduces the effect of SES (beta = .23 compared with .29) and the effect of a fundamentalist background slightly (beta = −.08 compared with −.10) but hardly alters the weights of a nondenominational background (beta = .07 compared with .06) and of mother's religiosity (beta = −.06 compared with −.05).

Finally, inclusion of family variables in the model very slightly reduces the disparity in scores attributable to race (beta = .12 compared with .13). Without family variables the mean difference in IQ scores between the races net of other variables was shown in Chapter 3 to be 3.9 points. That difference is reduced to 3.5 points when family variables are included in the model. And the overall explained variance in IQ increases 2 percentage points, or 25 percent compared with 23 percent. Thus it is evident that both differences in religious affiliation and religiosity *and* differences in family structure are sources of observed differences in measured intelligence between the races net of the effects of socioeconomic status.

The fact that sex of child is a significant predictor only of white children's

IQ scores suggests an interaction between race and sex on IQ scores.[22] With the races combined, the beta weight of race is .12, and sex of child does not enter the equation.

However, when the IQ scores of each sex are separately regressed on the same set of variables (Table 4-8), the weight of race becomes slightly lower among boys (beta = .11) and even lower among girls (beta = .10). Trivial race differences in IQ remain within each sex: 2.9 IQ points among boys and 2.7 points among girls. Within each sex the residual difference between the races is less than the residual difference of 3.5 IQ points found between the races with the sexes combined. Moreover, it becomes evident (Table4-8)

T A B L E 4 - 8 . Regression: IQ Scores of Boys and Girls on Structural Model with Race in the Equation

Variables	Standardized Coefficients (F's in Parentheses)		Raw Coefficients (Standard Error in Parentheses)	
	Boys	Girls	Boys	Girls
SES	.168 (10.46)*	.307 (46.36)*	.127 (.039)	.243 (.036)
Parent's demographic origins	.074 (2.62)	—	.459 (.074)	—
Parent's origin family size	—	—	—	—
White exposure	—	—	—	—
Fundamentalist	—	−.106 (5.69)*	—	−3.174 (1.33)
High Protestant	—	.056 (2.24)	—	2.470 (1.649)
Catholic	—	—	—	—
Nondenominational	.128 (9.21)*	—	6.887 (2.269)	—
Jewish	.093 (4.29)*	—	4.208 (2.031)	—
Religiosity	−.116 (7.89)*	—	−2.341 (.834)	—
Number of children	−.097 (5.11)*	−.137 (13.22)*	−.641 (.284)	−.909 (.250)
Marital status	—	.083 (5.35)*	—	3.194 (1.380)
Years employed	—	—	—	—
Mother's organizations	—	—	—	—
Race	.113 (6.16)*	.102 (5.84)*	2.912 (1.173)	2.677 (1.108)
Intercept	96.65591	84.09265		
R² =	22%	29%		
N =	512	590		

*p < .05

that the nature and the weight of variables that predict IQ scores of boys and girls are not the same. Thus, SES is a considerably stronger predictor of girls' than of boys' IQ scores (beta = .31 vs. .17). Family size is a somewhat stronger negative predictor of girls' than of boys' scores (beta = −.14 vs. −.10). Only these variables and race are significant predictors of IQ scores of both sexes. Girls from father-present homes net higher scores (beta = .08) than girls from father-absent homes, and girls from a Baptist/fundamentalist background net significantly lower IQ scores (beta = −.11) than girls from other religious backgrounds. Conversely, sons of nondenominational (beta = .12) and Jewish mothers (beta = .09) net significantly higher scores than sons of mothers from other religious backgrounds. Mother's religiosity is a negative predictor only of boys' IQ scores and exerts no independent effect on girls' IQ scores. Thus, five variables explain 29 percent of the variance in girls' IQ scores, while six variables explain 22 percent of the variance in boys' scores. Finally, it appears that the greater prevalence among blacks of large families of low socioeconomic status, of Baptist/fundamentalist religious affiliation, and of father absence is a more significant source of disparity in the IQ scores of black relative to white girls than of boys in the two races, and probably serves to explain the larger zero-order difference in IQ scores found between girls than between boys. The high degree of religious homogeneity and religiosity among blacks appears to be a stronger source of disadvantage in the development of intellectual competence of black males relative to white males.

Effects of Sex, Religious Affiliation and Religiosity, Measures of Family Structure, and Mother's Extrafamilial Participation

Adding measures of family structure and mother's extrafamilial participation to the model based on SES and religious variables and IQ scores slightly increases the vairance explained in black children's achievement scores but does not improve the prediction of white children's achievement scores.

Table 4-9 shows that net of IQ and SES, the two strongest predictors of children's achievement scores in both races, father presence and mother's organizational participation, each exert a weak positive effect on black children's achievement test performance. Separately, neither variable significantly increases the variance explained, but together they raise the variance explained in black children's achievement scores by about 1 percent.[23] None of the family structure variables enters the white equation, as Table 4-9 shows.

With the races combined, mother's organizational memberships exerts a weak but significant positive effect (beta = .05) on achievement scores independent of IQ (beta = .44), SES (beta = .23), race (beta = .21), a nondenomi-

TABLE 4-9. Regression: Achievement Scores of Blacks, Whites, and Races Combined on Structural Model with IQ

Standardized Regression Coefficients (F's in Parentheses)

Independent Variables	Blacks	Whites	Races Combined
IQ	.482	.479	.442
	(200.35)*	(172.99)*	(368.75)*
SES	.229	.250	.229
	(36.22)*	(41.70)*	(65.34)*
Parent's demographic origin	—	−.081	—
		(4.94)*	
Parent's family size	—	—	—
White exposure [a]	—	—	—
Fundamentalist	—	—	—
High Protestant	—	—	—
Catholic	—	—	—
Nondenominational	.081	.071	.061
	(6.10)*	(3.99)*	(7.57)*
Jewish	—	—	−.039
			(2.95)
Religiosity	—	−.080	−.045
		(5.06)*	(4.30)*
Number of children	—	—	—
Marital status	.057	—	—
	(3.11)		
Years employed	—	—	—
Organizational memberships	.063	—	.054
	(3.00)		(5.69)*
Sex of child	—	—	—
Race	—	—	.213
			(74.35)*
Intercept	−3.46461	−0.87914	−3.34555
R^2 =	43%	39%	55%
N =	579	523	1102

*p < .05
[a] not included for whites and races combined

national background (beta = .06), and mother's religiosity (beta = .04). With these variables taken into account, the net difference in achievement scores of the two races amounts to slightly over four-fifths of a Stanine, compared with a zero-order difference of 2.04 stanines. All told, these variables account for 55 percent of the variance in achievement scores of children in the combined sample.

Table 4-10 shows some interesting differences in the number and weights of significant predictors of boys' and girls' achievement scores. IQ is a slightly stronger predictor of girls' scores (beta = .45) than of boys' scores (beta = .43). SES is also a somewhat stronger predictor of girls' than of boys' scores (beta = .27 vs. .23) as is race (beta = .22 vs. .17). Daughters of nondenominational mothers tend to net higher scores, and Jewish daughters tend to net lower scores relative to other girls; although neither effect alone is significant, together they increase the variance explained in girls' scores by about 1 percent.

In the case of boys, sons of nondenominational mothers net significantly higher scores (beta = .09) than other boys; sons of more religious mothers net significantly lower scores (beta = −.10); and sons of mothers with more extensive organizational participation net higher scores (beta = .07).

It is interesting that as in the case of IQ scores, the zero-order race difference in achievement scores is slightly higher among girls (2.11 stanines) than among boys (1.91 stanines).[24] With the full set of structural variables in

TABLE 4-10. Regression: Achievement Scores of Boys and Girls on Structural Model with Race and IQ in the Equation

Variables	Standardized Coefficients (F's in Parentheses)		Raw Coefficients (Standard Error in Parentheses)	
	Boys	Girls	Boys	Girls
IQ	.430	.445	.063	.061
	(164.76)*	(196.61)*	(.005)	(.004)
SES	.231	.271	.025	.030
	(34.51)*	(58.55)*	(.004)	(.004)
Parents' demographic origins	—	—	—	—
Parents' origin family size	—	—	—	—
White exposure	—	—	—	—
Fundamentalist	—	—	—	—
High Protestant	—	—	—	—
Catholic	—	—	—	—
Nondenominational	.085	.044	.664	.328
	(7.16)*	(2.21)	(.248)	(.221)
Jewish	—	−.055	—	−.381
		(3.31)		(.210)
Religiosity	−.095	—	−.282	—
	(9.07)*		(.094)	
Number of children	—	—	—	—
Marital status	—	—	—	—
Years employed	—	—	—	—
Mother's organizations	.074	—	.103	—
	(4.94)*		(.046)	
Race	.174	.224	.653	.809
	(25.98)*	(49.80)*	(.128)	(.115)
Intercept	−2.68876	−3.70048		
R² =	55%	56%		
N =	512	590		

*p < .05

the model, however, the net difference in achievement scores between black and white boys is reduced to about two-thirds of a stanine, compared with a residual difference of four-fifths of a stanine between black and white girls' scores. Thus, it appears that taking into account social-structural differences—socioeconomic status, religion, and family structure—serves to reduce the disparity in achievement test performance of black and white boys more than of black and white girls. The reasons for this will become apparent when we compare the strategies of socialization that black and white mothers employ in relation to sons and daughters.

Summary

The foregoing analyses mark the conclusion of the first part of the study, which compared the effects of several components of socioeconomic status, mother's religious affiliation and religiosity, family structure, mother's extrafamilial participation, and sex of child on black and white children's performance on IQ and achievement tests. The analysis made it evident that social-structure and family-structure measures explain more of the variance in black children's scores than in those of white children and that the predictors of children's test scores often differ in the two races. Thus, 14 percent of the variance in black children's IQ scores is accounted for by mother's current social milieu, parents' socioeconomic origins, and mother's exposure to whites. Although parents' education enters the black equation, it does not significantly increase the variance explained in black children's IQ scores net of the aforementioned variables. In contrast, parents' education is the strongest predictor of white children's IQ scores. Parents' demographic origins is a weaker but also significant predictor, but occupational status of the higher-ranking parent does not add significantly to the variance explained in white children's IQ scores, which amounts to 12 percent.

Religious variables increase the variance explained in black children's IQ scores to 16 percent. Children of Baptist/fundamentalist mothers average lower scores and children of nondenominational/nonreligious mothers average higher scores than other black children even when social and family structure variables are controlled. Mother's religiosity is also a weak negative predictor of black children's IQ scores. White children of nondenominational mothers also net higher IQ scores than other white children. It was shown that among whites, sex of child increases the variance explained in white scores to 15 percent. White girls net 3.3 points higher than white boys.

Family-structural variables increase the variance explained in IQ scores in both races, but the weight and direction of their effects differ in the two races. The number of children in the family is a strong predictor of black children's IQ scores, second only to socioeconomic status. The more siblings, the lower the IQ scores of black children are likely to be. In contrast, mother's tenure in the labor force is a positive predictor of black children's IQ scores, and mothers' organizational participation also has a slight but not significant positive effect.

In contrast to blacks, mother's extended labor-force participation among whites is a negative predictor of children's IQ scores. Family size is a negative predictor of white children's IQ scores but a weaker one than in the case of black children. White girls net significantly higher IQ scores than white boys, and adding sex of child to the equation increases the variance explained in white scores by 1 percent. While white children from two-parent families tend to net higher scores, this variable does not significantly increase the variance explained in white scores and it does not even enter the black equation.

With the races combined, number of children is the only family-structure variable that is a significant predictor of IQ scores. While its effect is considerably weaker than that of socioeconomic status, it exerts as much weight as race. The effect of father presence is no stronger than that of mother's organizational participation, and neither variable by itself significantly increases the variance explained in IQ scores of the combined sample.

When the full set of structural variables is taken into account, the net difference between the races is reduced to 3.5 IQ points. Evidence that even this difference is inflated by the presence of an interaction between race, sex, and IQ is provided when IQ scores of boys and girls are separately regressed on the structural variables; the net race difference then becomes 2.9 IQ points among boys and 2.7 points among girls. In both instances the mean difference between the races is less than the residual mean difference between the sexes among white children. That is, the structural model tested in the foregoing pages accounts for more of the observed variance between the races than between the sexes among white children.

The social structures in which white girls and boys are reared are not different, although some variables impact differently on the two sexes. But the social-structural contexts in which black and white children are reared differ markedly. These differences profoundly influence socialization processes, which, it will be shown presently, directly influence the development of intellectual competence among children in the two races.

Notes

1. Female-headed families have markedly lower incomes than male-headed families; female heads have lower educational and occupational attainment, a higher proportion of absence of any wage earners, and a higher proportion below the poverty level (Johnson, 1978; McEaddy, 1976). Results of studies of the effects of father absence that do not control for these variables are likely to be misleading.

2. A recent multivariate analysis of black and white children aged 3–5 located in urban and rural areas reports similar results. Father absence exerted no significant effects, but each additional sibling is associated with a significant reduction in children's PPVT scores (Liebowitz, 1977). A comprehensive review of research on the effects of father absence on school achievement, juvenile delinquency, and masculine identity (Herzog and Sudia, 1973) concludes that the behavioral and psychological effects imputed to father absence are much less uniform and less uniformly adverse than is widely assumed.

3. It is important to report that while the difference between the races in the proportions of small families is small (25 percent among blacks and 30 percent among whites), the proportion of children from homes with 3–4 children is considerably greater among whites (55 percent) than among blacks (37 percent), whereas the proportion of large families (5 or more children) is over twice as large among blacks as among whites (38 vs. 15 percent).

4. IQ scores of black children vary more with family size ($F = 28.10$) than do white children's scores ($F = 4.92$). A weaker relationship exists between IQ scores and mother's labor force participation in both races, but the relationship between IQ and mother's labor force participation is stronger among black children ($F = 12.05$) than among whites ($F = 2.39$).

5. The mean years of employment are 3.7, 4.6, and 6.9, respectively, for black low-, middle-, and high-SES mothers ($F = 24.88$); the corresponding figures for white mothers are 1.8, 2.9, and 2.2 ($F = 4.18$).

6. For example, at the time mothers were interviewed, the proportion employed in the black middle class was 73 percent, compared with 40 percent in the white middle class; in the working class the corresponding proportions were 40 percent and 23 percent. In the sample overall, 57 percent of black and 36 percent of white mothers were employed at the time they were interviewed.

7. In 1972, among father-present families, 51 percent of black children under age 18, compared with 37 percent of white children, had a mother in the labor force. Among families headed by women, in contrast, 55 percent of white children compared with 44 percent of black children had employed mothers (Young, 1973). Black mothers heading families are twice as likely as their white counterparts to have three or more children (McEaddy, 1976), and higher fertility depresses labor-force participation. Higher fertility is also associated with early first births. Twice the proportion of black women as compared with white women had a first birth by age 20, and early births adversely affect the educational and occupational attainment of women (Waite and Moore, 1978).

8. A comparison of the mean number of children according to the number of years worked shows very little variation among whites: 3.4, 3.3, and 3.1, respectively, among those who have not worked since child's birth, those who worked 1–4 years, and those who worked 5 years or longer. Among blacks, however, the corresponding differences are very pronounced: 5.5, 4.6, and 3.6 children ($F = 26.49$).

9. An equally plausible interpretation, of course, is that the higher fertility of black women (compounded by the higher rate of father absence) inhibits participation in extrafamilial roles to a greater degree than is the case among white women.

However, some evidence from a recent longitudinal study suggests that young women who planned to work were more often employed and had fewer children at the time of the follow-up study and that this relationship holds both for presently married and never-married women (Stolzenberg and Waite, 1975).

10. When black mother's family size is regressed on the above variables plus SES, religion, and parents' origin family size, white exposure operates to significantly reduce family size net of other variables in the equation.

11. A .2 association between family size and southern origins is found among black women (and also their husbands), but virtually no association is found between these variables among whites.

12. It should be noted, however, that the sample contains only five cases of white Catholic children from father-absent homes, and consequently, this deviation from the general pattern, while suggestive, may not be reliable. Nevertheless, it is noteworthy that Catholics are the only white group in which mothers' average educational attainment matches that of their husbands (5.0). In all other white groups, mothers average somewhat lower educational attainment than their spouses (Table 3-2). Further, white Catholic husbands average the lowest socioeconomic origins and the largest origin family size relative to other husbands in the white sample.

13. Indeed, only one black nondenominational mother and three Jewish ones have large families, and the latter group is the only one in the entire sample where the mean IQ of children in large families is higher than that of children in small families; but since the case base is so small, it can hardly be treated as a significant finding.

14. With a single exception, white children from all religious backgrounds average higher achievement scores than their black co-religionists with the same number of siblings. Among children in small families, race differences in scores as a rule are smaller (around 1 stanine) than in medium-sized families (around 1½–2 stanines) except among Catholics, where white children average only half a stanine higher than their black co-religionists. In large families, white children score about 1½ stanines higher than black children among Baptists, Methodists, and Catholics and about 1 stanine higher among High Protestants. Virtual parity in achievement scores is found only between white nondenominational children and the one black denominational child growing up in a large family.

15. The only deviation from this pattern is among the nondenominational group, where the highest score is exhibited by children whose mothers had been employed 1–4 years.

16. With respect to achievement scores, white High Protestant children of nonworking mothers maintain higher scores than their co-religionists whose mothers had worked for a shorter or longer period. But their achievement scores are no higher than the scores of children of nondenominational mothers, whatever their labor-force participation, nor of children of longer employed Jewish mothers.

In contrast to whites, the positive association between work tenure and achievement scores is unequivocal among blacks. Children whose mothers had stayed out of the labor force average lower scores than their co-religionists whose mothers had held jobs, except among nondenominational children, where the mean achievement score is higher (6.8) of those two children whose mothers had not worked, compared with children of mothers who had worked for a shorter (6.1) or longer (6.4) time.

17. Mothers in these three groups have the highest educational attainment and are more apt to be engaged in professional careers than other mothers in the sample.

18. The F value for religiosity is just short of being significant at the .05 level. Neither is mother's organizational participation significant, but together these variables increase the variance explained in black children's scores by 1 percent.

19. This disparity may be due to the fact that a much smaller proportion of white children come from families with 5 or more children and that among blacks even an increase of 2 or 3 siblings tends to lower IQ scoress, whereas this is less often the case in the white sample.

20. The results of an analysis of variance aimed at testing for interaction effects between race, sex, and SES indicate the presence of a significant interaction (F = 21.03) between race and SES on mother's tenure in the labor force, confirming the results of the univariate and regression analyses which show a linear relationship between SES and years in the labor force among blacks, while among whites the relationship is nonlinear.

21. It is interesting to note that the net 3.3-point IQ advantage of white girls relative to boys (beta = .115) is very similar to the 3.5 net advantage of whites relative to blacks (beta = .123).

22. An analysis of variance reveals that while there is no significant race-sex interaction on the univariate level, with other variables in the equation the multivariate F becomes significant (F = 4.56).

23. Without IQ in the equation, family size and marital status are significant predictors of black children's achievement scores, and mother's organizational participation approaches significance. The fact that family size no longer enters the equation when IQ is included indicates that it has no *direct* effect on achievement scores. The weights of marital status and mother's organizational affiliation also are reduced and that of SES is substantially reduced (from beta = .33 to .23).

24. White girls' mean achievement score is 6.53 compared with 4.38 among black girls. The corresponding zero-order scores among boys are 6.22 and 4.30, respectively, for whites and blacks.

CHAPTER 5

Maternal Values, Investment in Children, and Intellectual Competence

The previous chapters presented a comparative analysis of the relationships of parents' religion, social and demographic origins, current status, and selected attributes of family structure to the intellectual competence of black and white children. A host of social-structural variables were shown to influence the intellectual and scholastic competence of children by the time they reach later childhood. In most cases the *direction* of these relationships, although not their magnitude, is the same for both races despite the very considerable differences in the structural locations of blacks and whites in American society.

The task undertaken in this part of the book is twofold. First, three dimensions of maternal role performance that have an important bearing on intellectual and scholastic competence will be identified, with special emphasis on describing the relationship between maternal values and practices in the two races and on comparing the relationships of each dimension of maternal role performance to variations in IQ and achievement test performance of black and white children. A major hypothesis guiding the study was that the beliefs mothers bring to child rearing and the practices they employ to implement their beliefs constitute major intervening variables between parents' location in the stratification system and the development of children's intellectual competence.

The second task addressed in this part of the study will be to identify the ways in which maternal values and strategies are influenced by the family's location in the stratification system, by selected aspects of family structure and by the sex of children.

It would be naive to assume that social-structural variables alone explain a great deal of variance in maternal role performance. Daily interpersonal relations, particularly the intimate exchanges that take place between mother and child, are the primary arenas for the expression of needs and interests that are idiosyncratic and infinitely varied, the products and residues not merely of women's prior life experiences and current situation but probably also of organic idiosyncrasies and of interactions of the latter with the former, in ways that as yet are little understood. Nevertheless, there is a considerable body of empirical evidence from past studies (Davis and Havighurst, 1946; Sears, Maccoby, Levin, 1957; Hess and Shipman, 1965; Kamii and Radin (1974), Pearlin and Kohn, 1966; Kohn, 1969 1977; Pearlin, 1971, Kagan and Moss, 1962; Douglas, 1964; Simpson, 1962) that maternal beliefs and behavior are indeed conditioned by women's location in the stratification system. This is not to say, of course, that no overlap in maternal values and behavior is found between black or white women or between middle- and working-class women. There probably is as wide a range of variation in maternal behavior and beliefs within the black working class as within the white middle class, but the modalities are very different between mothers located in these two quite different strata. For example, only a small proportion of white middle-class mothers report frequent use of physical punishment to control their children, and a large proportion hardly ever use this mode of control. In the black working class, a much smaller proportion of mothers rarely use this mode of control and a much larger proportion do so frequently. To state this another way, one could say that the black working-class mother who rarely spanks her child is deviant relative to other women in her own stratum. But in the white middle class, the mother who frequently employs physical punishment is deviant relative to her race and class peers.

Social class is a global concept which has been shown to be greatly confounded with a woman's educational attainment, with the character of her social milieu, with her religious and denominational affiliation, with her social and demographic origins, and with race in American society. The task of specifying more precisely the structural variables that influence maternal values and behavior will be reserved for later.

Maternal Values

Maternal values constitute my point of departure in seeking the linkages between socialization and intellectual competence in children. Child rearing can fruitfully be viewed as a goal-directed set of activities. Implicit in it are "theories" both about the nature of children and about the strategies necessary to gain children's conformity to parental objectives. Melvin Kohn (1969) in his excellent study of parental values observes: "From people's conception of the desirable—especially of what characteristics are desirable in children—one can discern their objectives in child rearing. Thus, conceptions of the desirable—that is, values—become the key concept of this analysis, the bridge between position in the larger social structure and the behavior of the individual" (from *Class and Conformity*, p. 7). I share Kohn's view that values include beliefs about the desirable. But I would also add that beliefs about the nature of children and about the nature of their own child mediate the behavior of men and women in the performance of the parental role. Their behavior in relation to their children operates, in turn, to reinforce the beliefs they initially brought to the parental role. The mother, as a rule, is the first being to interact regularly with her infant. Consciously or not, she tries in a multitude of subtle ways to teach it to respond in accord with her expectations. The ways in which she communicates her expectations are conditioned by her conceptions of the original nature of children and of effective strategies of gaining conformity to her values. Such conceptions do not originate with the individual but are *socially* derived. Her sources of reference are her own experiences in her family of origin as modified by subsequent sources of experience and influence—her early religious indoctrination, her formal education and reading, and her current associates: spouse, relatives, friends, and neighbors.

Philosophers explicate their theories about human nature and the human condition. Oridinary people label their "theories" common sense. These commonsense notions constitute the premises upon which they base their behavior toward their children.

The ongoing interplay between the aspirations and operational theories women bring to the maternal role, their behavior toward an infant, and the infant's developing responses lay the foundation of the patterns of response children develop toward other human beings and learning situations presided over by other authority figures.

Society invests in parents, particularly the mother, the responsibility for rearing their child but also bestows upon them the right to exercise their authority over the child in any way they see fit, short of the most extreme and overt abuse. The manner in which a mother goes about teaching her child and what and how much she wants and expects the child to learn are influenced not merely by her material resources but also by her values and beliefs about what constitute legitimate and effective ways of gaining conformity to the immediate and longer-term goals she envisions for the child's future.

Mother's Educational and Occupational Values

The aspirations and expectations that parents hold with respect to the future educational and occupational attainment of their children represent

one important bridge between the parents' position in the social stratification system of the larger society and their children's position in the
formal stratification system of the school, which is determined first and
foremost by the level of ability they demonstrate on written tests. It is well
known that economically and educationally more advantaged parents as a rule
have higher educational aspirations and expectations for their children, who
in turn average higher scores on all manner of school tests involving verbal
and numerical skills. This success reinforces their own and their parents'
aspirations and expectations with respect to their future educational attainment (Hyman, 1953; Kahl, 1957; Simpson, 1962; Rosen, 1956, 1959, 1961;
Sewell and Shah, 1968; Elder, 1962; Bordua, 1960; Chad Gordon, 1972).

On the basis of survey research alone it is not possible to demonstrate
conclusively the causal priority of parental aspirations in the process described above. Indeed, it could be argued that parents' aspirations become
adjusted to the level of scholastic ability demonstrated by their children, and
within broad limits that is probably true. Whatever their initial ambitions for
their child, middle-class parents of a retarded child will scale down their
ambitions and expectations for the future of that child. By the same token,
the aspirations of working-class parents of an unusually able pupil very likely
become elevated by the child's superior performance. But the evidence of
common observation as well as that provided by extensive longitudinal research carried out in Great Britain (Douglas, 1964; Douglas et al., 1968) is
that the level of educational aspirations parents hold for their children as a
rule antedates the knowledge they later acquire concerning the children's
scholastic ability. Middle- and working-class British mothers exhibited considerable disparity in the educational ambitions they held for their children
when the children were still in infancy. Even more interesting is the finding
that those working-class mothers who had high ambitions for their infants,
though they were the exception rather than the rule, afforded their infants
better care, qualitatively and quantitively, than did their less ambitious
social-class peers. Their children exhibited higher intellectual ability in
childhood and higher educational attainment in adolescence than were
characteristic of British working-class children of initially less ambitious
mothers.

The British study, as well as the large body of survey research carried out
in the United States on the relationship of parental and adolescent aspirations to educational attainment, is based largely on white samples. My
sample composition makes possible a comparison of the role that maternal
aspirations play in the development of intellectual competence among children in the two races, both directly and indirectly, through their effect on
other aspects of maternal role behavior.

The mothers in my sample were asked three questions designed to ascertain their level of aspirations for their children with reference to educational
attainment, scholastic excellence, and occupational attainment:

1. What is the least amount of education that you think would be enough for your (son or daughter)?[1]
2. Would you be satisfied if (child) were passing; at the middle of (his/her) class; above the middle; outstanding?
3. Would (child) be doing well enough if (he/she) had a job like ____? (Concrete examples of nonskilled, skilled, clerical, and professional occupations were provided.)[2]

Mothers were also asked about their educational *expectations,* as distinct from their aspirations: "How far do you really expect (child) to go in school—some high school, graduate from high school, post–high school training, some college, graduate from college, graduate or professional school?"

Several investigators have reported that black mothers voice aspirations for their children at least as high as, if not higher than, those expressed by white mothers, despite the fact that as a rule black children exhibit less scholastic ability (Gottlieb, 1966; Pettigrew, 1964).

The present study confirms the findings of these earlier studies. With respect to educational aspirations, for example, 69 percent of the black middle-class mothers, compared with 68 percent of the white middle-class mothers, consider anything less than some college education "not enough." Among the working classes, 45 percent of the black mothers but only 30 percent of the white mothers gave this answer.

Racial differences are even more pronounced with respect to mother's aspirations for excellence. Fully 22 percent of the black working-class mothers want their children to be outstanding, compared with only 4 percent of the white working-class mothers. Nineteen percent of the black middle-class mothers compared with 13 percent of the white middle-class mothers express such lofty ambitions.

A somewhat different pattern is observed with respect to occupational aspirations of black and white mothers. Among the middle classes, 55 percent of the black mothers and 63 percent of the whites aspire to professional careers for their children. Among the working classes, the pattern of differences is reversed; a third of the black mothers compared to 28 percent of the whites have professional ambitions for their children.

In response to the question tapping *expectations,* fully 83 percent of white middle-class mothers expect their children to attend college, compared with 74 percent in the black middle class; in the working classes, 46 percent of the black and 41 percent of the white mothers voice such high expectations.

A comparison of the correlations between aspiration level and educational expectations of mothers in the two races shows a higher association between these variables among white (.60) than among black mothers (.47). In short, it appears that when a white woman expresses high educational ambitions for her child, she is also more likely to expect her child to realize these ambitions, whereas black mothers, on the whole, are less confident that their ambitions for their children will be realized, first, because their economic resources do not, as a rule, equal those of whites;[3] second, because their children, as a rule, exhibit less scholastic proficiency, which makes it more problematic to sustain their motivation to seek higher education by the time they reach adolescence. Not to be gainsaid, furthermore, is the belief, more prevalent among black than among white mothers, that their children's scholastic performance is not up to par. Evidence of this are responses to the question "Do you think your child is doing as well as he/she can in school or do you think he/she could do better?" Fully 76 percent of the black mothers in both the middle class and the working class felt their child could do better. The corresponding percentage among whites was 60 percent, in both the middle class and the working class.[4]

Maternal Values and Children's Competence and Achievement Scores

White children's performance on IQ and achievement tests show higher correlations with maternal aspiration level (.36 and .38, respectively) than that of black children (.27 and .26, respectively). This finding would, of course, be anticipated in view of the fact that black mothers voice aspirations for their children as high as or higher than those of white mothers, but at the same time, their children average lower IQ and achievement scores than white children. Indeed, it is interesting that though a far higher proportion of black middle-class mothers (69 percent) than of white working-class mothers (30 percent) aspire to a college education for their children, the average IQ and achievement scores of children in these two groups are very similar. And though a substantially higher proportion of black working-class mothers (45 percent) than of white working-class mothers (30 percent) want a college education for their children, the white children average higher IQ and achievement test scores.

The two races differ less in the degree of association between mother's educational expectations and the IQ and achievement scores of children than in the association between aspiration level and children's performance. Thus, the correlations between mother's educational expectations and IQ are .33 among blacks and .36 among whites, and the correlations between educational expectations and achievement score performance are .36 among blacks and .41 among whites. This is because among whites the magnitude of correlations between maternal aspirations and IQ and achievement and those between maternal expectations and IQ and achievement are very similar. Among blacks, however, the correlation between educational expectations and achievement is higher (.36) than between aspirations and achievement (.26), an indication, perhaps, that the educational expectations voiced by black mothers are more influenced by their children's demonstrated scholastic ability than are their aspirations. The same tendency is observed among white mothers, but the difference in magnitude of correlation between maternal aspirations and achievement (.38) and maternal expectations and achievement (.42) is less.

It is not immediately apparent why and how maternal aspirations influence the development of intellectual competence in children. To be sure, children learn through observation, interaction, selective reinforcements, and identification what skills and activities their parents value, but the processes through which parents are more or less successful in transmitting their values or, more specifically, their ambitions to their children requires further exploration and explication. The problem is to identify the mechanisms through which internalization of a given value takes place so that values initially external to the child become incorporated in his or her personal system and thereby function independently as a source of self-motivation and self-governance.

This question, of course, Sigmund Freud (1933, 1949, 1960) dealt with brilliantly and repeatedly in his own work, and since his time it has been addressed by many other thinkers and writers, some operating within the psychoanalytic perspective, focused on the development of the ego, such as Heinz Hartmann (1958) and Erik Erikson (1959). Others, such as Jean Piaget (1952) and George Herbert Mead (1934), addressed the question using other theoretical perspectives, not necessarily inconsistent with the Freudian metaphor but different and also fruitful. Talcott Parsons, in a brilliant essay (1964a), integrated (very successfully, in my opinion) the perspectives of these earlier thinkers with a sociological analysis of the development of personality in the context of the family viewed as a social subsystem which lays the foundation for participation in more complex social systems, of which the school is the first encountered by the child.

All these theorists addressed generic issues and processes in the development of the self as an autonomous system but did not take as an object of systematic investigation the effects of variability in values and socialization strategies on the development of those basic skills and motivational orientations that equip the child to master the sequence of increasingly complex and abstract subject matter that comprises higher education.[5] Although attainment of higher education is not mandatory, college or university training and certification increasingly have become prerequisites for entry into the more prestigeful and renumerative occupations in complex societies. Failure to qualify for entry into institutions of higher education, therefore, usually bars the individual from the opportunity to compete for entry into a whole range of occupations that proliferate in advanced technological societies.

Maternal Aspirations and Investment in Children: A Process of Social Exchange

Between maternal aspirations and the child's demonstrated intellectual competence in later childhood lies an extended history of interaction between mother and child, the nature of which, I would be the first to admit, is possible to ascertain by the survey method only in a crude and approximate way.[6]

In an essay on the immigrant Jewish mother some years ago (Blau, 1967), I took as my point of departure the lofty educational aspirations such women held for their children and undertook to identify the attitudes and practices by which this largely working-class ethnic group characteristically implemented their ambitions. I proposed that Jewish immigrant mothers' heavy investment in their children of nurturance, care, and attentiveness to their health and general well-being was commensurate with their high ambitions and that together these constituted major factors in the exceptionally high mobility rates of their children compared with other immigrant ethnic groups, via the route of higher education.

That and other related propositions constituted a preliminary theoretical effort that guided the design of the present study, which was intended to test the general validity of my argument as it applies to non-Jews—black and white. For if, as I argued, it was not simply the traditionally high valuation that Jews place on literacy and learning but more directly the "unrealistically" high ambitions of Jewish immigrant parents *coupled* with a diversion of scarce resources of time, effort, and money from other possible goals to an uncharacteristically high investment of these resources in their children that led to the high intellectual aptitude exhibited by the children, then similar outcomes would also be expected among non-Jews—black and white—who exhibit a similar pattern of high maternal ambition *coupled* with a heavy investment of resources in their children from infancy through adolescence. Other elements, also identified as part of the socialization strategy of Jewish immigrant mothers, will be introduced and discussed in the appropriate context later on.

George Homans, over a decade ago (1962), observed that "of all our many 'approaches' to social behavior, the one that sees it as an economy is the most neglected, and yet it is the one we use every moment of our lives—except when we write sociology" (p. 293). Since this statement appeared, theories about human behavior couched in terms of social exchange have gained wide currency among sociologists (cf. Peter Blau, 1964; Scott, 1971), but this perspective has not, to my knowledge, been employed in the study of children's intellectual competence in relation to maternal values and behavior.

> Social behavior is an exchange of goods, material goods but also nonmaterial ones, such as the symbols of approval or prestige. Persons that give much to others try to get much from them, and persons that get much from others are

under pressure to give much to them. This process of influence tends to work out at equilibrium to a balance in the exchanges. For a person engaged in exchange, what he gives may be a cost to him, just as what he gets may be a reward, and his behavior changes less as profit, that is, reward less cost, tends to a maximum. Not only does he seek a maximum for himself, but he tries to see to it that no one in his group makes more profit than he does. The *cost* and the *value* of what he gives and of what he gets vary with the quantity of what he gives and gets. Homans, 1962, p. 292].

If it is true that "persons that give much to others try to get much from them," the obverse also appears to be true with respect to the relationship between maternal aspirations and the extent of maternal investment of resources in children. Mothers who voice high aspirations for their children's future educational and occupational attainment in effect "try to get much" from their children, because it takes a great input of effort over an extended period of time for a child to achieve competence in the skills and knowledge offered in the school. Such mothers are also more likely to "give much" to their children—that is, to invest more in their children in ways that cost them more in time, interest, effort, money, or other resources.

To test this proposition, several components of investment in children were constructed.

The first component measure, positive interaction during infancy and early childhood, derived through a principal components analysis, is based on measures of the frequency with which the child was taken along by mother when shopping or visiting friends and the frequency with which mothers reported singing songs, telling stories, reading to their child, answering their questions, and naming objects during the child's preschool years. The correlation between early interaction scores and maternal aspiration level is .29 among blacks and .26 among whites.[7]

A second component of maternal investment in child deals with an indirect form of investment: namely, whether a mother had read Dr. Benjamin Spock's book *Baby and Child Care* and/or other literature by child-rearing experts.

Exposure to Spock and other child-rearing "experts" is, to be sure, strongly and independently related to race and social-class position of mothers (Blau, 1964), but it is not a simple function of a woman's social characteristics. It is also an expression of interest and concern in performing the maternal role well. Not all white middle-class women, for example, have read Spock, although the overwhelming majority have. Conversely, while a majority of black working-class women have not read Spock, a substantial minority have. Regardless of their race or class position, women who are willing to expend money, time, and effort—to incur the *cost* of reading experts and to incur the risk of exposing themselves to recommendations contrary to their own beliefs or practices—do so because, among other things, they believe they can enhance their performance as mothers and thereby provide better care to their child. In that sense, exposure to experts represents the mother's investment of time and effort in the child. It would be expected that such an investment would more readily be made by mothers with high aspirations for the future achievement of their children than by those with more modest aspirations. Among whites, the data clearly support these expectations: the correlation between maternal aspirations and reading child-rearing experts is .31 among whites. Among blacks, the association is considerably weaker, only .13.

A third measure that reflects the investment of time and attention in the child is the extent of mastery of verbal and numerical skills achieved by the child before school entry. Mothers were asked which skills their child knew before entering school or learned only afterward—ABC's, identification of colors, numbers up to ten, counting of small change, and reading. Earlier mastery of these skills probably reflects inputs into the child not solely by the mother, of course, but also by other members of the family.

It goes without saying that the middle-class home provides more opportunities for early learning of verbal and numerical skills, which is part of what Strodtbeck (1964) describes as the "hidden curriculum" of the middle-class home. The more elaborated language and the greater conceptual complexity (Bernstein, 1961) employed by better-educated parents constitute a source of continuous and inadvertent instruction for the child. Moreover, parents who are themselves articulate probably encourage and respond more to the efforts of their children to master those skills that allow them to participate more fully and freely in the interactional system within the home. However, it is also to be expected that working-class parents who have high aspirations for their children, though not well educated themselves, will also exert more effort to teach their children basic skills such as the ABC's, counting, and naming colors, and will reward the children with demonstrations of pride and approval for mastery of these skills, thereby reinforcing the children's sense of efficacy and motivation to master such skills.

Indeed, in both races maternal aspirations and early mastery of basic skills are moderately related; the association of these variables among whites is $r = .22$ and among blacks $r = .26$.

The final component of extent of investment in the child is a score based on three items: whether or not the child attended nursery school, was given lessons on a musical instrument, and was sent to a summer camp; in short, an indicator of the extent to which families allocate economic resources to provide culturally enriching experiences for the child in early and later childhood. To be sure, the provision of culturally enriching experiences is related to socioeconomic status, educational attainment of parents, and other social characteristics in both races. For families with greater economic resources the relative "cost" of providing experientially broadening experiences above and beyond the free formal instruction provided by schools is lower than for families with very meager resources. Indeed, it has been estimated that such input into middle-class children affords them almost a year's advantage in scholastic ability over less-advantaged children (Mosteller and Moynihan, 1972). Nevertheless, financial ability is not the sole determinant of this form of investment in children. Many middle-class families do not choose to allocate economic resources to the cultural enrichment of children but prefer instead to invest more heavily in expensive consumer goods. By the same token, among working-class families, black and white, one finds some parents who deem it more important to allocate their resources to enriching experiences for their children, even though this means sacrificing the purchase of other desirable goods. A notable example of just this pattern are Eastern Jewish immigrant parents who, precisely because they had inordinately high ambitions for their children, invested in such "luxuries" as music lessons and summer camp to a much greater extent than other low-status ethnic immigrant groups in the same urban communities. There is humor to be found in the "self-sacrificing *yiddishe Mama*" and in the slogan of immigrant Jews, "*Alles far die Kinder*" (Everything for the children), but it is also true that this pattern was a distinguishing characteristic of Jewish immigrants (Blau, 1967). Indicators of the sacrifices made to provide enrichment are the markedly lower birth rates in the earlier decades of this century among Jews compared with non-Jews (Seligman and Antonovsky, 1958) and their lower rates of home ownership compared with non-Jews (Goldberg and Sharp, 1958).

In the present study, maternal aspirations are also associated with the parents' provision of culturally enriching experiences to children, although the association is stronger among whites ($r = .39$) than among blacks ($r = .23$). Interestingly, the relationship between provision of cultural enrichment and mother's educational *expectations* is stronger among blacks ($r = .37$) and, indeed, approximates the association found among whites ($r = .41$).

The racial difference in the magnitude of the association of aspirations to the allocation of resources for cultural enrichment is undoubtedly due in some degree but not altogether to their pronounced differences in socioeconomic status. But when socioeconomic status is controlled, the correlations between maternal aspirations and cultural enrichment remain higher among whites than among blacks—among whites, .33 in the imiddle class and .27 in the working class; among blacks, .20 and .12, respectively. Although the black middle class is of considerably higher SES and educational attainment than the white working class (and also has higher mean aspirations for children), the provision of cultural enrichment does not increase with maternal aspirations to the same degree in the black middle class as in the white working class. Further explication of these differences is reserved for later discussion.

In the foregoing discussion evidence was offered to support the proposition that in both races mothers who voice higher aspirations for their children's future educational and occupational achievements are likely to also invest more heavily in intrinsically rewarding and stimulating forms of socialization. Each form of investment, in turn, is shown to be related to children's performance on IQ and achievement tests.

Thus, high maternal aspirations promote higher investment in the child of positive and stimulating experiences. This, in turn, engenders higher intellectual motivation and competence in children. Here, the role of reciprocity comes into play in two ways. The child who gets more encouragement *and* more rewards, measured by positive, stimulating inputs, comes to the school better prepared experientially to learn the formal content of the school. Equally important, the child who has been the frequent recipient of pleasurable, rewarding attention and response feels an obligation to live up to the aspirations and expectations of his or her benefactors. The psychoanalytic concepts of identification and internalization and the sociological concept of reciprocity can be seen in this context to be related to each other. All parents seek to instill their values in their children, but they differ in the means they employ to accomplish their ends and in the extent to which they are successful in gaining internal as against merely external conformity to behaviors they value. There are many areas of behavior in which parents can gain conformity from a child by force or even the threat of force. Thus, children can be made to go to school whether or not they wish to go. But the will to learn the content offered by the school cannot be promoted in a child solely through exhortation or coercion. Inner motivation in this realm is a product not of punishment but of stimulation and teaching buttressed by conditional rewards, such as interest, encouragement, praise, and approval bestowed on the child throughout the early years of life both when he or she struggles to master a word, a concept, or other behavior and when the child successfully masters a skill. The sense of efficacy thus gained is the reward that stimulates further initiative to learn (Piaget, 1952; White, 1963; Erikson, 1959). This process, endlessly repeated from earliest infancy, underlies the development of intellectual motivation in children.

Jean Piaget (1952) has documented in painstaking and beautiful detail the very earliest sequence of learning by his own three children, starting from birth. There is every reason to suppose that any normal child, black or white, *given the same investment of time, attention, stimulation, and rewards from birth onward,* would exhibit the same sequence of mastery of basic intellectual conepts, although, of course, individual variations in the time it takes children to master such basic concepts would be expected. For Piaget was not merely an observer of the processes that constitute the "origins" of intelligence; he was at the same time an agent in the evolution of the processes of exploration, trial and error, and eventual mastery and consolidation of understanding that he has described in such fascinating detail. Probably very few families, however, provide the kind of conditions for the intellectual development of children that the Piagets apparently did, where not only the mother but also the father engage heavily in stimulating interaction with the children.

Piaget's description focuses on the ways in which his children went about solving "intellectual" problems virtually from birth on. The investment of time and positive forms of stimulation that served to establish and reinforce the behavior being observed he takes as given. However, it is precisely the effects on intelligence of *variations* of such forms of investment by mothers which are the objects of investigation in the present study.

In the foregoing pages it has been shown that a certain degree of consistency obtains between mothers' valuation of educational and occupational achievement and their willingness to invest the resources at their disposal, over and above the culturally obligatory task of providing children with the physical nurturance and care necessary to ensure survival and growth.[8]

Summary

In this chapter, I have described the two components—aspirations and expectations—that combined form the single dimension *maternal valuation of education.* Next, I described four measures of maternal behavior—early interaction with child, exposure to child-rearing experts, early mastery, and cultural enrichment—that were combined to form the second dimension of socialization, *investment in child.*

In the next chapter, I discuss the components and their interrelationships that were combined to form the third dimension of socialization on which my analysis focuses—mother's orientation to and use of aversive discipline. The modal socialization strategies of black and white mothers are then compared and discussed. The chapter concludes with a multivariate analysis of the predictive value of the socialization model based on my three dimensions of socialization and sex of the child as compared to the social structural model presented in Chapter 4.

Notes

1. Codes were 1 = some high school, 2 = complete high school; 3 = post–high school training; 4 = some college; 5 = graduate from college; 6 = post-college education.
2. Responses to questions 2 and 3 were coded on a scale of 1 to 4. The combined responses to these three questions form a Guttman scale, and the resulting scores constitute the measure of mother's level of aspiration for her child.
3. Evidence that mothers with fewer economic resources, regardless of race, are more pessimistic about their children's chances of obtaining higher education is provided by answers to the question "How good would you say (child's) chances

would be of getting admitted to college if he/she wanted to go?" Only 10 and 11 percent, respectively, of white and black middle-class mothers answered "not very good" or "not good at all"; among working-class mothers, however, the proportions giving these answers were 22 percent among whites and 21 percent among blacks.

4. Significant differences between the races on this question remain even after a host of variables are covaried. See Richard Appelbaum, 1971.

5. Freud broadly defined a healthy personality as constituting two basic elements—the ability to love and the ability to work, that is, to perform the socioemotional and instrumental components of at least those social roles that the individual is culturally obligated to perform. Implicit in much of Freud's writing is the recognition of the connectedness of these two sets of functions. In Erikson's work (1950, 1999), particularly in his delineation of the critical nuclear conflicts that confront the developing person and the enduring effects of earlier resolutions on the resolutions effected in later stages, the articulation between the socioemotional and instrumental components of the developing personality is made somewhat more explicit.

6. Nevertheless, the survey method constitutes the most viable means of testing propositions concerning modal relationships between values and behavior in different subgroups of large populations. When evidence from longitudinal and from observational studies agree with the results obtained from survey analysis, confidence in results is of course, strengthened.

7. The correlation between mother's educational expectations and early interaction is .34 among blacks and .28 among whites.

8. Table A-6 (page 235) summarizes the correlations found among blacks and whites between maternal aspirations and expectations and positive forms of investment in the child, on the one hand, and between the relationships of each component measure of investment in children and the children's IQ and achievement-test scores, on the other hand.

CHAPTER 6

Modes of Control, Socialization Strategies, and Intellectual Competence

A considerable body of theoretical and empirical literature exists describing the relationship of authoritarianism and fatalism to a variety of behaviors and outcomes, such as racial and ethnic prejudice (Adorno et al., 1950), political behavior (Lipset, 1959), religious *Weltanschauung* (Weber, 1958), scholastic competence of black and white children (Coleman et al., 1966), and occupational roles and child-rearing values (Kohn, 1969; Pearlin, 1971).

While they constitute analytically distinct entities, there is some evidence of a relationship on macroscopic levels of analysis between a felt sense of powerlessness or fatalism, the endorsement of authoritarian values or movements (Fromm, 1941 and in Lipset, 1960), and commitment to punitive as opposed to restitutive legal forms and modes of societal control (Durkheim, 1964). Toleration of diversity and valuation of individuality and autonomy as a rule increase with the technological complexity and urbanization of a society, (Durkheim, 1964; Weber, 1958; Simmel, 1950), and within technologically advanced societies, the better-educated, intellectually more cultivated strata, whose conditions of work afford them more autonomy and self-direction, express a greater sense of control over their lives (Kohn and Schooler, 1973, 1978) as opposed to a sense that they are subject to the control of external forces (Rotter, 1966; Seeman, 1967). Higher strata are also found to place greater emphasis on the cultivation of self-direction and a lower valuation on conformity or obedience in rearing their children than the lower strata in the society (Kohn, 1969; Pearlin, 1971).

Thus, Leonard Pearlin, in a cross-national comparative study utilizing Italian and American data, observes:

> Occupational self-direction . . . explains much of the class difference in paren-
> tal values. Middle-class men are more likely to work at jobs that require self-
> direction, and this occupational condition is associated with high valuation of
> self-control for children. Working-class men, however, are more likely to be
> required to comply with the direction of others and this is associated with valuing
> obedience for one's children. Social class is thus determinative of the extent of
> occupational self-direction, and this aspect of occupational experience, in turn,
> molds conceptions of good and proper behavior—not only for one's self within the
> occupational setting, but also for one's children in the family. [Pearlin, 1971, p.
> 188–189]

Analysis of the structural sources of variations in fatalism and authoritarianism among the mothers in our sample will be reserved for later
discussion. A necessary preliminary is to define operationally the concepts of
fatalism and authoritarianism; to describe the relationship between them in
the two races and their relationship to maternal ambition, on the one hand,
and to maternal investment in negative modes of gaining conformity from
children, on the other; and finally, to report and interpret the relationship of
fatalism and authoritarianism to the development of intellectual competence
and motivation.

Maternal Fatalism

The responses of mothers to three questions that form a Guttman scale[1]
constitute a measure of maternal *fatalism*.

1. Children should be taught not to expect too much out of life so that
   they won't be disappointed.
2. Children should learn early that there isn't too much you can do about
   the way things are going to turn out in life.
3. Children should learn that planning only makes a person unhappy,
   since your plans hardly ever work out anyhow.

This measure taps a dimension similar to what social psychologist Julian
B. Rotter (1966) defined as "generalized expectancies for Internal versus
External Control of Reinforcement." That is, it indicates the extent to which
individuals perceive reinforcements received as contingent on their own
efforts or skills as opposed to the belief that reinforcements are controlled by
forces external to the self, such as chance, luck, fate, or dieties.[2]

On the basis of results of his own research and the work of many other investigators using his instrument, Rotter concludes:

> A series of studies provides strong support for the hypothesis that the individual who has a strong belief that he can control his own destiny is likely to (a) be more alert to those aspects of the environment which provide useful information for his future behavior; (b) take steps to improve his environmental condition; (c) place greater value on skill or achievement reinforcements and be generally more concerned with his ability, particularly his failures; and (d) be resistive to subtle attempts to influence him. [Rotter, 1966, p. 25]

Robert K. Merton (1957) made some astute observations about the functions and dysfunctions of the belief in luck which corresponds to Rotter's concept of external orientation and to my measure of fatalism. The belief in luck "serves the psychological function of enabling people to preserve their self-esteem in the face of failure." But Merton goes on to suggest that a dysfunctional aspect of the belief is that it may also serve to "curtail sustained endeavor." Rotter's work on external orientations, Seeman's work linking this concept to a sense of powerlessness (Seeman, 1959, 1967), and the concept of alienation found in the works of the great classical theorists Weber and Durkheim all have in common the perception that generalized orientations toward the world, whatever their structural origins, once established, not infrequently operate as a "self-fulfilling prophecy" (Merton, 1948).

In the present study, which deals only with the orientations of mothers and not with those of their children, it is not possible to test the hypothesis that mothers often transmit such generalized orientations as fatalism to their children and thereby inhibit the children's development of a sense of intellectual efficacy. It is, however, possible to ascertain the relationship of maternal fatalism to children's IQ and scholastic achievement and to other beliefs and practices held by mothers.

For example, following Rotter's and Merton's lead, a negative relationship would be expected between maternal fatalism and level of aspirations for the child. Fatalism and ambition are antithetical to each other. It is precisely the risk of failure to realize aspirations and plans that prompts a mother to teach her child "not to expect too much," that "there isn't too much you can do about the way things turn out," and that "planning only makes a person unhappy."

And indeed, in both races, a negative association is found between maternal aspirations and fatalism: among blacks the correlation is $-.30$, among whites $-.31$. A somewhat stronger negative association between educational expectations and fatalism occurs among whites ($-.39$), but among blacks the association of fatalism to expectations is much the same ($-.34$) as to aspirations. In both races, mothers with low fatalism scores are inclined, as Rotter predicts, to "place greater value on skill or achievement reinforcements" with respect to their children.

Besides inhibiting maternal ambitions for their children, fatalism has an adverse effect on all measures of positive investment of time and resources in children and is negatively associated with children's IQ and achievement test scores in both races. Table 6-1 shows a somewhat stronger negative association of fatalism with early interaction and preschool mastery of skills among blacks, whereas among whites a stronger negative association is observed between fatalism and exposure to experts and to the provision of culturally enriching experiences. In both races, fatalism shows a stronger negative association with achievement scores than with IQ scores, which suggests that the communication of a fatalistic orientation is more damaging to children's progress in school as the tasks they are called upon to learn become more difficult.[3] A two-step process by which maternal fatalism may inhibit scholastic ability of children is hypothesized. First, a mother who perceives life's outcomes as externally governed rather than as resulting from the cultivation of skill and effort is likely to invest less time, effort, and other resources in rearing her child. Only to the extent that one believes one's own actions make a difference—that is, only if they offer the promise of a return commensurate with the cost—is such an investment rational. As shown earlier, positive forms of investment in the child appear to promote intellectual development. To the extent that maternal fatalism inhibits investment in the child, it may inhibit intellectual growth. In contrast, mothers with a sense of efficacy who invest care, attention, and stimulation in their children provide positive reinforcements for learning. Extension of the child's skills, in turn, promotes a sense of efficacy and an interest in and appetite for the mastery of new skills. In short, it seems plausible that here, as in so many realms of social life, the "Matthew Effect"—"to those who have will be given"—(Merton, 1968) begins to operate; that is, those children who have been given to more are more capable intellectually when they enter school, and their early competence enhances their confidence that they can successfully master the more difficult tasks they encounter as they pass on to higher grades.

TABLE 6-1. Correlations of Fatalism with Component Measures of Investment in Child and Children's Test Scores

	Blacks	Whites
Early interaction	−.25	−.18
Read experts	−.19	−.35
Mastery	−.17	−.12
Cultural enrichment	−.22	−.29
IQ	−.21	−.18
Achievement	−.27	−.29

Further explication of the process through which maternal fatalism inhibits the development of scholastic ability must wait upon the introduction of a strongly related but analytically distinct value orientation, namely authoritarianism.

Maternal Authoritarianism

Maternal authoritarianism in this study is measured by responses to four items that also form a Guttman scale:[4]

1. Obedience and respect for authority are the most important virtues children should learn.
2. Children need some of the natural meanness taken out of them.
3. It is sometimes necessary for the parent to break the child's will.
4. It is often necessary to drive the mischief out of a child before he or she will behave.[5]

A strong association is found in both races between mothers' scores on the fatalism and authoritarianism scales: among blacks the correlation is .49 and among whites .56.

The family is the only institution outside the state in which superordinates—that is, parents—as a rule are socially accorded the right to use force, short of severe physical injury, to gain conformity of children to norms, whatever they may be.[6] And just as states, from antiquity on, have been dichotomized as authoritarian or democratic, so too can parental values and behaviors employed to gain children's conformity be used to classify modes of control found within families or other social groups (Lippitt and White, 1947). Many parallels have been drawn between the manner in which the state exercise authority over citizens and the way in which parents exercise authority over their children. Indeed Plato, in his *Republic*, delineated the relationship between these two institutional spheres. A contemporary political thinker, Harold Lasswell (1951), has also done so. He writes: "The state is a symbol of authority, and as such is the legatee of attitudes which have been organized in the life of the individual within the intimate interpersonal sphere of the home and the friendship group" (p. 173) and "Children are always brought [up] in relation to a system of interferences and indulgences... and they always perceive an order of some kind" (p. 256).

Lasswell's intention in these passages is to relate the effects of the early upbringing of individuals to adults' choice of political ideologies, political styles, and political behavior. Adorno and his associates (1950) empirically established a link between the mode of authority under which individuals are reared in childhood and the evolution of authoritarian character structure as a factor in the development of hostility and prejudice against members of minority groups in the democratic context of American society. My interest in the present context is in the relationship between maternal authoritarianism and fatalism and the process through which this dual orientation inhibits the development of intellectual motivation and ability in children.

Underlying a high valuation of obedience in children is a more general "theory" about the original nature of the human being, traditional in the Western world. Originally fostered by the dogma of the church, it later was elaborated by Hobbes and his followers as justification for the investment of absolute power in the monarchy. Essentially, this view holds that the original nature of man is sinful, untamed, agressive, and antisocial and that strong measures are necessary to counter and suppress these evil tendencies in both the private and public realms. It is not merely the right but also the responsibility of those in authority to "train" subordinates, first and foremost, to respect and obey authority, whether it is exercised by parents, by the church, by the sovereign, by an officer over his men, or by the master over his slaves. Such "training" was and still is thought to necessitate prohibitions and extensive restrictions imposed in earliest childhood, when the individual is weakest, most dependent, and most vulnerable. Since "natural meanness," "willfulness," and "mischievousness" are perceived as constituting the basic nature of the child, he or she can be expected initially to defy and resist parental authority. Therefore, the child must be taught to *fear* the consequences of disobedience more than the pleasure it might afford. Precisely because such a view recognizes the powerful reinforcement value of pleasure, it preceives punishment—i.e., the induction of *pain*—as all the more necessary to counter the "natural" impulses of the child to resist restriction and restraint. To exorcise the "devil" requires powerful antidotes by those who believe themselves to be the representatives of God, and indeed, as will be shown presently, mothers who embrace such a fundamentalist world view score highest on authoritarianism and use coercive forms of punishment most frequently to gain conformity to their norms. In short, the parent for whom obedience in children is a paramount value is inclined to invest more time and effort in taming, curbing, and suppressing inclinations toward autonomy in the growing child. Instead of cultivating the capacity for inner control or self-direction, such a parent repeatedly reinforces the child's sense of powerlessness, his or her consciousness of being subject to *external* forces and powers outside the realm of control. And just as the authoritarian state seeks to ensure obedience by a heavy investment of its resources in restrictions on the freedoms of its citizenry, reinforced by punitive rather than restitutive sanctions, so authoritarian parents rely more on prohibition, threats, and actual punishment than on positive reinforcements to instill conformity in children.

In contrast to the authoritarian's view of the original nature of the child is a democratic "theory" that has gradually gained ascendency among more enlightened circles in modern democratic states over two centuries, but which was also part of the heritage of two ancient cultures—Judaic and Chinese: the delineation of the child's original nature as neither good nor bad but rather as *tabula rasa.* An ancient Chinese saying gracefully conveys the essence of the democratic view: "The child is born as a white linen cloth, and the design which eventually appears upon it is due to the kind of training that he has had" (Sollenberger, 1968).[7]

Parents who embrace the latter theory are inclined to veiw their responsibility as being that of a teacher who conveys moral precepts to the child and who, through dialogue and example, gradually leads the child to internalize the desired norms and thereby develop the capacity of self-control.[8]

Earlier, a strong association between fatalism and authoritarianism was reported among both white and black mothers. The relationship of fatalism and intellectual ability in children has been more extensively and sytematically investigated than the relationship of authoritarianism to intellectual ability. Thus, one study reports that children of mothers with a low sense of control have lower IQ scores than other children, and this difference was found to persist even when mothers' own IQ and other variables of their behavior are controlled (Bear, Hess, Shipman, 1966).

The Coleman study (1966) provides no data on mothers' attitudes but found that variations in *children's* sense of control over the external environment strongly differentiated achievement scores of white, black, and other minority children. White children more frequently expressed a sense of control over the environment than black and other minority children, and they also had higher achievement scores. In all groups, however, children who exhibited a sense of control over the environment—i.e., who believed "hard work" helped in achieving success—scored higher on achievement tests than children within their own group who did not share this belief. Indeed, minority students who exhibited a high sense of control scored higher on achievement tests than white students with a low sense of control.

In the present study maternal fatalism and maternal authoritarianism are each negatively correlated with IQ scores and even more with achievement scores of children in both races. Thus, among blacks, the relationship of maternal fatalism to IQ is $-.21$ and to achievement scores $-.27$; the correlation of maternal authoritarianism to IQ is $-.19$ and to achievement $-.32$. Among whites, the correlation of maternal fatalism with IQ is $-.18$ and with achievement $-.29$; the correlation of maternal authoritarianism with IQ is $-.22$ and with achievement $-.30$. In both races, in short, maternal falalism and authoritarianism show a similar negative association with children's IQ and achievement scores. This is not surprising, since the two are strongly associated with each other. This being the case, the two measures will be combined in the multivariate analyses later in the study.

At this point in the discussion, however, it seems worthwhile to seek an understanding of the processes through which each of these maternal orientations inhibits the development of intellectual and scholastic ability in children.

The findings of Coleman and his collaborators concerning the importance of a sense of personal control in the prediction of scholastic ability raises the question of how the socialization process fosters or undermines this very important orientation to the environment. Erikson (1950, 1959), elaborating the theories of Freud, sees the conflict between autonomy and self-doubt as a critical developmental issue that arises in what Freud calls the anal phase, when the child is called upon to learn self-control over its eliminatory processes. To establish self-control entails gaining the cooperation of the child. Parents go about this task either through the use of positive inducements and reinforcements or through negative, fear- or pain-producing ones. The process of toilet training is seen by Freud and Erikson as paradigmatic of the interaction between parent and child in a whole range of socialization experiences where the parental objective is to gain the child's conformity to social rules.

Parents, particularly the mother as a rule, are the first authority figures in the child's life, and the manner in which they exercise their authority and the extent to which they control the child's range of activities as his or her capacities for independent action expands are important differentiating factors in the development of a sense of inner control and a sense of autonomy or efficacy as opposed to a sense of being subject to external, arbitrary forces, to feelings of helplessness or self-doubt.

In the *Authoritarian Personality*, Else Frenkel-Brunswick makes a distinction between "ego-destructive discipline which applies negative sanctions for the violation of 'primarily moralistic'" rules that "force[s] the child into submission and surrender of his ego, thus preventing his development, and a form of control concerned with 'rationalized'" principles that "contributes to the growth of the ego." She discusses further the implications of these alternative forms of control.

I propose that a direct source of fatalism or a sense of control is the manner in which parents, as the first authorities or control figures in a child's life, exercise their authority over the child. Repressive, "ego-destructive" discipline "forces the child into submission and surrender of his ego, thus preventing his development." Such discipline is described as "threatening, traumatic, overwhelming." Contrasted with ego-destructive discipline is "assimilable, and thus non-ego-destructive discipline which contributes to the growth of the ego; it is similar to a therapy in which the therapist becomes an ally of the patient's ego, helping him to master his id. This second type of discipline seems an important condition for the establishment of an internalized superego, and thus crucial for the development of an unprejudiced personality. This category proved differentiating at a high level of significance" (Adorno, et al., 1950, p. 372).

Else Frenkel-Brunswick, as a preamble to the passage quoted above, makes a distinction between discipline for violation of *rules,* "primarily moralistic," and discipline for the violation of *principles.*

> The choice between these two opposite alternatives on the part of parents would seem to be crucial for the establishment of the child's attitude toward what is considered right or wrong; it probably decides the externalization vs. internalization of values. These two types of discipline further imply different resultant attitudes toward authority. In the first case, discipline is handled as "vis major," as a force outside of the child to which, at the same time, he must submit. The values in question are primarily the values of adult society; conventions and rules helpful for social climbing but rather beyond the natural grasp of the child. At the same time, this type of value lays the foundation for an attitude of judging people according to external criteria, and for the authoritarian condemnation of what is considered socially inferior. The second type of discipline invites the cooperation and understanding of the child and makes it possible for him to assimilate it. [Adorno, et al., 1950, p. 372]

It is possible to further elaborate the concomitants of authoritarian versus democratic modes of control by comparing the implications of each for maternal responses to criticism and expressions of negative affect on the part of the child.

It is not surprising that mothers who are more authoritarian—that is, who lay heavy stress on obedience training—are decidely more inclined than nonauthoritarian mothers to deny their children the right to criticize their parents or express negative affect toward them and tend to treat such behavior as a transgression, subject to the same form of punishment as any other offense. This is not to say that a nonauthoritarian mother enjoys or invites dissent or outbursts of temper. Parents aim to transmit their own values to their children, just as democratic states aim to instill conformity to democratic norms in their citizenry. But just as the democratic state accords legitimacy to dissent and protest and provides mechanisms for citizens to exercise that right, within limits, without harassment, so also does the democratic parent respect the child's right, within limits, to express criticism and hostility. The authoritarian parent, in contrast, views such behavior as a transgression and seeks to suppress it by threats or punishment. The authority and discretion are vested in parents to define within the domain of home what the rights of children are, to decide what acts constitute transgressions and what sanctions to invoke when these occur.

Suppression of Autonomy

Melvin Kohn (1969) makes a distinction between two parental values—conformity and self-direction. That distinction is an ambiguous one, for all parents, even the most permissive, value conformity to norms they seek to instill in their children. What distinguishes a democratic parent from an authoritarian one, rather, is the dedication of the democratic parent to the *principle* of self-direction—that is, to the establishment of internalized controls, whereby the child assumes responsibility for his or her own acts instead of relying on the exercise of control by external authorities, whether they be parents, teachers, or representatives of the law. Learning self direction is a protracted process wherein the child gradually develops the ability to exercise his or her own judgment by being allowed the opportunity to form and express independent opinions, subject, of course, to parental review and discussion. Thus, parents who value self-direction are also concerned with gaining conformity to their own values, but they attempt to do so through an ongoing dialogue characterized by a considerable measure of reciprocity and exchange, through persuasion and explanation, and through approval and criticism. They forgo coercive forms of control as a rule, although they may recognize them as efficient means of gaining conformity quickly, for fear of endangering the development of self-direction and self-control in their child. They perceive these as important qualities underlying high educational and occupational achievement. In short, they forgo the immediate reward of external compliance for the long-range objective, which they recognize requires self-motivation and effort, not external control and coercion, particularly after the constraint of compulsory schooling is removed in adolescence.

A measure of the extent to which mothers suppress autonomous behavior in their children is based on a combined score of mothers' answers to three questions:

1. Do you allow (child) to criticize your views when (he/she) disagrees with them or not?
2. When (child) gets angry with you and expresses it, do you usually punish (him/her) for that or not?
3. Do you let (child) express anger toward (his/her) father or not?

The higher the score,[9] the more likely a mother is to negatively reinforce verbal expression of dissent, thereby teaching the child as she or he develops to suppress the exercise of critical faculties in order to avoid disapproval or punishment by parents and, later on, by other authority figures. Passive compliance is likely to be equated with virtue, with being "good," while the expression of doubt and dissent are earmarks of "badness" of the sort that gets one into trouble with authority figures.

A similiar magnitude of association is found in both races between maternal authoritarianism and fatalism, on the one hand, and the suppression of autonomy, on the other. Among blacks the correlations are identical (.36). Among whites the correlation between authoritarianism and suppression of autonomy is higher (.46), and the latter's association with fatalism is (.41). Thus, in both races, suppression of autonomy rises with both maternal authoritarianism and fatalism.

Use of Physical and Nonphysical Punishment

Variations in types and frequency of punishment used to control children have been a subject of extensive empirical study, both as they relate to social-structural variables (Kohn, 1969; Pearlin 1971; Sears, Maccoby and Levin, 1957) and as they relate to various forms of problem behavior, such as aggression (Bandura, 1959), delinquency (Aichorn, 1955), and authoritarianism and prejudice (Adorno et al., 1950).

In the present study, two measures were constructed to assess the extent and types of negative reinforcement used by mothers to control children's behavior.

> When you were toilet-training (child), how often did you spank (him/her)—very often, once in a while, or hardly ever? [The same question was asked with respect to the frequency of "bawling out" and shaming the child during toilet training.]
> When (child) was 3 or 4 and (he/she) wouldn't mind you, how often did you do any of the following things? For each, could you tell me if you did it very often, fairly often, once in a while, or hardly ever? Spank or whip (him/her); threaten to spank, if (he/she) didn't mind; punish (him/her) by taking some privilege away; give (him/her) a good talking to or scolding; tell (him/her) you don't like (him/her) when (he/she) acts like that?[10]

At a later point in the interview, mothers were asked about their use of punishment in later childhood:

> I'll read some ways that parents use to punish children for bad behavior at this age. How often do you use the method of... depriving (child) of something (he/she) wants, like TV, movies, candy? Spanking or whipping? Isolating (child)? Telling (him/her) how disappointed you are? Telling (him/her) you don't like (him/her) when (he/she) acts like that? Explaining to (him/her) why you disapprove?[11]

Two additional questions related to the mothers' frequency of conflict with and criticism of their child were asked:

> How often do you and (child) have disagreements because (he/she) wants to do something you think (he/she) is too young to do? Does this happen very often, fairly often, once in a while, or hardly ever?
> How often do you criticize (child) when (he/she) is not doing something as well as you think (he/she) could? Very often, fairly often, once in a while or hardly ever?

A principal components analysis of responses to all these questions yielded two composite measures. One component, on which severe methods of toilet training and frequency of spanking in early and later childhood had high loadings, constitutes a measure of the frequency with which mothers used coercive forms of discipline in rearing their children. A second measure, on which frequency of deprivation of privileges, criticism, and conflict with the child had high loadings, constitutes a measure of the frequency with which mothers used disparagement as a mode of control.

In addition to these two measures, two measures of father's use of physical discipline in relation to the study child in early and later childhood were constructed. Since the administration of physical discipline has traditionally been seen as more characteristically a paternal than a maternal function (Parsons et al., 1955), a more accurate assessment of the extent of use of physical punishment in the home is gained by measures based on both parents rather than simply on mother's behavior alone.

A significant association between maternal authoritarianism and frequency of coercive discipline is found in both races. Correlations of coercion with maternal fatalism are only slightly lower. However, the use of coercive discipline is more strongly correlated with authoritarianism among whites (.33) than among blacks (.22), and it also varies more with maternal fatalism among whites (.30) than among blacks (.15). These differences between the races suggest that somewhat greater consistency exists between the values articulated by white mothers and their modes of control than is the case among black mothers. Less association between the use of disparagement and maternal orientations is found among whites, and among blacks there is virtually no association between these variables.[12]

Despite the differences in magnitude of association between maternal values and the use of aversive modes of control, and in the degree of consistency between mothers and fathers in the use of physical punishment in the two races, the magnitude of association between the use of coercive discipline and disparagement by mothers is much the same among blacks (.33) as among whites (.27).

These findings suggest that the values mothers espouse influence the manner in which they exercise authority over their children. The more authoritarian and fatalistic a mother is, the more likely she is to use negative and punitive sanctions with her child. She seeks to coerce the child into the *habit* of obedience by the application of force in the belief that pain and shame are the only effective countermeasures to the "natural meanness and mischief" of children. Such mothers rely on the memory of the pain induced and the child's fear of being subjected to it again to operate as inhibiting forces against further transgression. They further seek to subjugate the child by denying him or her the right to voice criticism and negative feelings, thereby further inhibiting the development of an active stance toward the environment. Under such a regimen of control, strivings for autonomy are viewed as transgressions that need to be firmly suppressed if parental authority is to be maintained. Opportunities for verbal exchanges in which the child learns to articulate his or her own thoughts and feelings are denied. Some children respond to such restrictions by becoming submissive in the presence of authority; others develop a sullen stance, verbalizing and acting out hostility when not under the surveillance of parents. Whatever the response, an authoritarian regimen is likely to produce external conformity but at the cost of undermining the growing child's sense of control as opposed to the infantile sense of being controlled by powerful, external forces.

In short, authoritarian modes of socialization tend to breed a fatalistic orientation in children; that is, a sense of powerlessness and a sense that they are not responsible for events but are mere instruments of fate subject to arbitrary, external, and unpredictable forces.

Abraham Maslow (1943) years ago identified the tendency to avoid responsibility for one's own fate as an attribute of authoritarian character. The strong association between authoritarianism and fatalism found among mothers of both races in our sample provides some empirical confirmation of his proposition.

Coleman et al. (1966) in their important study of the sources of variance in black and white achievement provided convincing evidence of the dysfunctional effects of having a low sense of control on children's achievement.

A low sense of control has been found repeatedly to be more prevalent among black children than among white children (Battle and Rotter, 1963; Coleman et al., 1966; Lefcourt, 1966). Coleman and his colleagues report that the variable "fate control" accounted for about three times more of the variance in the achievement test scores of black children than of white children at *higher* grade levels, even with family background characteristics controlled.

These investigations deal with the effects of a low sense of control in children but not with the sources of such attitudes nor with the processes through which they become established and impede intellectual development in childhood.

The source, as I have suggested in the foregoing pages, lies in the value orientations and modes of control employed in the early socialization of the child. It remains to provide an account of *how* authoritarian maternal values and practices impede the development of the conceptual thinking and language skills which are critical elements in the development of verbal intelligence. For this purpose, it is necessary to go beyond my own data and draw upon the work of other investigators.

Basil Bernstein (1961, 1964) has identified important differences in the language styles of British middle-class and working-class parents that he believes help account for differences in intellectual ability exhibited by their children. Language is viewed by Bernstein as a form of social behavior that determines and is determined by the nature of social relations and control systems operative in the family (as well as in other social groups). He distinguishes between two types of family control—status-oriented and person-oriented[13]—and two types of language codes—restricted and elaborated—that respectively express and reinforce each mode of control.

"Restricted" verbal codes are limited, stereotyped, and lacking in specificity and precision of conceptualization and communicated meaning. Sentences are simple and short, and there is little elaboration of content. An "elaborated" code, in contrast, is more particularized with respect to its referents, more differentiated, and more precise, and discriminates more between cognitive and affective content, permitting the expression of a wider and more complex range of meanings.

Status-oriented modes of parental control of children utilize more restricted speech patterns and rely more on status-oriented, imperative forms of address. Behavior tends to be regulated more in terms of status attributes and external criteria. Person-oriented modes of parental control, in contrast, utilize more elaborate language codes, are more cognizant of and concerned with the individual characteristics of a child and with the effects of parental communications on the internal thoughts and feelings of children, and are characterized by less imperative modes of interaction and communication.

Two important recent observational studies confirm and elaborate the theoretical work of Bernstein and of Maslow and provide concrete illustrations of the interactional processes through which authoritarian modes of maternal control and restricted language codes combine to impede children's cognitive development and sense of efficacy. They also are consistent with my interpretation of the negative associations reported in the present study between authoritarian-fatalistic orientations of mothers and children's performance on IQ and achievement tests.

Minton, Kagan, and Levine (1971) observed mothers' interactions with their 27-month-old children (49 boys and 41 girls, first-born and white) in their homes on two separate occasions, as part of a longitudinal study based on observational data which began when the children were in early infancy. A major aim of the study was to determine to what extent mothers' control behavior with respect to their two-year-old children was influenced by the characteristics of the child in early infancy. A major dimension of difference between mothers was "distrustful" and "trustful" modes of control, which the authors themselves equate with distinctions made in an earlier longitudinal study of controlling and democratic homes (Baldwin, Kalhorn, Breese, 1945, 1949) and with the "authoritarian versus equalitarian" dichotomy used by many other investigators. They found a markedly greater use of authoritarian modes employed by mothers with less than a college education. As will be shown later, this is consistent with my own findings.

The authors sum up their findings as follows.

> The pattern of correlations reveals one group of mothers, typically high school graduates, who prohibit their child frequently, physically punish him, and do not bother to explain these socializing practices. This cluster is reminiscent of Baldwin's authoritarian parent and in accord with other work indicating that the lower middle class parent is directive and convinced that the child has to be told what to do. . . . The better educated, more egalitarian mother, who allows the child more freedom, acts as if she believed the child were capable of controlling his behavior. During the home interview, these parents described their children

as thinking before they acted. . . . The relative independence of the child's tendency to obey immediately from the mother's tendency to punish or explain suggests that difference among mothers in the disposition to explain or punish is related to a psychological dimension within the mother, and is not primarily a function of whether she has an obedient child. We are not denying that the child makes a contribution to the mother's tendency to punish, but these data argue that at this age most of the variance is coming from the mother. [pp. 1889–1891]

The authors found better-educated mothers to be less authoritarian, less intrusive, less inclined to expect mischievous behavior, and more tolerant of mild misdemeanors in their children. They also found, interestingly, that the children of these mothers were markedly more inclined to invite their mothers to play with them than the children of less-educated, more authoritarian mothers. The authors interpret this not as an indication of greater dependency but rather as evidence of a more trusting and companionate orientation toward the mother, in contrast to one where she is an object of fear. Even at this early age, positive, stimulating experiences produce pleasure and gratifications that promote identification with the mother. This in turn facilitates internalization of her aspirations and normative standards, thereby providing the leverage to influence her child even after the range of alternative social resources at the child's disposal are extended in later childhood and adolescence.

The authoritarian mother, in contrast, is much more inclined toward the traditional view "Spare the rod and spoil the child." She believes that fearing her will instill the habit of obedience in her child, including compliance to her demand for good school performance. However, the will and the ability to master intellectual skills are not in the realm of behavior that can be established through fear and coercion. Instead, an authoritarian regimen often has a "boomerang" effect over the long run, particularly after the child has the capability of finding alternative and more gratifying activities and social resources. In short, the net result as the child grows older is avoidance of the mother *and* of her strictures, further diminishing her influence (Furstenberg, 1971; Winch and Gordon, 1974).

A vivid and precise account of how authoritarian, status-oriented modes of interaction combine with restricted language styles to impede children's intellectual growth is reported by Robert Hess and Virginia Shipman (1965). Their research, based on interviews with 163 black mothers from four social status level and on systematic observation of how they taught their four-year-old children several simple assigned tasks, revealed marked and consistent differences between status groups in maternal teaching styles and in their children's styles of information processing and learning.

Upper-middle-class mothers exhibited markedly greater verbal output and used a higher proportion of abstract words and more complex syntactic structures, which employ more coordinating and subordinate clauses. Their communications were less prohibitive, less imperative, and more instructive. Upper-middle-class mothers gave more explicit verbal information to their children about tasks and about what was expected of them; they offered more support and help of various kinds. They criticized no less than other mothers, but they praised their children's efforts more. As a result, marked differences were observed between upper-middle-class children and children from lower classes in what they were able to learn from their mothers.

Hess and Shipman conclude:

> The picture that is beginning to emerge is that the meaning of deprivation is a deprivation of meaning—a cognitive environment in which behavior is controlled by status rules rather than by attention to the individual characteristics of a specific situation and one in which behavior is not mediated by verbal cues or by teaching that relates events to one another and the present to the future. This environment produces a child who relates to authority rather than to rationale, who although often compliant, is not reflective in his behavior, and for whom the consequences of an act are largely considered in terms of immediate punishment or reward rather than future effects and long range goals. [p. 136]

A concrete example offered by Hess and Shipman of maternal behavior which "is not mediated by verbal cues or by teaching that relates events to one another and the present to the future" would be a mother who watches her child's efforts to perform a task and who punishes him when he makes an error. Another mother, instead, will offer verbal and nonverbal cues to help the child avoid the mistake, thereby encouraging preliminary reflection and anticipation of consequences.

Implicit in this illustration is the confounding of the meaning and consequences of error and transgression by the more authoritarian mothers. What is communicated to the child who is punished for making an error in the same manner in which he or she is punished for committing a transgression is that any act which is labeled "wrong" will result in disparagement or more coercive forms of punishment.

The term "wrong" precisely used refers to a normative violation, but it is frequently used by parents and teachers as a synonym for "incorrect." The difference in meaning is probably quickly discriminated by the child whose mother elaborates her meaning when she communicates with him or her, but the discrimination of meaning is more problematic for children growing up in homes where restricted speech codes and status-oriented modes of interaction prevail.[14]

If error is perceived as equivalent in its consequences to being "bad"— that is, that it evokes a disparaging or punitive response—the motivation and ability to *solve* problems which are basic characteristics of intellectual work is inhibited. As Hess and Shipman comment:

> A problem-solving approach requires reflection and the ability to weigh decisions, to choose among alternatives. The effect of restricted speech and of status orientation is to foreclose the need for reflective weighing of alternatives and

consequences; the use of an elaborated code, with its orientation to persons and to consequences (including the future), tends to produce cognitive styles more easily adapted to problem-solving and reflection.

The passive compliance, based on fear of punishment, that authoritarian mothers aim to instill with respect to parental norms is also likely to be established with respect to formal learning situations and to other authority figures, notably teachers, particularly if they also exercise their role in an authoritarian manner. And the same boomerang effects may be expected with respect to formal learning—sullen defiance rather than passive compliance—as the child grows older and more hardened to punishment.

Authoritarian modes of control and restricted modes of communication impede intellectual development of the child long before formal schooling begins. Early deficits in the mastery of basic concepts and skills become cumulatively greater handicaps as the child is called upon to master increasingly complex content. Frustration and failure ensue. Instead of a growing sense of efficacy, children reared under such a regimen develop feelings of inadequacy and of futility about exerting effort.

Evidence, previously cited, shows that such an orientation, once established, becomes a further impediment to learning, for it operates as a self-fulfilling prophecy. Those who do not believe that their own efforts are of any avail are less inclined to make attempts to succeed at any activity that depends on intellectual knowledge or skills.

Seeman (1967) has provided empirical evidence that a sense of helplessness leads not only children but also more mature individuals to delay or avoid seeking information or knowledge that is associated with anxiety about control.

In these ways, authoritarian modes of control are linked to restricted and restrictive modes of communication. Their combined effect is to impede the understanding and mastery of the most basic concepts and their articulation in language, leading to a cognitive deficit established long before the child begins formal schooling. In addition, authoritarian modes of control undermine and delay the development of the sense of self-efficacy that normally follows in the wake of growing physical and linguistic dexterity in children reared in families that value, cultivate, and encourage the growth of individuation and autonomy. In authoritarian homes, these very qualities are viewed negatively, and significantly greater time and energy are devoted to suppressing them because they are perceived as antithetical to continued conformity to the exercise of arbitrary power. According to the authoritarian view, this obedience is the role behavior appropriate to children and other dumb animals. Such a mode of control deprives the growing child of a sense of inner responsibility and instead prolongs an infantile orientation toward the world, in which ego is the victim, not the master, of its own destiny. Once established, such an orientation operates as a self-fulfilling prophecy, particularly in the realm of intellectual work, in which effectiveness depends on the expectation of gain through the input of effort. For the person who comes to learning already cognitively handicapped, a low sense of control further reinforces intellectual disability. Thus, early cognitive disability and a low sense of control exert reciprocal effects that increase over time and help account for the pattern repeatedly observed among working-class and black children of decrements in test scores with increasing years of schooling as opposed to the increments in scores generally exhibited by white middle-class children (Douglas, 1964; Coleman, et al., 1966).

Race and Socialization Strategies

Three dimensions of socialization have been identified and described. The remainder of this chapter presents a comparison of the relationships among these dimensions found among black and white mothers in order to arrive at some estimate of the prevalence of maternal strategies that promote and hinder the development of intellectual and scholastic competence in the two races. The chapter concludes with a multivariate analysis of the three dimensions of socialization to determine the independent contribution of each to the explanation of variance in children's test scores in each race and in the scores of the races combined.

A very substantial correlation is found between mother's valuation of education and the investment of resources in rearing children in both races, although the magnitude of correlation is slightly higher among white (r = .55) than among black mothers (r = .50).[15] In both races, the modal pattern of mothers with a low valuation of education is to invest least in child-rearing activities of a positive and stimulating character. As mothers' valuations of education rise, the proportions who invest more resources in rearing their children also rise in both races. Mothers who place a high valuation on their children's future education most frequently exhibit a high level of investment in the kinds of activity that promote intellectual development. To that extent blacks and whites are similar. But marked differences are observed between the races in the extreme categories. Thus, a markedly higher proportion of white (66 percent) than of black mothers (44 percent) who value education highly fall in the upper third with respect to their level of investment in their children. Even among mothers who place a low value on educational attainment, far fewer white mothers (46 percent) than black ones (64 percent) exhibit a low level of investment in activities and experiences that promote measured intelligence.

The marked differences in the strategies of socialization of black and white mothers become even more evident when their use of aversive discipline is compared, controlling for valuation of education and investment in child.

In both races investment in the child *increases* and aversive discipline *decreases* as maternal ambitions rise. However, even white mothers who place a low value on educational attainment but exhibit a high degree of investment typically score low on the use of aversive discipline (57 percent), compared with only 18 percent of their black counterparts. In short, whatever their level of ambition, white mothers who exhibit a high level of investment in rearing their child *typically* forgo aversive discipline, whereas black mothers, whatever their level of ambition and the amount of investment in their child, *typically* use more aversive discipline to control their children. Thus, even among black mothers with high levels of ambition *and* high investment in their child, only two-fifths score low on the use of aversive discipline, compared with three-quarters of their white counterparts.

This difference in the socialization strategies of black and white mothers is a significant source of difference in the scholastic ability of black and white children.

Table 6-2 provides evidence for the proposition that a strategy of high investment and low use of aversive discipline optimizes achievement of children in each race, although it does not, nor would it be expected to, eliminate the differences in scores between black and white children since maternal strategies of socialization are only *one* source of disparity in children's scholastic ability. Nevertheless, it is interesting to note the similarities in the size of the increments in children's achievement scores in the two races with rising levels of maternal investment and declining use of aversive discipline. Under a nonauthoritarian regimen, increments of investment in the child yield the highest return. That is, the increment of difference in achievement scores in both races is greatest between the mean achievement of children of low "investors" and high ones—a difference of 1.7 stanines among blacks and 2.0 among whites. Conversely, the lowest increment in children's achievement scores with level of maternal investment occurs among mothers with high aversive-discipline scores in both races, 0.8 stanine in each race. Under conditions of moderate use of discipline, the increment in achievement with rising levels of investment is somewhat higher for white children (1.6 stanines) than for black ones (1.1 stanines), which suggests that even a moderately authoritarian regimen undercuts the "return" on her investment more in the case of a black mother than in the case of a white one, perhaps because, as a rule, she has fewer resources to invest in her child.

Black mothers express higher ambitions for their child's future educational attainment than white mothers, other things being equal (Appelbaum, 1971), and in both races, the extent of a mother's investment in child rearing rises with valuation of education. From all the evidence at hand, this is productive for promoting both intellectual development and the motivation to do well in school. Indeed, it is fruitful to postulate that maternal strategies of socialization govern the sort of transactions that develop between child

TABLE 6-2. Mean Achievement Scores by Maternal Investment, Use of Aversive Discipline, and Race

Level of Aversive Discipline

Level of Investment in Child	Low				Middle				High			
	BLACK	N	WHITE	N	BLACK	N	WHITE	N	BLACK	N	WHITE	N
Low	4.2	(14)	5.4	(37)	3.9	(72)	5.0	(44)	3.7	159	5.2	(38)
Middle	5.1	(31)	6.7	(74)	4.7	(80)	6.2	(68)	4.0	81	5.5	(34)
High	5.9	(47)	7.4	(164)	5.0	(57)	6.6	(48)	4.5	38	6.0	(16)
Difference between low and high	+1.7	(92)	2.0	(275)	+1.1	(209)	+1.6	(160)	+0.8	278	+0.8	(88)

114

and mother. The mother who invests more of the resources at her disposal—time, effort, money—to provide experiences that promote growth of the child's skills and sense of efficacy becomes an important source of gratification for her child, who thereby is put under an obligation to reciprocate or repay that investment. Such exchanges are not calculated or even necessarily conscious. But it is a matter of common observation that whenever individuals are the beneficaries of pleasant and gratifying interaction from another, they are inclined to invest more time and effort in activities valued by that other (Homans, 1962; Blau, 1964). Conversely, when they are recipients of actions and experiences that are unpleasant or demeaning from another, they are not under the same obligation to *voluntarily* exert effort to comply with the other's wishes or expectations. Instead, if they have any choice in the matter, they will seek to withhold gratification and to distance themselves from that other.

Mothers who have high ambitions for their children's future *and* implement these ambitions by investing in stimulating and pleasurable interaction, but who at the same time utilize a good deal of aversive discipline, engage in a strategy that is counterproductive in that it minimizes rather than maximizes the return on their investment. What they give to the child in terms of stimulation and gratification with one hand, so to speak, they take away with the other. Thus, mothers who are a frequent source of demeaning and unpleasant experiences lose some of their influence over their child, because he or she does not feel the same obligation to reciprocate for positive benefits when there are frequent negative interludes. It is as though an authoritarian mother, by exacting relatively frequent expiation from her child for transgressions real or imagined, discharges the child from the obligation to repay positive benefits received from her. The necessity to suppress expressions of pain and anger are costs imposed by an authoritarian mother on her child, whatever her level of positive investment. But if the level of authoritarianism is high at the same time that positive investment in the child's growth is low, the return in terms of scholastic performance is likely to be very low. Children of mothers who follow such a strategy have the lowest achievement scores in both races. Conversely, the highest scores in both races are exhibited by children whose mothers follow a strategy of high investment and low aversive discipline. The mean score of black children with such mothers is 5.9 and that of white children 7.4, as Table 6-2 shows.[16]

It has been shown that mothers in both races who value educational attainment more also invest more of their resources in stimulating forms of interaction and utilize aversive modes of control less. Furthermore, it appears that a strategy that combines high positive investment and a low use of aversive control optimizes scholastic ability, whereas the reverse strategy has the opposite effect in both races. However, the optimal strategy of socialization has been shown to be far more prevalent among white than

among black mothers in the sample. Evidence that this difference is a significant source of disparity in the test performance of black and white children
will be presented in the following pages.

Effects of Socialization on Black and White Children's IQ and Achievement Scores: A Multivariate Analysis

Sociologists, as a rule, focus mainly on the social-structural antecedents
of the phenomena they seek to explain, although some recent stratification
studies have incorporated parental aspirations as well in their theoretical
models (Sewell and Shah, 1968; Gordon, 1972). Social psychologists, in contrast, have been mainly concerned with assessing effects of variations in
parental beliefs and practices on children without extensively delineating
their social-structural antecendents (Sears, Maccoby, Levin, 1957; Kagan
and Moss, 1962).

The first part of the study assessed the effects of social structural variables
on IQ and achievement test performance.

Some findings of considerable interest emerge when the predictive value
of the socialization model and the structural model are compared.

The three dimensions of socialization explain 16 percent of the variation
in black children's IQ scores. However, the predictive power comes mostly
from mother's valuation of education (beta = .22) and investment in the child
(beta = .21). Use of discipline has a weak negative effect (beta = −.07) but
does not significantly increase the variance explained by the other two variables in the equation. In the case of white children's scores, the discipline
variable does not even enter the equation. Mother's valuation on education
(beta = .25) and investment in the child (beta = .24) are almost equally
strong predictors of white children's IQ scores; together they account for 19
percent of the variance in IQ scores, or 3 percent more than socialization
variables account for in black children's IQ scores. Sex of child raises the
variance explained in white children's scores by 1 percent to 20 percent but
does not enter the black equation.[17]

With the races combined and with race in the equation[18] as well as the
three socialization measures, the variance explained in IQ scores amounts to
28 percent. The net effects of mother's valuation of education (beta = .22), of
being white, (beta = .23), and of investment in the child (beta = .21) are very
similar. Discipline has a negative effect on IQ scores which is weaker (beta
= −.08), though significant. The remaining difference in IQ scores of the two
races is 5.9 points after socialization measures are controlled.

It is interesting to note that this remaining difference between the mean
scores of black and white choldren is higher than that observed when IQ
scores were regressed on socioeconomic-status, religious, and family var-

iables (beta = 3.5). However, the variance explained by the "socialization" model (28 percent) is greater than that explained by the structural model (25 percent).

Thus, the socialization model explains 3 percent more of the variance of IQ scores in the combined sample than is explained by the structural model. At the same time, the residual difference in mean IQ scores between the races is higher (5.9) with the socialization model than with the structural model. This results from the fact that the socialization model increases by 5 percent the amount of variance explained in white children's IQ scores but decreases by 2 percent the variance explained in black children's scores. Social and family structural variables, in contrast, account for more variance in black children's IQ scores (18 percent) than in those of white children (15 percent). These differences in the predictive power of structural and socialization variables in the two races suggests that a model that takes into account both differences in structural factors and socialization strategies may have more predictive and explanatory value than a model based solely on one or the other set of variables. A test of this proposition is reserved for Chapter 8.

The socialization model explains slightly less of the variance in black children's achievement scores (41 percent) than is explained by the structural model (43 percent), but it explains more of the variance in white children's achievement scores (43 percent as compared with 39 percent). Further, with the socialization model, IQ score becomes a substantially stronger predictor of black children's achievement scores (beta = .50) than of white children's scores (beta = .42), whereas with social-structural variables, IQ scores are equally predictive of black and white children's achievement scores (beta = .49). That socialization variables have the effect of reducing the weight of IQ as a predictor only of white children's scores suggests that socialization processes are stronger mediators of the effects of social structure on achievement test performance in the case of white than in the case of black children because of the greater prevalence among white mothers of optimal strategies of socialization.

The differences in the beta weights of two socialization dimensions in the two races support this interpretation. First, mother's valuation of education is a markedly stronger predictor of white children's achievement scores (beta = .21) than of black children's scores (beta = .10). Second, use of aversive discipline is a weaker predictor of white children's achievement scores (beta = −.10) than of black children's scores (beta = −.15). Investment in child, in contrast, is virtually as strong a predictor of black children's achievement scores (beta = .09) as of white children's (beta = .10). These results of the multivariate analysis are consistent with evidence presented earlier that the relatively heavy reliance on aversive discipline even by black mothers who value education highly undercuts the positive effects that a high valuation of education normally has in promoting scholastic achievement. It is also noteworthy that only with the socialization model does sex of the child enter the prediction equation of black children. It appears that black boys' achievement scores tend to exceed those of black girls (beta = .06) when socialization variables and IQ scores are controlled. Although this effect does not significantly increase the variance explained, it is a suggestive finding that will be discussed further when the sexes are analyzed separately.

The socialization model does not alter the amount of variance explained in achievement scores of the combined sample, which remains 55 percent when IQ is included in the equation. Mother's valuation of education is only a slightly stronger predictor of achievement scores (beta = .14) than aversive discipline (beta = −.13). Again, the effect of aversive discipline is to lower achievement test performance in contrast to the positive effect that mother's valuation of education has on scores. Investment in child is a weak positive predictor (beta = .05) of achievement scores.

With the socialization model the remaining difference between black and white children's achievement scores is slightly greater (beta = .93 vs. .87) than with the model based on social structural variables, but the increment of difference in achievement scores of the two races is less than observed in IQ scores. These disparities in results with the two models, as already indicated, result from the fact that structural variables account for more variance in black children's scores, whereas socialization variables account for more variance in white children's scores.

Summary

Three dimensions of socialization have been identified and described— mothers' valuation of education, investment in the child, and belief in and use of aversive control. Mothers in both races who place a high valuation on their children's education generally exhibit a higher level of investment in activities that promote intellectual development. But a markedly higher proportion of white than of black mothers who highly value education exhibit a high level of investment in the child. And even among mothers who place a low value on educational attainment, far fewer white than black mothers exhibit a low level of investment in the child.

Whatever their level of ambition, white mothers who exhibit a high level of investment in the child typically forgo aversive discipline, whereas black mothers, whatever their level of ambition and the amount they invest in the child, typically use more aversive discipline to control their children.

These differences in the socialization strategies of black and white mothers are a significant source of difference in the scholastic ability of their children. A strategy of high investment and low use of aversive discipline optimizes the scholastic achievement of children in each race. That is, under a nonauthoritarian regimen, the increment of difference in achievement scores is greatest between the mean achievement scores of children of low and high "investors." Under an authoritarian regimen, the increment of difference in achievement scores is smallest between children of low and high investors.

In sum, mothers who have high ambitions for their children's future and implement these ambitions by investing in stimulating and pleasurable interaction with their children, but who at the same utilize a good deal of aversive discipline, engage in a strategy that is counterproductive in that it minimizes rather than maximizes the return they command on their investment. Mothers who utilize high aversive control and exhibit low investment in the child command the least return on their investment, and children of mothers in both races who follow such a strategy have the lowest achievement scores.

A comparison of the predictive value of the socialization model and of the structural model presented in Chapter 4 reveals, first, that the socialization model accounts for more variance in white than in black children's IQ scores (19 vs. 16 percent) and, second, that sex of the child raises the variance explained in white scores by the socialization model to 20 percent, but this variable does not enter the black equation.

With the races combined and with race in the equation, the socialization model explains 28 percent of the variance in children's IQ scores: the independent positive effects of mother's valuation of education, of investment in the child, and of being white are very similar. Aversive discipline has a weaker, but still significant, negative effect. The remaining difference in IQ scores of the two races is 5.9 points after socialization measures are controlled.

Thus, the socialization model explains 3 percent more of the variance in IQ scores than is explained by the social structural model, but the residual difference in mean IQ scores between the races is higher with the socialization model than with the social structural model (5.9 vs. 3.5). This results from the fact that the socialization model increases by 5 percent the amount of variance explained in white children's IQ scores, but it reduces by 2 percent the variance explained in black children's scores. Social and family structural variables, in contrast, account for more variance in black than in white children's IQ scores (18 vs. 15 percent). These differences in the predictive power of structural and socialization variables suggests that a model that combines structural and socialization variables may have more predictive and explanatory value than one based solely on one or the other set of variables.

The socialization model explains slightly less variance in black children's achievement scores and somewhat more variance in white children's scores than the structural model does. Moreover, with the socialization model, IQ becomes a stronger predictor of black than of white children's achievement scores. This suggests that socialization processes are stronger mediators of the effects of social structure on achievement test performance in the case of white than of black children because of the greater prevalence among white mothers of optimal strategies of socialization. That mother's valuation of education is a markedly stronger predictor of white than of black children's achievement scores, whereas aversive control is a stronger predictor of black than of white children's scores, is further evidence that the relatively heavy reliance on aversive discipline by black mothers undercuts the positive effects normally exerted by a high valuation of education on children's scholastic performance.

The evidence presented in this chapter strengthens the case for the proposition that significant differences observed in the socialization strategies of black and white mothers are independent sources of the disparity in their children's performance on IQ and achievement tests. That proposition will be further explicated and tested in Chapters 8 and 9.

The next chapter compares the extent to which black and white mothers' socilization goals and practices are conditioned by their socioeconomic status, religious affiliation, and familial and extrafamilial roles.

Notes

1. Coefficient of reproducibility = .94; coefficient of scalability = .77. With respect to each statement, "Agree" was coded 1 and "disagree" was coded 0. The higher the score, the lower (it is assumed) is a mother's sense of control over her life and the greater the likelihood that she teaches such an orientation to her child.

2. Rotter's I-E scale consists of 29 paired items, one couched to elicit agreement from subjects "externally oriented," the other to elicit disagreement from subjects with such an orientation. The total of "externally" oriented items endorsed constitutes a subject's score on this measure (Rotter, 1966, p. 12).

3. In sharp contrast to the process described above is the example of Muhammad Ali, the heavyweight boxer. When, as a child, he was beaten in a fight and came home crying to his mother, she told him that he could learn to fight and could accomplish "anything he wanted to." That assurance exemplifies the antithesis of the response that a mother with a high fatalism score would have made. (From an interview with Mrs. Cassius Clay, Sr., by Sandra Pressman, *Chicago Daily News*, Oct. 22, 1971.)

4. "Agree" to each statement was coded 1 and "disagree" was coded 0. The range of summated scores was 0 to 4 (Coefficient of reproducibility of the scale is .87 and coefficient of scalability is .67).

5. The first item in the authoritarianism scale, "obedience and respect for authority are the most important virtues children should learn," is very similar to the measure employed by Melvin Kohn (1969) and to an item that constituted part of the "F" scale constructed by Adorno and his associates (1950) in their classic study of the authoritarian character. The remaining three items in my authoritarianism scale are from the PARI instrument constructed by Schaeffer and Bell (1958).

6. The right of school officials to administer corporal punishment to children is more variable and is associated with the character of the state. But even within the United States, which subscribes to democratic principles, some states still countenance the use of corporal punishment in schools.

7. Still a third view, originally espoused by Rousseau and embraced by libertarian anarchists in the eighteenth and nineteenth centuries and more recently by such influential writers as Paul Goodman (1960), is that the basic nature of the child is benign, selfless, and innocent, but in the course of socialization, this basic goodness of the child becomes subverted and the child learns ambition, avarice, aggression, etc. Advocates of this view tend to advocate a laissez-faire strategy of socialization in which the role of parents is merely to provide nurturance and freedom to grow unfettered; the child will then grow into an open, good, and creative human being. William Golding's novel *Lord of the Flies* (1964) portrays a very different vision of what a society might be like if governed solely by children.

8. An example of such an orientation is provided by Sollenberger (1968) in his analysis of Chinese child-rearing practices. Teachers reported to him that if a note was sent home about a child's infraction of school rules, "almost invariably the father will appear the next day and apologize for *his* failure in the proper upbringing of the child" (p. 21). In short, the onus for failure is not externalized by laying it upon the young child but instead responsibility is internalized, suggesting an association between such an orientation and a high sense of inner control, which is the antithesis of a fatalistic orientation.

9. Allowing criticism is scored 1 and denial of right to criticize is scored 2. Nonpunishment of expression of anger is scored 1 and punishment is scored 2. Allowing child to express anger with or without reservation is scored 1 and denial to this right, with or without reservation, is scored 2. The range of summated scores is from 3 to 6.

10. These two questions were followed by the question, "How often did your husband do this?"

11. "How often does your husband do this?" was asked after each of the questions regarding mother's behavior.

12. The same pattern of differences between the races is observed in the relationship between maternal and paternal use of coercive discipline: among whites the correlation between these variables is considerably higher (.43) than among blacks (.23). Similarly, while a moderate correlation is found between maternal authoritarianism and maternal suppression of autonomy (.26) and between maternal authoritarianism and paternal use of physical punishment among whites (.26), among blacks virtually no relationship is found between maternal authoritarianism and paternal use of coercive discipline (.05), and only a very slight relationship is observed between mother's suppression of autonomy and paternal use of coercive discipline (.13). All correlations among components of aversive control and IQ and achievement test scores are shown in Table A-7, page 236.

13. This distinction is strongly reminiscent of the delineation by Maslow (1943) of authoritarian character structure, characterized by a hierarchical view of social relations, a concern for status and power over people, and the use of power to assuage psychological needs engendered by the thwarting of such basic needs as

safety, love, and a sense of belonging. From the latter arises a "world view" wherein each individual appears pitted against others and where the visible alternatives are to fear or to be feared. When the authoritarian is in a dominant status, he or she will tend toward cruelty and sadism; in a subordinate status he or she will tend to be submissive or masochistic. The authoritarian person tends to identify kindness, sympathy, and generosity with weakness, and cruelty, self-ishness, and hardness with strength. In contrast, the democratic personality values and respects diversity and individuation, and instead of being threatened by them, seeks mastery over things and tasks rather than power over people. Judgment of others is on the basis of internal rather than external criteria, on specific achievements rather than on generalized status and power.

14. Piaget (1948), in his studies of the development of moral judgment in children, has shown that judgments based solely on consequences of acts are characteristic of young children, but that in later states of development, this primitive view is gradually supplanted by judgments of acts also in terms of an actor's intent as the child masters the more complex comcepts and language entailed in more differentiated judgments. Lawrence Kohlberg (1966) has shown a relationship to exist between children's IQ scores and their level of moral development.

15. A lower negative correlation is found in each race between use of aversive discipline and valuation of education (blacks, $r = -.38$; whites, $r = -.42$) and between aversive discipline and investment in child (blacks, $r = -.36$; whites, $r = -.37$).

16. The same pattern of findings, with one exception, is observed when IQ scores are the dependent variable. The lowest average IQ score of black children (92) occurs when mothers follow a low investment–high aversive discipline strategy. The highest average score among blacks (106) is exhibited by children of mothers who follow a strategy of high investment and low discipline. The former strategy also produces the lowest IQ among white children (97). The highest mean IQ score (115) is found among white children of mothers who exhibit high invest-ment and a moderate use of aversive discipline. Children of mothers, with high investment and low aversive discipline scores score slightly lower (112).

17. With sex of child in the equation, the effect of mothers orientation to education is slightly strengthened (beta = .28), while the effect of investment in the child is slightly reduced (beta = .21). The reason for this will become clearer when the sexes are analyzed separately in Chapter 9.

18. Sex of the child does not enter the equation for the whole sample.

CHAPTER 7

Social Sources of Variation in Socialization

The previous chapter revealed differences between the socialization strategies that black and white mothers typically employ to implement their ambitions for their children and suggested that these differences are a significant source of disparity in the measured intelligence and scholastic ability exhibited by children in the two races. This chapter seeks to assess the extent to which observed variations in the maternal socialization strategies of black and white mothers arise from differences in the social-structural location and family situations of mothers in the two races. A multitude of social characteristics have been shown to differentiate black and white mothers in our sample, particularly the religious and socioeconomic composition of the two samples and also their family size, marital status, and work histories.

Socioeconomic Composition of Religious Groups

In both races, Baptist and other fundamentalist groups contain the largest proportion of low-SES members, but the only groups in which low-SES individuals constitute a clear majority are black Baptists and other fundamentalists (64 percent). Among whites with the same denominational affiliations, mothers of low SES also constitute the modal group (47 percent), but the majority is either of middle (29 percent) or high status (24 percent). Thus it is apparent that black Baptist and other fundamentalists constitute the most homogeneously lower-status religious group in the sample. At the other end of the spectrum, white Jewish, nondenominational/nonreligious, and High Protestants are predominantly of high socioeconomic status (83, 84, and 71 percent respectively). Nondenominational and nonreligious blacks are the only group in the black sample in which high SES families constitute the majority (53 percent). Black Catholics in my sample are predominantly middle status (73 percent) and the only black religious group with a higher SES constituency than their white co-religionists (50 percent). In contrast, next to the fundamentalists, white Catholics contain the highest proportion of low SES members (32 percent) in the white sample. In all *Protestant* denominations, the proportion of the membership that is of low SES is markedly higher among blacks than among whites.

The first task is to determine the extent to which a woman's location in the three distinct but related stratification hierarchies influences maternal values and socialization practices.

A comparison of valuations of education between black and white mothers who are of the same religious affiliation and similar socioeconomic status (Table A-8, page 237) strikingly reveals the remarkable consistency with which black mothers' ambitions for their children exceed those of their white counterparts. The only exception is among high-SES nondenominational/nonreligious mothers, where the mean scores of blacks and whites are identical (16.5).

Among blacks as among whites, maternal valuation of education rises with SES level within each religious and denominational group, but the largest differences between black and white mothers occur at the low SES level and the smallest differences are at the high SES level, with two exceptions. Among Catholics, black scores exceed white ones by as much in the high-SES (13 versus 11) as in the low-status group (17 versus 15). Indeed, black Catholics and fundamentalists of high SES do not value education less than the nonreligious mothers (17). In contrast, white Catholic mothers of high SES value education less (14.5) than all other groups in their stratum—blacks and whites. At the low-SES level, white Catholic mothers as well as white fundamentalists and Methodists value education least (11), whereas black Catholics value education more (13) than all other low-SES mothers, black as well as white, except black High Protestants (14).

The other interesting exceptions are the Jewish mothers in the sample, all of whom are white and none of whom is of low SES. Middle-status Jewish mothers value education just about as much as their high-status co-religionists (16). Jewish mothers exhibit the highest ambition, on the average, at the *middle*-SES level, compared with their black and white class peers of other religious backgrounds.[1]

Overall, it is clear that the previously noted differences in the social-class composition of religious groups do not fully account for variations in maternal orientations to education among religious groups. Among blacks of low SES, Baptists and other fundamentalists value education least (12), Methodists and Catholics scores are somewhat higher (13), and High Protestants are the highest (14). Among whites of low SES, Baptists, Methodists/Lutherans, and Catholics are all about equally low (11) and lower than High Protestants (12). At the middle-SES level, black Baptists, Methodists, and Catholics on the average value education somewhat less (14) than High Protestants and nondenominational/nonreligious mothers (15). Baptists voice the lowest ambitions among whites (12); Methodists/Lutherans and Catholics are somewhat higher (13); High Protestants and the nondenominational mothers score still higher (14); and Jewish mothers score highest (16). At the high-SES level, differences in valuation of education all but disappear among blacks of different religious backgrounds (16.4 to 16.8). But among high-SES whites, Catholics score lower than all Protestants (14.5), and nondenominational and Jewish mothers, as a rule, value education most (16.5 and 16.2, respectively).

The pattern with respect to investment in the child and socioeconomic status is different. At the low-SES level, black mothers average slightly lower scores (19.5) than their white counterparts (20.1); at the middle-SES level, the mean scores of white and black mothers are identical (21.4); and at the high-SES level, black mothers invest slightly more (24.0) than whites (23.6) in rearing their children. Thus, the extent of investment in child differs more by socioeconomic status than by race.

When religious affiliation as well as socioeconomic status is taken into account (Table A-9, page 237), some differences between the races emerge. The investment in their children of black *low*-SES Baptist and other fundamentalist mothers (19) is lower than that of any other subgroup in the sample—black or white. However, black low-SES mothers with other religious affiliations—Methodists, High Protestant, and Catholic—tend to invest slightly more in their children than their white co-religionists (21 vs. 20). Since 83 percent of black mothers at the low-SES level are Baptist or other fundamentalist, this means that in the large majority of cases, black, lower-SES mothers' average investment in their children is lower, as a rule, than that of white mothers of comparable socioeconomic status.

It is interesting, however, that at higher SES levels, black Fundamentalist mothers invest in their children to the same extent as their white co-religionists; at the middle-status level the scores of fundamentalists of both races is 21 and at the high-SES level, the mean score of both is 24, which suggests the presence of an interaction effect. The combination of being black, of low socioeconomic status, and fundamentalist has a particularly adverse effect on maternal investment, and children in this particular group as a rule are the most deprived in terms of maternal inputs that promote intellectual growth in infancy and early childhood. Other factors that operate to depress fundamentalist mothers' investment in their child will be identified presently.

At the middle-SES level, black fundamentalist and Methodist mothers average less investment (21) than High Protestant (23), Catholic (23), or nondenominational/nonreligious peers (22). Among whites in the same stratum, fundamentalist, High Protestant, and Catholic mothers invest least in their child (21): Methodist-Lutherans score somewhat higher (22), and nondenominational and Jewish mothers average the highest mean scores (23). Thus, it appears that in the middle-SES stratum, black High Protestant and Catholic mothers and white nondenominational and Jewish mothers exhibit the highest investment in children, whereas black and white fundamentalists, black Methodists, white Catholics, and white High Protestants invest least.

At the high-SES level, interestingly, black and white fundamentalists invest as much in their children (24) as Jewish and white nonreligious mothers, black Methodists, High Protestants, and Catholics. White High Protestants and Methodists average slightly lower scores (23), while Catholics score lowest (22). Black nonreligious mothers average the highest mean investment in their child (25) in the entire sample, which is surely an important source of their children's intellectual and scholastic proficiency. It would seem that just as there is an interaction between being poor, black, and fundamentalist that has the effect of inhibiting maternal investment, so there is also an interaction between being black, of high socioeconomic status, and nondenominational or nonreligious that promotes high investment in children.

To summarize, the strongest effect on variations in maternal investment appears to come from mothers' socioeconomic position. But some of the variance also is due to race and religious effects, and to complex interactions between these three structural variables. The use of aversive discipline, in contrast, varies more with race than with religion or socioeconomic status.

At each SES level, black mothers use more aversive discipline than white mothers; race differences are smallest at the low SES level (16 versus 15) and become larger at the middle- (14 versus 12) and high-SES levels (11 versus 9). In both races mothers of low SES use the most discipline. The decline in the use of discipline is steeper among white mothers of middle SES than among blacks. High-SES black and white mothers use the least discipline, but black mothers' scores remain considerably higher than those of white mothers.[2]

Religious affiliation does not alter the general pattern of differences noted above except in one interesting case. In all comparisons (Table A-10, page 000), black mothers use more authoritarian modes of control than their white co-religionists at a similar SES level except in the case of Catholics. White Catholics of low and middle SES have slightly higher mean discipline scores (16 and 13, respectively) than their black counterparts (15 and 12, respectively). But at the high-SES level, black Catholics' scores exceed those of white Catholics (12 vs. 11). Indeed, among black Catholics there is virtually no decrement in the use of discipline by high-SES mothers compared with those of middle SES (12), but a considerable decline is observed among white Catholics (13 vs. 11).

Low-SES black Fundamentalist and white Catholic mothers exhibit the highest mean discipline scores (16) closely followed by black Methodist, High Protestant, and Catholic mothers (15). These groups, on the average, employ more aversive discipline than any other subgroups in the entire sample. The most marked difference at the low SES level between black and white co-religionists is among high Protestants: black mothers average a score of 15 compared with a score of 11 among whites, which makes the latter the lowest users of discipline at the low-SES level in both races.

At the middle-SES level, black fundamentalist and Methodist mothers use the most discipline (14), followed by white fundamentalist, Catholic, and nondenominational mothers (13). Black High Protestants and white Methodists use less discipline (12) and white Protestants a bit less (11), followed by Jewish mothers (10). The lowest use of discipline is found among white nonreligious women at the middle- (9) and high-SES level (8).

At the high-SES level, black fundamentalists characteristically continue to exhibit the highest use of discipline (13), followed by black Catholic mothers (12); white Catholics and black Methodists (11); white Methodist/Lutheran, black High Protestant, and black nondenominational mothers (10). Interestingly, white fundamentalists of high SES average discipline scores no higher than those of white High Protestants or Jews (9). The lowest users of aversive discipline, however, are white nondenominational mothers (8).

Family Size and Socialization

When race, religion, and SES are simultaneously controlled, it becomes evident that differences in family size are a product more of race and socioeconomic status than of religious and denominational affiliation (Table A-11, page 000). For example, among mothers located in the lowest third of the SES distribution, black mothers average five children compared with an average of four children among whites. Within each race there are only minor variations in family size for different religious affiliations. At the middle-SES level, black women average four children, compared with three children among whites, and this difference persists even when religion is controlled, *except* among the nondenominational/nonreligious mothers, who in both races average the fewest children (2.4 among blacks and 2.5 among whites). At the high-SES level, the average number of children is three in each race. However, black High Protestant mothers average only two children; black Methodists and white Jewish mothers also tend to have fewer children than average (2.5 and 2.6, respectively). White Methodists/ Lutherans in contrast average 3.6 children. In short, religious affiliation exerts some effects on family size independent of socioeconomic status. Interestingly, Catholic mothers do not have larger families than other women in their own race and stratum, despite the church's official opposition to the use of mechanical means of contraception and abortion.[3]

Black mothers voice higher ambitions for their child as a rule than white mothers of similar SES level and religious affiliation. At the same time black Baptists, Methodists, and Catholics of low and middle SES have larger families as a rule than their white counterparts. Only among High Protestants and nondenominational women at the middle-SES level is family size the same in the two races. At the high-SES level, race differences in family size disappear, and among Methodists and High Protestants they even become reversed, but the proportion of such women in the black sample is small (7 percent).

A rational strategy for a group that is economically and socially disadvantaged and at the same time values higher education as the major route of upward mobility for its children would be to sharply limit family size so as to make it possible for parents to invest more of their limited resources in each individual child. Such a strategy was successfully followed by Jewish Eastern European immigrants (Blau, 1967, 1974b) who also had a high level of ambition but limited resources with which to effect their lofty goals.[4]

There is, to be sure, a negative relationship among blacks as among whites between maternal ambition and family size. In both races mothers with large families are less ambitious than those with smaller families. But whatever their family size, black mothers as a rule voice higher ambitions for their children than their white co-religionists.[5]

Whatever the material and nonmaterial resources at her disposal, a mother with a few children can make a greater investment in each child than one with many children. To be sure, an ambitious mother will exert herself more and invest more of her resources in a child even if she has several offspring. But there is a limit to how much any woman, whatever her level of ambition, can invest in a particular child if she carries the responsibility of rearing five or more children. Indeed, a less ambitious mother with only a few children may well be able to invest more of her available resources in each child than a more ambitious woman with a large family, particularly if the former also has more resources at her disposal. Thus, although the ambitions of black mothers often exceed those of their white counterparts, they have as a rule fewer resources of virtually every kind and *in addition* have more children as a rule among whom they must divide their more meager resources.

The proportion of mothers with five or more children is more than twice as high among blacks (38 percent) as among whites (15 percent). Except at the high socioeconomic level and except among High Protestant and nonreligious women of middle socioeconomic status, black mothers, as a rule, have larger families than their white co-religionists of similar status.

Almost invariably, within each religious group maternal investment scores decline as the number of children in the family rises.[6] It is noteworthy, however, that black women with *small* families in most comparisons invest *more* in rearing their children than their white co-religionists.[7] This pattern of differences is reversed among Baptist and other fundamentalist and non-denominational mothers who have three of four children and in all religious groups of women with five or more children. White mothers as a rule invest more in their child than their black co-religionists. The sole exception occurs among Catholics; black Catholic mothers invest more than their white co-religionists as a rule, whether the comparison is between women with small, medium, or large families.[8]

The amount of time and other resources mothers invest in their children varies not only with family size and socioeconomic status but also with religious and denominational affiliation. With family size controlled, it is evident that among blacks, Baptist and other fundamentalist mothers average the lowest investment scores whether they have small (21), medium (20), or large families (19); Methodists score somewhat higher (23, 22, and 20, respectively); and High Protestants (24, 23, 21), Catholics (25, 22, 22), and nondenominational mothers (24, 23, 23) score highest. Among whites, Catholic and Baptist mothers with small families average lower investment scores (21) than Methodists (22), High Protestants (23), nondenominational (25), or Jewish mothers (24). Among women with medium or large families, Catholics investment scores are lower (21 and 19) than those of Baptist mothers (22 and 20, respectively), Methodists (22), High Protestants (23 and 22, respectively), nondenominational (24 and 23), or Jewish mothers (24 and 23).

In both races, the use of aversive discipline rises with the number of children in the family, but black mothers rely more on aversive controls than their white co-religionists regardless of family size, with one exception. Among Catholics virtually no differences are observed between blacks and whites with three or four children (13). Black Catholic mothers with small families use slightly more discipline than their white co-religionists (14 vs. 13); white Catholics with large families use a good deal more discipline than their black co-religionists (15 vs. 12).

While in all other comparisons black mothers use more discipline than their white counterparts, there appears to be more variation with family size among black than among white mothers. Thus, among white fundamentalists only trifling differences occur between mothers (13), whatever the size of their family, but among their black co-religionists the use of discipline markedly increases as the number of children rises (14 to 15 to 16).

Among Methodists, black mothers with large families tend to use somewhat more discipline than blacks with smaller families (14 vs. 13) and the same is true for whites (12 vs. 11). Indeed, white Methodists with large families use virtually as much discipline as white fundamentalists.

Among white High Protestants the use of discipline rises only slightly according to family size (9.3, 9.4, 9.6), but in the case of their black counterparts the use of discipline rises markedly with rising family size (10 to 12 to 16).

Among nonreligious black mothers, it is possible to compare only those with small and medium families (since there is only one woman with a large family in this group). But only a trifling rise in the use of discipline is observed among mothers with three or four children (11.6) as compared with those with smaller families (12.1). The same is true, among nonreligious whites, but in large families there is a tendency to use more punishment (9 vs. 8). This group, however, uses less discipline than any other group in the entire sample regardless of family size. The other two groups that use aversive discipline most sparingly are white Jewish (9) and High Protestant mothers (9).

In sharp contrast, over the whole sample, black fundamentalists (16) and High Protestant (16) and white Catholic mothers (15) with large families use aversive discipline most. In these three groups also, the level of maternal discipline increases most markedly with large family size.

Fundamentalists of both races and white Catholic mothers with large families, it will be recalled, are also the groups which score lowest on investment in their children. The strategy that combines a low level of investment and a high level of discipline has been shown to yield the lowest return as measured by children's IQ and achievement scores. The use of such a counterproductive strategy appears to be conditioned more by the size of a woman's family in religious contexts where a strategy of low investment and high aversive control is relatively prevalent than in contexts where it is relatively rare.

Thus, fundamentalist mothers of both races and white Catholics invest less in their children even when they have only one or two children to rear, whereas nondenominational mothers of both races and Jewish mothers average the highest scores regardless of family size. Black Catholic and High Protestant mothers with one or two children also have very high investment scores, but they do not maintain that level of investment if they have more children to rear, although even with large families they score higher than black Baptists, Methodists, and white Catholics.

Just as white nondenominational, High Protestant, and Jewish mothers are consistently high on investment in their children, so they are consistently low on the use of discipline regardless of family size. Black denominational women are consistently lower than other black mothers in their use of discipline, but they are higher on this score than the aforementioned white groups. Black Catholics exhibit a curious pattern of variation with family size: those with small families have among the highest investment scores and high discipline scores as well. Indeed, on the latter score they are as high as black fundamentalists. As the size of family increases, black Catholics show a decline in investment in each child but also a decline in their use of discipline, a pattern just the opposite of that exhibited by white Catholics, who, even with small families, match fundamentalists in their low investment and high use of discipline.

Marital Status and Variations in Maternal Socialization Strategies

The proportion of mothers rearing children without husbands in the home is higher among blacks than among whites. Within each race no significant differences in father absence are found according to SES level in my sample.[9] Protestants have a higher incidence of father absence in both races (28 percent among blacks and 10 percent among whites) than Catholics (24 percent among blacks and 5 percent among whites) or Jews (4 percent). The proportion of nondenominational/nonreligious mothers without husbands is very similar to that among Protestants (29 percent among blacks and 10 percent among whites).

When Protestant mothers are broken down by denomination, markedly greater differences are found among whites in the proportion of father-absent families: 6 percent each among white Baptists and Methodists/ Lutherans and 18 percent among High Protestant whites. Among blacks the corresponding proportions are 29 percent among Baptists, and 26 percent among Methodists and High Protestants.

Married black mothers express significantly higher valuations of education (13.7) than those without husbands (13.0), but there is no significant variation on this score among white mothers (14.4 vs. 14.6). It is also worth noting that white mothers, whether married or not, have higher mean scores than black mothers, which is a reversal of the pattern reported earlier when valuation of education was broken down according to mother's SES and religious affiliation. The reasons, of course, are that marital status is associated with race and that the composition of the two races with respect to socioeconomic status and religion is markedly different. The much larger proportion of low-SES mothers and the much higher proportion of Baptist mothers among blacks markedly lowers the scores of both married and non-married black women relative to whites. Indeed, when religious affiliation is controlled, in virtually all comparisons of black and white mothers of the *same* religious affiliation, black mothers, currently married or not, have higher ambitions for their children than their white counterparts.

There are also some interesting interactions between religious affiliation, marital status, and maternal valuation of education. Thus, among Baptists and other fundamentalists without husbands (of which there are 105 blacks and only 4 whites) black mothers have considerably higher ambitions (12) for their children than their white nonmarried co-religionists (9). The difference between the races virtually disappears among the currently married because of the markedly higher valuations of education exhibited by white married Baptists (13) compared with nonmarried ones (9). Among black Methodists/ Lutherans, there is virtually no score difference between married and nonmarried mothers (14), but among their white co-religionists married mothers have slightly higher ambitions than (14) the nonmarried (13). In short, the differences favoring blacks are larger in the nonmarried than in the married group. A similar pattern is observed among High Protestants; black nonmarried mothers tend to be more ambitious (15) than their white counterparts (14), but this difference between the races virtually disappears among married mothers (15).

Among Catholic mothers in both races and nondenominational white mothers, ambition for their children is *higher* among *nonmarried* mothers than among the married (16 vs. 14 and 15 vs. 13 among black and white Catholics, respectively, and 17 vs. 16 among nondenominational whites). In contrast, nondenominational black mothers voice higher ambition if they have husbands (16 vs. 15), a pattern also exhibited by Jewish women (16 vs. 15).

Investment in children is also significantly higher among married (21) than among nonmarried black mothers (20), but there is virtually no difference in investment in child among white mothers according to whether they have a husband (22.5) or not (22.2).

When religion is controlled, married mothers exhibit higher mean investment scores than mothers without spouses among black (20 vs. 19) and white (22 vs. 18) Baptists; white High Protestants (23 vs. 22) and black nondenominational women (24 vs. 23). No differences in investment in child according to marital status are observed among Methodists in either race (21) or among black High Protestants (23). Interestingly, Catholic mothers without spouses, who, it will be recalled, value education more, also average higher investment scores than their married co-religionists both among blacks (24 vs. 22) and among whites (23 vs. 22).[10]

It is also worth mentioning that both race and religion condition the relationship between father absence and maternal investment in children. In father-absent homes, black mothers invest more in children than their white counterparts in three groups: Baptists (19 vs. 18), High Protestants (23 vs. 22), and Catholics (24 vs. 23). In father-present homes, black mothers invest less in children than their white co-religionists only among Baptists (20 vs. 22). Among Catholics, black mothers score higher (22 vs. 21), and in other religious groups no significant differences in mean investment scores are found between the races.[11]

The use of discipline does not vary significantly by marital status in either race. Black mothers, as I have already indicated, resort considerably more to aversive controls, whatever their marital status. However, when religion is controlled, an interaction is observed that is worth reporting.

Black Baptist/other fundamentalist mothers (16 vs. 15) and white Methodist/Lutheran (13 vs. 11) and High Protestant mothers (11 vs. 9) without husbands use more discipline than their married co-religionists. The use of discipline by mothers does not vary appreciably with marital status among black Methodists (14) and High Protestants (12), nor among white nondenominational (8) and Jewish mothers (9). But black (12 vs. 13) and white (12 vs. 14) Catholics without spouses use *less* discipline than their married co-religionists, and the same pattern of differences is found among black nondenominational mothers (10 vs. 12).

In sum, the effects of father absence on maternal socialization patterns are not uniform. As a rule, married mothers tend to voice higher ambitions for their children than mothers without husbands. The exceptions to this prevailing pattern are found among Catholic mothers, both black and white, and white nondenominational mothers. Catholics in both races and black nondenominational women exhibit the same reversal with respect to strategies of socialization: mothers without husbands invest more in their children and use less aversive discipline than their married co-religionists. It is interesting that the typically large differences between the races in their use of discipline disappears between black and white Catholic mothers without husbands (12) and is reversed among the married: white Catholic mothers with husbands tend to use more discipline (14) than their black co-religionists (13).

One can only speculate about the meaning of these results. It is possible that a selection process operates and that in a religious context which strongly condemns divorce, separated and divorced Catholics may differ in important ways from the general run of Catholics. Such women may be less inclined to follow the traditional view of the church on the sanctity and permanence of marriage and, being less traditional in this respect, they may hold more liberal views about rearing children as well. This hypothesis seems more plausible than the alternative hypothesis that the absence of a husband in the home leads them to compensate for this loss by investing more ambition and time in their child. While I believe that such compensatory strategies can be found among mothers without spouses, I can think of no good reason why it would be more frequent among Catholics than among mothers in other religious groups.

Maternal Employment and Socialization Strategies

With the sharp rise in the proportion of mothers of school-age children in the labor force in recent decades (Oppenheimer, 1970; Hapgood and Getzels, 1974), assessment of the effects of gainful employment on maternal values and practices becomes more important than ever before. Moreover, in view of the pronounced differences in the rates of gainful employment among black and white mothers, reported in Chapter 4, a pertinent question is the manner and extent to which employment influences maternal values and strategies of socialization in various religious contexts in the two races.

The duration of mothers' employment since the birth of her child varies with SES and religious affiliation as well as with race (A-12, page 239). At the low-SES level, black mothers' average length of employment is 4 years in all religious groups except High Protestants, who average 3 years. White mothers' average length of employment among Methodists/Lutherans and Catholics is 1 year; and among Baptists/fundamentalists and High Protestants, 2 and 4 years, respectively. At the middle-SES level, black Catholic mothers' average years of employment is longer (6 years) than among Baptist, Methodist (5 years), High Protestant (4 years), or nondenominational mothers (2 years). Among whites, nondenominational and Baptist mothers had worked longer (4 years), on the average, than other Protestant and Catholic (3 years) or Jewish (2 years) mothers.

The differences between the races in mothers' length of employment are largest at the high-SES level, whatever the religious affiliation. Among blacks, nondenominational and Catholic mothers' average work tenure was longer (8 years) than Methodists, High Protestants (7 years), or Baptists (6 years). Among whites, Baptist mothers had worked somewhat longer (3 years) than High Protestant, Jewish, and nondenominational women (2 years) or Catholics (1.5 years).

Among blacks in all religious groups, mothers' length of labor-force participation rises directly with SES; among whites in all religious groups except High Protestants, mothers at the middle-SES level average somewhat longer tenure in the work force than either their low- or high-SES co-religionists. Among white High Protestants, low-SES women had worked somewhat longer than their middle-SES co-religionists.

Among blacks, maternal ambition rises significantly and monotonically with the years mothers have worked: those who have remained outside the labor force since the birth of their children average somewhat lower scores (12.6) than those who have worked for a limited period, and these in turn average lower scores (13.3) than mothers who have worked half or more of their child's lifetime (14.1). Among whites there are no significant differences on maternal ambition according to years worked, but the direction of the relationship tends to be opposite to that found among blacks: mothers who have not worked since the birth of their child (14.7), or who have worked a shorter time (14.6), tend to average higher scores on ambition than those who have worked for a longer period (14.1).

It is also noteworthy that among mothers who have not worked at all or who have worked for only a short period, whites have higher ambitions, on the average, than their black counterparts, but the difference between the races disappears altogether among women who have worked 5 years or longer.

In every religious group, black mothers with the longest tenure in the labor force value education more than their co-religionists who have remained out of the labor force during their child's lifetime. Among black mothers who have held jobs 5 years or longer, Baptist mothers value education least (13.5) and nondenominational mothers value education most (17). High Protestant (11), Catholic (15), and Methodist (15) mothers' scores fall between the two extremes. Among mothers who have worked a short period, High Protestant and Methodist mothers average higher scores (15) than mothers of other religious groups, and Baptists again score the lowest (13). Among mothers who have not held jobs since their child's birth, Baptists and Catholic mothers value education least (12), Methodist and High Protestant mothers score higher (13), and nondenominational mothers score highest (16). Among white mothers valuation of education does not vary to any significant degree with years of employment within most religious groups except in two cases. High Protestant and nondenominational mothers who have not worked during their child's lifetime value education more (16 and 17, respectively) than their co-religionists with an extended employment history (13 and 15, respectively). But even nondenominational mothers with extended years of employment, as a rule, value education more than their counterparts in other religious groups. High Protestant mothers with extended employment, in contrast, score as low as Baptist mothers (13).

It is often assumed that mothers who do not hold jobs invest more time and other resources in rearing their children, but suprisingly little research exists on this issue (Kanter, 1977). A comparison of the extent of investment in their children between women in my sample who have not worked since the birth of their children and women who have held jobs for a shorter or longer period shows significant differences only among black mothers, but in the opposite direction to what might be expected: black mothers who have remained out of the labor force altogether invest slightly *less* in their child, on the average (20.1), than those who have worked four years or less (20.4). The highest mean scores, however, are found among black mothers with five or more years of employment (21.3). Among white mothers, the differences are small and nonsignificant but tend to be in the opposite direction. In all three comparisons, white mothers on the average invest more in rearing their children than black ones. One reason for this difference between the races has, of course, to do with the differences in their material resources. Black parents, as a rule, have fewer resources of education and income than whites, and one important means of reducing that disparity has been for black mothers to hold jobs. Among black mothers it is women at the low-SES level who most often have stayed out of the labor force since the birth of their child. Among whites, in contrast, mothers at the high-SES level, with far more ample economic, educational, and social resources, as well as mothers of low socioeconomic status exhibit fewer years of employment than mothers of middle SES.

Moreover, black mothers who have not worked at all average markedly more children (6) than their white counterparts (3). Indeed, only among blacks is there a definite decline in family size with years of employment: women who have worked four years of less average five children and those employed longer average four children. White mothers, in contrast, average three children, whatever their employment history.

The depressing effects of large families on the extent of investment in a child have already been shown. Thus, any benefits gained from having the mother at home are offset by the larger family size and more limited resources of black mothers who are full-time homemakers. The differences between the races in the extent of investment in their children is greatest among the mothers who have remained outside the labor force since the birth of their child. That a mother stays out of the labor force, in short, does not in and of itself promote greater investment in children in either race, and this is particularly not the case in the black sample.

In all religious groups, black mothers with an extended employment history invest *more* in their children than their co-religionists who have not worked during their child's lifetime (Table A-12, page 240). The single exception to this pattern is found among black Catholic mothers: investment in children is somewhat lower among mothers with extended work histories (23) than among those who have not worked since their child's birth (24).[12] Among mothers with extended employment, black nondenominational and High Protestant mothers invest more in their children than their white counterparts (25 and 23 vs. 23 and 22). In fact, the mean scores of black nondenominational mothers with extended employment is virtually the same (25) as that of white Jewish mothers with an extended employment history. That these two groups have the highest mean investment score in the entire sample constitutes evidence against the assumption that full-time homemakers necessarily invest more time and resources in children than working mothers. Among black mothers, in fact, just the opposite is true in most cases. Among whites, maternal employment has no uniform effects on the extent of investment in children. In three religious groups—High Protestant, Catholic, and nondenominational—white mothers who have been full-time homemakers since their child's birth average higher investment scores (23, 21, 25) than their co-religionists with extended labor force participation (22, 20, 23). Among Jewish mothers, in contrast, those with extended work-force participation invest more in their children (25) than full-time homemakers (24). And among Baptists (20) and Methodists (22), no significant variations are found in the extent of maternal investment between full time homemakers and working mothers.

Use of aversive discipline does not vary significantly with mothers' work tenure in either race, although black mothers who have not been in the labor force during their child's lifetime tend to use more aversive discipline (15) than those who have worked for a lengthy period (14).

When religion is controlled, it becomes evident that black mothers, as a rule, use more aversive discipline than their white coreligionists, whatever their work history except among Catholics. White Catholic mothers who have been full-time homemakers or who have worked for a limited time average considerably higher scores than their black counterparts (14 and 13 vs. 12). Only among Catholics with extended work tenure is the mean discipline the same (13) in the two races.

Among white mothers, High Protestants are the only group that exhibit a linear rise in discipline scores with mothers' years of work tenure (9, 10, 11).[13] White Baptist, Catholic, and Jewish homemakers tend to use more discipline (13, 14, 10) than working mothers of the same religious background (12, 13, 8). Methodist mothers with limited work experience exhibit a higher aversive control score (12) than either homemakers or mothers who have worked five years or longer (11).

Social Sources of Variation in Socialization: A Multivariate Summary

Race, religious affiliation, and socioeconomic status each appear to exert some influence on family structure and the extrafamilial participation of mothers. The latter factors, in turn, are associated with variations in maternal socialization. The nature of these relationships can be clarified by a multivariate analysis of the contribution that stratification and family-structural variables make to each of the three dimensions of socialization that have been identified. Such an approach also makes possible a summary comparison of the social sources of variation in the ways black and white mothers rear their children and an estimate of the extent to which observed differences are due to socioeconomic, religious, and familial differences that currently characterize blacks and whites in American society.

Valuation of Education

Six variables account for 32 percent of the variance in black mothers' valuation of education (Table A-13, page 239), of which SES is the strongest predictor (beta = .37). The number of children in the home is the second strongest (beta = −.18) and exerts a negative effect. Black mothers value education more for daughters than for sons (beta = .13), and mother's organizational memberships is a significant positive predictor of valuing education (beta = .10). Being married (beta = .06) and exposure to whites (beta = .06) each exert a weak positive effect, but neither variable by itself significantly increases the variance explained.

Seven variables constitute significant predictors of white mother's valuation of education and explain somewhat more variance (37 percent) in white values than in black ones. SES is also the strongest predictor of white mother's value orientation (beta = .47), and its net effect is stronger on white than on black mothers' values. The number of children in the family is a weaker negative predictor of white mother's valuation of education (beta = −.12) than of blacks'. White mothers value education more for sons (beta = −.10) in contrast to black mothers. Jewish (beta = .10) and non-denominational white mothers (beta = .09) value education more than mothers from other groups even after other variables are taken into account. Among black mothers, in contrast, religious affiliation does not exert an independent effect on mother's valuation of education after other variables are controlled. Organizational memberships enhance valuation of education among white mothers (beta = .09) just as among black mothers. Finally, length of work-force participation is a negative predictor of white mother's valuation of education (beta = −.08), but this variable does not enter the equation for black mothers.

The same variables that are significant predictors of mother's valuation of education in each race also predict mothers' values when the races are combined (Table A-13, page 240). SES (beta = .47) exerts the strongest effect. Black mothers value education more than white mothers (beta = −.17) after other variables are controlled. Family size remains nearly as strong a negative predictor (beta = −.15) for the whole sample as it is among black mothers. Organizational membership (beta = .11) is about as predictive of mothers' values for the whole sample as it is for each race separately, and Jewish (beta = .07) and nondenominational (beta = .06) mothers value education more than mothers of other religious persuasions in the whole sample, as was found to be the case for whites alone. Mothers with husbands show a weak tendency to value education for their children more than husbandless mothers (beta = .04), but this variable does not add significantly to the variance explained by the other variables in the equation.

Together these seven variables explain 34 percent of the variations in mothers' orientation to education. It will be noted that sex of the child did not enter the equation when the races are combined, which could have been expected since black mothers value education more for daughters and white mothers value education more for sons.

Investment in the Child

Most of the variables that predict mother's valuation of education also predict maternal investment in children (Table A-14, page 241). SES (beta = .27), number of children (beta = −.21), and membership in organizations (beta = .21) have the strongest effects on investment in children among black mothers. That blacks invest more resources in rearing daughters than sons (beta = .10) is consistent with their tendency to value education more for girls than for boys. Black Catholic mothers invest more in their children (beta = .08) than other black mothers when other variables are taken into account, and Baptist and other fundamentalist mothers tend to invest less (beta = −.08). Finally, exposure to whites promotes investment in children (beta = .07) among black mothers.

These variables account for 37 percent of the variance in black mothers' investment in their children, a somewhat larger proportion than is accounted for by the same model in black mother's valuation of education.

While the amount of variance explained in white mothers' investment in their children is the same as that for black mothers (37 percent) and several of the same variables predict this dimension of maternal behavior, there are also some differences in the nature and magnitude of the predictors in the two races. For example, SES (beta = .33) is a stronger predictor of white mothers' investment in their children than of blacks', but the number of children is a weaker predictor (beta = −.15) of this dimension of socialization. Sex of the child conditions white mothers' investment in their children (beta = .12) very slightly more than it does that of black mothers, although in both races mothers tend to invest more time and resources in daughters than in sons.[14] Organizational memberships has a weaker positive effect on investment in their child among white (beta = .10) than among black mothers.

Longer tenure in the labor force is a weak but significant negative predictor of white mothers' investment in their children (beta = −.09) but does not enter the black equation. Finally, religious background exerts a stronger independent effect on white mothers' investment in children than it does among black mothers. Jewish mothers and nondenominational white mothers invest more in their children (beta = .16) and Catholic white mothers invest less (beta = −.09) than other white mothers. While these differences were observed and reported earlier in the chapter, the regression analysis shows that there are real subcultural variations on this dimension of maternal behavior that are not simply the product of the variations in SES and family size that exist between Jews and nondenominational families, on the one hand, and Catholics, on the other.

The model being tested explains slightly more of the variance in mothers' investment in their children (Table A-11, page 238) in the whole sample (39 percent) than it does in either race taken alone.

SES continues to be the strongest predictor (beta = .34) of how much time and other resources mothers invest in their children. The number of children in the family exerts the second strongest effect (beta = −.20), and, of course, it is a negative one. Organizational memberships have a positive effect (beta = .15) independent of other variables in the equation and a much stronger one than the contribution made by marital status (beta = .04), which does not add significantly to the variance explained in mothers' investment in their children.[15] Nondenominational and Jewish mothers tend to invest more in their children (beta = .09) and Baptist and fundamentalist mothers invest less (beta = −.08) than mothers of other religious backgrounds even when other variables are controlled. Mothers invest more in daughters than in sons (beta = .10) when the races are combined as in each race taken separately.

Interestingly, when all these variables are taken into account, the difference between the races is reversed: black mothers invest more time and other resources in their children than white mothers (beta = −.08). I take this finding to mean that if the conditions under which black and white mothers rear their children were equalized, if the size of their families were smaller, and if the religious composition of the two races were the same, black mothers would invest at least as much time and other resources in rearing their children as white mothers do. In short, whatever racial differences currently exist on this score appear to be the result of social-structural variables and not of indigenous or enduring cultural differences.[16]

Orientation to Use of Discipline

The variables in the model under examination explain considerably less of the variance in black mothers' belief in and use of aversive modes of control in child rearing than of the variance in the other dimensions already discussed. The model also accounts for less variance in the use of discipline among black than among white mothers (Table A-15, page 242).

Seven variables explain 22 percent of the variance in the use of discipline by black mothers. Socioeconomic status again is the strongest negative predictor (beta = −.32), and sex of the child (beta = −.17) carries more weight than other variables. Boys receive more discipline from mothers than girls. Mothers' organizational memberships reduces the inclination to rely on aversive forms of control (beta = −.08), as does a High Protestant (beta = −.08), Catholic (beta = −.07), or nondenominational religious affiliation (beta = −.06). The one positive predictor of black mothers' use of discipline is the size of their family of origin (beta = .07). However, neither this variable nor the religious variables increase significantly the amount of variance explained over and above that explained by SES, sex of the child, and mother's organizational memberships.

A considerably larger amount of variance in the use of discipline by white mothers is accounted for by the model (34 percent). While SES is also the strongest predictor of the use of discipline by white mothers, it exerts a stronger independent effect (beta = −.44) than it does among black mothers (beta = −.32). Sex of the child, however, conditions white mothers' use of discipline less (beta = −.08) than it does that of black mothers (beta = −.17), although aversive forms of control are directed more toward boys than toward girls in both races. Being Catholic exerts quite a strong positive effect on the use of discipline among white mothers (beta = .18) but has the opposite effect among black mothers (beta = −.07) and in fact serves as a weak negative predictor of discipline. White Baptist mothers (beta = .09) and more religious mothers generally (beta = .07) use more discipline, but these two effects are weaker than the effect of a Catholic affiliation. Finally, white mothers without husbands in the home tend to use more discipline (beta = −.07) than married mothers, with other variables controlled.

With black and white mothers combined (Table A-15, page 242) the model accounts for 39 percent of the variance in discipline. SES is by far the strongest single predictor (beta = −.44) of maternal modes of control, but small significant effects are also exerted by other variables: boys are disciplined more than girls (beta = −.11); nondenominational (beta = −.09), Jewish (beta = −.09), and High Protestant mothers (beta = −.08) tend to use less discipline even with all other variables considered; the size of the families in which parents grew up promotes the use of more discipline (beta = .05). While mother's religiosity (beta = .04) and being husbandless (beta = −.04) are variables that enter the equation, they do not make any significant additional contribution to the variance explained.

With all these variables in the equation, the significantly greater proclivity toward the use of aversive forms of control by black mothers compared with white (beta = −.07) persists.[17] Training children to be obedient, particularly male children, was, I believe, viewed as necessary for their survival by black parents during slavery and the postreconstruction era, when blacks were subject to the arbitrary exercise of authority and coercion by whites without the possibility of legal protection or redress. That situation still obtained when black mothers in my sample were growing up.[18] Thus, greater reliance on aversive forms of control of children persists as part of a cultural tradition of adaptation to subjugation which has ceased to have adaptive value and, indeed, becomes counterproductive under conditions of expanding educational and occupational opportunities.

Summary

It was shown in Chapter 4 that the social structural model accounts for more variance in black than in white children's IQ scores, and in Chapter 6 it was shown that the socialization model accounts for more variance in white than in black children's IQ scores. Sex of the child is an independent predictor of white but not of black scores: white girls average higher IQ scores whether structural variables or socialization variables are controlled.

With structural variables controlled, the racial difference in IQ scores is reduced more than it is when socialization variables are controlled. The smallest mean IQ racial differences are found when the sexes are analyzed separately and social structural variables are controlled.

These findings constitute evidence that interactions between race, sex, and IQ scores, on the one hand, and interactions between race, social structural, socialization variables, and IQ scores, on the other, are significant sources of the disparity in black and white children's IQ scores.

Chapters 5 and 6 identified three dimensions of maternal socialization that influence the development of intellectual and scholastic competence in childhood and provided evidence that a counterproductive socialization strategy of low investment and high use of aversive control which impedes the development of such competence is considerably more prevalent among black than among white mothers. An optimal strategy of high investment and low use of aversive control is considerably more prevalent among white mothers.

This chapter compared the social sources of variation in each of the three dimensions of socialization among black and white mothers and showed that social structural variables account for the same amount of variance in the two races only in mother's investment in the child, but account for more variance in white than in black mothers' valuation of education and use of aversive controls. Moreover, black mothers manifest higher ambitions and use more aversive control even when all social structural variables under consideration are controlled.

Although socioeconomic status is the strongest predictor of each socialization dimension in both races, it exerts greater weight in the case of white than of black mothers. A similar pattern of differences is found with respect to religious variables. These findings indicate that variations in socioeconomic status and religious affiliation are stronger sources of variation in the socialization beliefs and practices of white than of black mothers.

Family size is a stronger source of variation in black mothers' valuation of education and in investment in the child than among white mothers, and sex of the child is a stronger predictor of black than of white mothers' values and use of aversive control. Black mothers value education more for daughters than for sons; white mothers tend to value education more for sons; but such values are conditioned more by the sex of the child among blacks than among whites. Similarly, while in both races mothers employ more aversive controls in rearing sons than daughters, more sex differentiation on this score is exhibited by black than by white mothers.

Inasmuch as sex of the child turns out to be an independent predictor of each of three socialization dimensions among both races, further exploration is needed of the social sources and consequences of sex differentiated maternal expectations and practices. The next chapter addresses these issues.

Notes

1. This finding of the relative unimportance of SES as a source of the high valuation of education among Jews is consistent with evidence from other studies (McClelland, 1961; Blau, 1967) and suggests that a high valuation of education arises out

of a long cultural tradition stressing the importance of scholarship for perpetuating Jewish heritage and identity.

2. The differences between the races described above are reflected also in the considerable difference in the magnitude of correlation between SES and use of aversive discipline: among blacks the correlation is $-.41$; among whites it is $-.55$.

3. It is interesting to compare the family size of mothers with the size of their origin families. Among blacks, in each stratum fundamentalist mothers and their husbands came from the largest families, on the average; black Catholic low-SES mothers and their husbands come from the *smallest* families, and they along with Methodists also come from the smallest families at the middle-SES level. Among whites, Jewish women and their husbands at high-SES levels come from the smallest families; at the middle-SES level, nonreligious women and their husbands come from smaller families than Jewish women in their own stratum. Fundamentalists and their husbands, in contrast, in all strata, but most particularly those of low SES come from the largest families.

4. Every benefit also entails a cost. In the case of the Jews, for example, the rates of individual upward social mobility were high and there were commensurate gains in status and power for the Jews as a whole. At the same time, the size of the Jewish community has been declining, and many Jewish leaders have expressed concern about the implications of that decline for the position of Jews vis à vis other groups in the political arena. Some militant black leaders oppose efforts to lower the birth rates of the black population on political grounds. They believe that blacks have more to gain at the ballot box or through revolution if they maintain high birth rates. But they dangerously underestimate the negative consequences not only to the general community but to blacks themselves of such a policy. My study documents the nature of some of these costs, and it would not be difficult, I believe, to show other costs imposed on *blacks* by high fertility rates in a context of rising expectations and expanded opportunities for mobility for this long oppressed people.

5. A reversal of this pattern is found in only four comparisons. White Baptist and nondenominational mothers with medium-sized families and white Methodist and High Protestant mothers with large families value education more than their black counterparts. The differences among the Baptists (13.5 vs. 13.2) and among the Methodists (12.8 vs. 12.4) are small, but those among the nonreligious (16.4 vs. 14.5) and among the High Protestants (14.3 vs. 12.4) are more substantial.

6. The only exception to this pattern among blacks is the one nondenominational mother with a large family whose investment score is as high as that of her co-religionists with three or four children. Among white Methodist, High Protestant, Catholic, and Jewish mothers there is virtually no difference in the mean investment scores of mothers with three or four children as compared with those who have one or two children. In all other cases there is a monotonic decline in investment scores as family size increases.

7. The sole exception to that pattern is among nondenominational women. White mothers with small or medium-sized families invest somewhat more than their black co-religionists (25 and 24 vs. 24 and 23, respectively).

8. Catholics, to be sure, are the only group in my sample where black mothers average socioeconomic status is higher than that of their white co-religionists.

9. Interestingly, no significant differences were found within each race between socioeconomic status groups in the amount of time mothers reported that their husbands spent with their children when they were not working. But at each SES level white scores are higher than black scores on a measure that combined mother's marital status and time father was reported to spend with his children. The subject of father's input in the socialization of children urgently merits more systematic investigation than it has yet received. The length of my interview with mothers precluded the inclusion of a satisfactory battery of questions aimed at ascertaining the *quality* of fathers' interaction with their children.

10. A similar pattern is found among white nondenominational and Jewish mothers. Those without spouses have slightly higher investment scores in both groups (24.5) than their married co-religionists (24.1).

11. It should be noted, however, that my sample contains only 4 cases of white nonmarried Baptist women and only 9 black and 5 white nonmarried Catholic mothers. Consequently, one must reserve judgment about the reliability of the findings reported above until they can be tested on samples containing larger N's of nonmarried black and white Catholic and white Baptist mothers.

12. The latter are the only group of black homemakers whose investment score exceeds that of their similarly situated white co-religionists.

13. Although not linearly related, nondenominational white mothers with extended work tenure also use more discipline (10) than their co-religionist homemakers (8).

14. This stronger tendency of white mothers to invest more in daughters may be one source of the significantly higher IQ scores of white girls compared with white boys and to black children of both sexes.

15. While in both races women who are married belong more to organizations than mothers who are rearing children without husbands in the home ($r = .19$), extrafamilial participation appears to be a stronger determinant of how mothers rear their children than marital status. For example, with only SES and family size in the equation, the partial r between marital status and investment in child while weak (.07) is significant ($F = 5.86$). However, when organizational membership enters the equation, the partial r becomes smaller (.05) and nonsignificant ($F = 2.61$). In short, having a marital partner facilitates a mother's participation in optional activities outside the home, but the exposure to networks of information and influence that such participation affords mothers, not the partner per se, has the stronger effect on the amount of time and other resources invested in the child.

16. The presence of Jews primarily in the white population and very rarely in the black population, the higher proportion of nondenominational and nonreligious women among whites, and the very heavy presence of fundamentalist mothers among blacks are facets of social structure perpetuated by discimination and social segregation that contribute to the variance between races. In earlier comparisons it was seen that nondenominational black mothers invest as heavily in their children as nondenominational and Jewish white mothers, but they constitute a very tiny proportion of the sample compared to the combined proportion of Jewish and nondenominational mothers in the white sample.

17. Richard Appelbaum (1971), who used multivariate analysis to determine the sources of variance in authoritarianism and in the use of physical punishment, two components of the dimension of discipline, obtained similar results using the same data but employing separate components of the discipline dimension.

18. In my sample, for example, mothers who were reared in the South hold more authoritarian beliefs about rearing children than those reared in the North regardless of whether they are now in the middle class or in the working class. They also rate their mothers as having been stricter and as having used physical punishment more while they were growing up than women who grew up in the North.

CHAPTER 8

Sex of Child and Maternal Socialization Strategies

More than ever before, the differences in the socialization of male and female children and in the consequences of these socially structured differences for the performance of various social roles by the two sexes have become matters of public controversy and discussion. Under pressure engendered first by the reemergence of the women's movement in the latter part of the 1960s, a pervasive reexamination is under way of the traditional assumptions concerning the biological basis for the differences in role assignments to the two sexes.

IQ scores and scholastic achievement are acknowledged to be important predictors of educational attainment, but since traditionally only males, as a rule, were obligated to prepare for and perform the occupational role over the entire span of adulthood, and since educational attainment is a major source of variations in occupational status, stratification studies in prior decades dealt almost exclusively with males, most frequently *white* males. During the 1970s some comparative work has appeared, most notably that of Treiman and Terrell (1975). Their research provides evidence that educational attainment plays as significant a role in the occupational achievement of gainfully employed women as of men.

Studies of IQ and achievement test performance, in contrast, frequently include sex as a variable and repeatedly have found that girls score higher on IQ tests than boys in the preschool years and in elementary school (Maccoby, 1966; Maccoby and Jacklin, 1974). In high school the findings are less consistent. Thus Eleanor Maccoby (1966) states that boys tend to score higher on IQ tests in high school, but in an extensive study of students in ten high schools, Coleman (1961) found that girls averaged higher scores. With respect to achievement as measured by school grades, girls do better than boys throughout their schooling, even in subjects, Maccoby notes, in which boys score higher on standard achievement tests.

Girls average higher scores on most aspects of verbal performance. "They say their first word sooner, articulate more clearly and at an earlier age, use longer sentences and are more fluent. . . . Girls learn to read sooner, and there are more boys than girls who require special training in remedial reading programs; but by age ten, a number of studies show, boys have caught up in their reading skills. Throughout the school years, girls do better on tests of grammar, spelling and word fluency" (Maccoby, 1966, p. 26). Boys, on the other hand, appear to perform better on tests of arithemetic reasoning and on spatial tests.

The race of the children studied, at least in the body of empirical literature reviewed by Maccoby, is not mentioned, but it seems that the findings reported were based largely, if not entirely, on white samples.

It is often claimed that in the early years of life girls mature more rapidly than boys, and this conclusion is based to some degree on the kind of evidence cited by Maccoby. Often these very early differences between the sexes are believed to have a biological basis, but very little controlled observation of maternal and paternal interaction with newborns and infants exists as yet, and it may well turn out that many of the observed differences between the sexes thought to have biological origins may result from differences in expectations and modes of rearing boys and girls. Some recent studies suggest that some of the variance between the sexes is produced by differential responses of mothers to male and female infants and that when mothers' responses are controlled for, sex differences in infant behavior become attenuated (Goldberg and Lewis, 1969).

Comparisons of the IQ scores of boys and girls in the present study reveal significant differences between white boys and girls but not between blacks. White girls' mean score (109) is significantly higher than that of white boys (105), but there is only a one-point difference, favoring girls, among blacks (97 versus 96). White girls also tend to average higher achievement scores (6.5) than white boys (6.2), but this difference only approaches statistical significance ($F = 3.68$). Among blacks there is virtually no difference in the average achievement scores of boys (4.3) and girls (4.4).

That the sex of a child conditions mothers' valuations of education in opposite ways in the two races was shown in the preceding chapter. Black mothers express significantly higher ambitions for daughters (14) than for sons (13), whereas white mothers tend to express higher ambitions for sons (15) than for daughters (14). But the latter difference only approaches statistical significance (F = 3.21).

In both races, however, mothers invest more in rearing daughters than in rearing sons. Thus, the average score of black mothers of boys (20) is significantly lower than that of mothers of girls (21). Similarly, white mothers of boys average significantly lower investment scores (22) than those of girls (23). However, the differences between the sexes within each race are smaller than those between the races when sex is controlled.

The use of discipline also varies with the sex of the child. In both races, mothers employ more aversive discipline with sons than with daughters. Among blacks, for example, the average score of boys' mothers is 15 compared with 14 among girls' mothers; among whites the corresponding scores are 11 and 10. As in the case of maternal investment in the child, so in the use of discipline, the differences between the races are greater than those between the sexes within each race.

Further findings of interest emerge when mother's SES level is controlled (Table A-16, page 243). Among blacks, sex of child conditions maternal ambition considerably more at the low-SES level than at higher-SES levels. Thus, 72 percent of low-SES mothers of sons and 56 percent of mothers of daughters register low ambition scores. High ambitions are held by 16 percent of the mothers of girls, compared with only 5 percent among mothers of boys. As SES level rises, these differences in maternal ambition become attenuated. At the high-SES level, 63 percent of boys' mothers and 69 percent of girls' mothers exhibit high ambition for the educational future of their child. This small persisting difference, however, is not statistically significant.

A rather different pattern is found among whites (Table A-16, page 243). Sex of child does not significantly differentiate maternal ambition at any SES level among whites. However, the differences favoring boys are largest at the low-SES level. While 60 percent of the mothers of sons exhibit low ambition, 81 percent of mothers of daughters do so. These differences in maternal ambition according to the child's sex diminish at the middle-SES level and become further attenuated at the high-SES level. Nevertheless, such differences as do persist tend to favor boys. Thus 62 percent of boys' mothers compared with 58 percent of girls' mothers register high ambition. The level of ambition of white mothers for their sons is very similar to that of blacks at similar SES levels, but the proportion of white mothers with high ambitions for daughters is lower (58 percent) than that of their black counterparts (69 percent).

In both races mothers tend to invest more of their time and other resources in daughters than in sons, but the extent to which sex of child differentiates this dimension of maternal behavior varies with race and socioeconomic status (Table A-17, page 244). Among black mothers at the low-SES level, low investment in both sons and daughters is the modal pattern, but it is more frequently exhibited by mothers of boys (63 percent) than by mothers of girls (56 percent). At the middle-SES level, low investment continues to be the modality for rearing sons (42 percent), but medium or high investment in daughters is more characteristic (37 percent each average, medium, and high scores), and only in this stratum are the differences by sex of child statistically significant. At the high-SES level differences in maternal investment according to sex of child are small, and a high level of investment is typical for boys (66 percent) as well as for girls (69 percent). The rise in the extent of maternal investment in sons is markedly greater among mothers at the high-SES level than among those at the middle-SES level (an increase of 47 percent), compared with the increment exhibited toward daughters (32 percent).

Among whites, as in the case of blacks, at every SES level the proportion who exhibit high investment is higher among girls' mothers than among boys' mothers, but the magnitude of differences according to sex of child is very much smaller at the low-SES level than at higher-SES levels (Table A-17, page 244). Thus at the low-SES level virtually the same proportion of white mothers exhibit low investment in sons as in daughters (48 percent and 49 percent, respectively); high investment in either sex is rare indeed in the case of sons (5 percent) and somewhat more frequent in the case of daughters (10 percent), a pattern very similar to that found among low-SES-level blacks. But the latter compared with their white counterparts register low investment scores for sons (63 percent vs. 48 percent) considerably more often than for daughters (56 percent vs. 49 percent).

At the middle-SES level among whites as among blacks, sex of child conditions maternal investment considerably more than in the lower stratum. Forty-three percent of boys' mothers average low investment scores, compared with 23 percent of girls' mothers; high investment, in contrast, is considerably higher for girls (31 percent) than for boys (18 percent). Sex of child conditions maternal investment to about the same degree in the case of blacks and whites at the middle-SES level.

At the high-SES level among whites, in contrast to blacks, sex of the child continues to exert a considerable effect on the extent of maternal investment. Although high investment is the modal pattern for both sexes, the proportion of mothers who score high is larger in the case of girls (69 percent) than boys (55 percent). The magnitude of this difference is larger among high-SES whites (14 percent) than among high-SES blacks (3 percent). Indeed, the proportion of mothers of girls in this stratum who register high investment is the same for the two races (69 percent), but in the case of sons, black mothers exhibit high investment more frequently (66 percent) than white mothers (55 percent).

The use of discipline as a mode of control, it has been shown, is relied on more heavily by black than by white mothers, as a rule, at all SES levels. When sex of child is introduced into the analysis, it becomes evident that the extent to which mothers use discipline is also governed more by sex of child among blacks than among whites at low- and middle-SES levels (Table A-18, page 245). However, the reverse is true among women at the high-SES level.

Among low-SES blacks, fully 71 percent of boys' mothers compared with 51 percent of girls' mothers register high discipline scores. Low-SES white mothers of boys far less frequently score high on aversive control (43 percent) than black mothers of boys. With respect to girls, in contrast, the difference between the races is small; 52 percent of black compared with 49 percent of white mothers register high discipline scores. No marked difference in the use of dscipline according to child's sex is evident among low-SES whites as it is among blacks at a similar SES level.

At the middle-SES level, pronounced differences persist in the use of aversive discipline according to sex of child among blacks. Fifty-seven percent of boys' mothers score high on discipline, compared with 31 percent of girls' mothers. Thus, extensive use of discipline continues to be the modal pattern with respect to boys, whereas a moderate use of discipline is the modal pattern with respect to girls. Among whites of middle SES, differences in the use of discipline according to sex of child are small and nonsignificant. Moderate discipline levels are the modal pattern with respect to both sexes.

At the high-SES level, differences in the use of discipline according to sex of child diminish among blacks; a moderate use of discipline is the modal pattern in relation to boys (51 percent), and low discipline is the modal pattern (51 percent) in relation to girls. Even at high-SES levels, however, the proportion of white mothers with low discipline scores is substantially higher than among black mothers. Thus, 43 percent of black mothers of boys compared with 63 percent of white ones score low on discipline, while among mothers of girls the corresponding proportions are 51 and 79 percent. Among whites at the high-SES level, mothers of boys use significantly more discipline toward sons than toward daughters. Indeed, only a minuscule proportion of white mothers of daughters (3 percent) score high on discipline. The proportion of black mothers of daughters who score high on discipline is substantially higher (21 percent). Further, in this stratum alone the proportion of black mothers who score high on discipline is higher in relation to daughters (21 percent) than in relation to sons (6 percent). Interestingly, black high-SES mothers of sons score high on discipline even more rarely than their white counterparts (10 percent), which makes this group the only one where the proportion with high discipline scores is lower among blacks than among whites. This is not to say, however, that black high-SES mothers use less discipline with their sons as a rule than their white counterparts; a moderate use of discipline is the modality for black high-SES mothers of sons (51 percent), whereas among their white counterparts, low discipline is more typical (63 percent).

In the foregoing pages, sex of child has been shown to condition maternal values and role performance to a varying degree in different SES levels in the two races.

In both races, mothers' ambition for their children is conditioned most by the child's sex at the low-SES level, and sex differences on this variable diminish with rising SES level. Among whites, mothers voice higher ambitions for sons; among blacks, mothers tend to express higher ambitions for daughters.

In both races mothers tend to invest more time and resources in rearing daughters than sons. Among blacks, sex differences are most pronounced at the middle-SES level and least pronounced at the high-SES level. Among whites, sex differences on this dimension of maternal behavior are more pronounced at the middle- and high-SES levels. At the low-SES level the differences are small and nonsignificant.

In both races, finally, more aversive discipline is employed by mothers in rearing sons than daughters. Among blacks, sex differences are least pronounced at the high-SES level. Only in the latter stratum is there a very considerable attenuation in maternal use of discipline in rearing sons, so much so that the proportion of mothers of girls with high discipline scores exceeds that among mothers of boys, but these last differences are not statistically significant.

Among whites, in contrast, sex of child conditions maternal use of discipline most at the high-SES level. Although low discipline is typical in relation to both sexes, it is particularly characteristic in relation to daughters. Sex differences are least marked among whites at the low-SES level, where high discipline is the modal pattern in relation to both sexes.

In the light of these findings it is interesting to compare the IQ and achievement scores of boys and girls in each race at various SES levels. For if the higher IQ of white girls compared with white boys were due to inherent biological differences between the two sexes, one would expect no variations in the magnitude of differences between the sexes at different SES levels. By the same token, it would be difficult to explain why sex differences in IQ are found among white children in our sample and not among black children.

In the black sample, when SES is controlled, a significantly higher proportion of girls (37 percent) than of boys (22 percent) score in the highest third of the IQ continuum in the *middle*-SES stratum, whereas a higher proportion of boys (39 percent) fall in the the middle third of the IQ continuum compared with girls (24 percent) (Table A-19, page 246). No significant sex differences in IQ scores are found in the low- and high-SES strata in the black sample. It is in the middle-SES group that the most pronounced sex differences were found with respect to investment in the child, girls being more advantaged on this score, and in this stratum are also found the most pronounced sex differences with respect to discipline, more discipline being used in rearing sons than daughters.

It seems reasonable to conclude, therefore, that a causal connection may exist between sex-differentiated maternal practices and the higher average IQ scores exhibited by black girls in this stratum. Being the objects more frequently of higher investment and lower discipline, girls also average higher IQ scores than boys. In short, differences in the strategy of rearing sons and daughters rather than biology seem to be the source of sex differences in this stratum of the black sample. No significant sex differences are found in the low-SES group because while black mothers have higher ambitions for daughters than for sons, they do not implement their ambitions by investing more in rearing daughters than sons. And while they use significantly less discipline in rearing daughters, a majority (52 percent) of girls' mothers nevertheless score high on discipline. Low investment and high use of discipline, I have already suggested, is a strategy that inhibits intellectual development in both races.

At the high-SES level among blacks no significant sex differences in IQ are found, very possibly because no significant sex differences were revealed with respect to maternal ambitions, investment in the child, or use of discipline.

In the white sample, a significantly higher proportion of girls score in the upper third of the IQ continuum (61 percent compared with 47 percent among boys) only in the high-SES group, which constitutes a far larger proportion of the white (56 percent) than of the black sample (13 percent) (Table A-20, page 247). Among high-SES whites, it will be recalled, no significant sex differences are found with respect to maternal ambitions, but maternal investment is significantly higher and aversive discipline is less frequently employed in relation to daughters than in relation to sons. The early advantage in intellectual development reflected in the higher IQ scores of girls may well be due to the fact that they are more frequently the beneficiaries of an optimal socialization strategy than are their male peers.

The advantage that girls enjoy on early IQ tests, at the middle-SES level among blacks and at the high-SES level among whites, apparently does not carry over to achievement test performance in the fifth and sixth grades. Among blacks no significant differences are found between boys' and girls' achievement levels in *any* of the three SES strata (Table A-20, page 247). Among whites no significant sex differences in achievement test performance are found in the low- and high-SES strata, but at the middle-SES level a significantly higher proportion of girls compared with boys (51 percent vs. 28 percent) average scores in the highest third of the achievement score continuum. Since no significant sex differences were observed in this stratum with respect to either maternal ambition or use of discipline, it seems plausible to attribute the higher average achievement level of girls to the significantly higher investment in daughters as compared with sons by white mothers at the middle-SES level. What may be operating in this stratum is the phenomenon of the "sleeper effect," first described in the empirical literature on the effects of mass communications (Hovland, Lumsdaine, Sheffield, 1949) and to my knowledge not yet satisfactorily explained. In the present context it occurs to me that the advantages girls derive from higher material investment in them comes to fruition more slowly in middle-SES than in the case of high-SES girls, who, I suggested, scored higher on IQ tests than boys in their stratum because of higher maternal investment. The white lower-middle-class home does not ordinarily offer as stimulating a milieu as the upper-middle-class home. Moreover, it will be remembered that white middle-status mothers have worked longer as a rule than either low- or high-SES white mothers. Consequently, children from upper-working-class or lower-middle-class homes may well start off more slowly than children from upper-middle-class homes, but, sustained by high maternal investment and exposed to a broader range of formal knowledge offered by the schools, girls in this stratum may "pick up steam" as their years of schooling increase, which becomes manifested in their achievement scores in the fifth and sixth grades.

In the present context it is interesting to note that though white high-SES girls have the highest mean IQ in the entire sample (113), the mean IQ score of white middle-SES girls (106) is almost as high as that of high-SES boys (108). In other words, the difference between the sexes at the high-SES level (5) is nearly as large as that between *girls* of middle- and high-SES levels (7).[1] But the difference in mean achievement scores between the sexes at the high-SES level is very small (7.1 vs. 6.9). At the middle-SES level the sex difference is larger (girls' mean score is 6.2 compared with boys' mean score of 5.5). Moreover, the increment in IQ and achievement scores among white middle-SES girls compared with low-SES girls is substantially greater than in the case of boys: middle-SES girls' average IQ score is 106 compared to a mean score of 96 among low-SES girls. Similarly, they score a whole stanine higher (6.2 vs. 5.2) on achievement tests. The gain among middle-SES compared with low-SES boys is substantially *smaller*. Their mean IQ is 103 compared with 100, and their mean achievement score is 5.5 compared with 5.2 among low-SES boys.

There is not much difference between the sexes in the increment in maternal valuation of education among middle-SES white children compared with those at the low-SES level. But there is a substantially larger increment in *investment* in girls than in boys in the middle as compared to the low stratum and a larger decrement in *discipline* in the case of girls than in that of boys in the middle- as compared to the low-SES stratum. In short, among whites, the optimal strategy of high investment—low aversive discipline is more frequently adopted toward girls than toward boys with a rise from the low- to the middle-SES group, thereby enabling mothers to more effectively implement their rising ambitions in the case of daughters than in the case of sons.[2]

Religion and Sex Differences

The way in which religious and denominational differences of mothers in American society condition their strategies of socializing daughters and sons is an issue that, to my knowledge, has not been the subject of systematic empirical investigation. It became a matter of interest when I discovered in a comparison of IQ scores of boys and girls, controlled by race and religion, that while in most religious and denominational groups, mean differences between the sexes were small, mostly favoring girls, among black *and* white High Protestants these differences were considerably larger. Indeed, the differences between the mean IQ scores of boys and girls within each of these two groups are as large as or larger than the differences between the races (Table A-21, page 248). Thus, the mean score of High Protestant black boys is 99, compared with 107 among black girls of the same denomination, a difference of eight points. The corresponding scores of boys and girls among High Protestant whites is 105 and 112, respectively, a difference of seven points, which is nearly as large as the zero-order difference between black and white boys of nine points.

Among all religious subgroups the mean IQ scores of girls are higher than those of boys with two exceptions: among whites, Jewish boys and girls have identical scores (110), and among blacks, *sons* of nondenominational/nonreligious mothers have a slightly higher mean score (110) than daughters (108); indeed, the mean score of boys in this group, the highest in the black sample, is identical to that of Jewish children. The next highest mean scores in the black sample are exhibited by nondenominational girls (108) and High Protestant girls (107), the same two groups which exhibit the highest mean scores among whites (113 and 112, respectively), exceeding slightly the scores of sons of white nondenominational mothers (111) and Jewish children of both sexes (110).

The three groups in which the differences between the races virtually disappear are Catholic children of both sexes and nondenominational boys; in all other groups, there is a five- to six-point difference between black and white children of the same sex within each religious group, except in the case of Baptist girls, where whites' mean score of 103 exceeds black girls' (95) by eight points.

Finally, it is of interest to note that, almost without exception, race differences in the case of both sexes are larger among the various Protestant denominations than between non-Protestants. But even among Protestants there is no group of white boys or girls whose mean IQ scores exceed those of their black counterparts by as much as 10 points, let along the 15 points which Jensen (1969) reports.

There can be little doubt that the very different denominational constituency of blacks and whites, which is never taken into account in IQ comparisons of children in the two races, accounts for the discrepancy between Jensen's figure (1969) and my data. Thus, if in the present sample, black Baptist children (who would constitute the larger majority in every sampling of the general population of blacks) are compared with white High Protestant children (who in any white probability sample would probably constitute a larger proportion than in the present sample, at least in northern urban regions), the magnitude of difference between races (approximately 12) approaches Jensen's much-quoted figure. But when religious and denominational affiliation and sex of child are controlled, there is as much variation in IQ scores between the sexes within each race in some groups as between the races.

In general, sex differences are less pronounced in achievement test performance than in IQ test performance in both races, particularly among blacks (Table A-22, page 248). The mean achievement score of black boys is 4.3, compared with 4.4 among black girls; the corresponding scores for white boys and girls are 6.2 and 6.5. In all except two religious groups in both races, where there is any difference between the sexes at all, girls tend to have slightly higher scores. All three white Protestant denominations show somewhat larger differences than other groups, favoring girls, but the largest difference is found among white High Protestants; girls' mean score is 6.9, compared with 6.2 among boys.[3]

In contrast to other groups, sons of black nondenominational mothers tend to average higher achievement scores (6.6) than daughters (6.1), and a similar pattern of differences, slightly attenuated, is observed among Jews in the white sample; boys' average score is 6.8 and girls' is 6.5. While these differences are small, they are interesting because they are the exception rather than the rule and therefore the question arises why reversal of the general pattern is found only in these two groups. The boys in these groups, it should be noted, average higher achievement scores than boys in every other group except sons of white nondenominational/nonreligious mothers, whereas the achievement test performance of girls in these two groups is lower than that of High Protestant white girls. Indeed, daughters of black nondenominational mothers, though they average the highest scores among girls in the black sample, are on a par with white Baptist girls, and Jewish girls' average score is identical to that of daughters of white Methodist/Lutheran mothers.

It is interesting that the only two groups in which achievement scores of the two sexes are identical are black Baptists, the lowest-scoring group in the entire sample (4.0), and white nondenominational/nonreligious children (7.4), who exhibit the highest scores in the sample.

Finally, it is evident that differences in achievement test performance vary less by sex of child than by race and mother's religious affiliation. Within each race there is a difference of about two stanines between children of each sex in the lowest and highest achieving groups. For each sex within each religious group, the race difference amounts to approximately one stanine in most cases, but among the daughters of Baptists and other fundamentalist mothers there is a difference of two stanines; black girls average a score of 4, while white girls' average score is 6.1.

Religious Variations in the Socialization of Boys and Girls

In the remainder of this chapter, a comparison of values and practices that mothers of different religious backgrounds employ toward sons and daughters will help to explicate the sources of sex variations in IQ and achievement test performance.

It was reported earlier that black mothers express higher ambitions for daughters than for sons, whereas the reverse tendency is found among white mothers. But when mother's religious affiliation is controlled, variations in these overall patterns are found within each race. Among blacks, for example, higher valuation of education for daughters than for sons is voiced by Baptist/other fundamentalist (13.5 vs. 12), High Protestant (16 vs. 14) and nondenominational mothers (17 vs. 15). The sex differences among Methodists, while in the same direction, are less pronounced (14.6 vs. 14.1). Black Catholic mothers, in contrast, tend to express higher ambitions for sons (15) than for daughters (14). Indeed, their ambitions for sons are as high as those voiced by black nondenominational mothers of sons. With respect to daughters, in contrast, black Catholic mothers' valuations of education (13.7) are virtually as low as those of Baptist mothers of daughters (13.5), whose scores are the lowest with respect to girls in the black sample.

Among whites, mothers express higher ambitions for sons than for daughters in three groups—Baptists (13 vs. 12), Catholics (14 vs. 12), and Jews (17 vs. 16). Among the three other groups—High Protestants, Methodists/Lutherans, and nondenominational mothers—ambitions are less differentiated according to sex of the child. But to the extent that differences are found, they tend to favor girls.[4] This lack of consistency between religious groups with respect to ambitions for daughters and sons probably accounts for the fact that overall sex differences with respect to valuation of education are found to be not significant among whites.[5] Among blacks, in contrast, the one group in which mothers' ambitions as a rule are higher for sons than for daughters are Catholics, who constitute only a small proportion (6 percent) of the black sample.

Given the pattern of reversals found among religious groups with respect to valuations for boys and girls, it is not surprising to also find more marked differences between the races in some religious groups than in others. Thus, among Baptists, white mothers have higher ambitions for boys (13) than black ones (12), whereas black mothers have higher ambitions for girls (13.5) than white mothers (12).

Among Methodists/Lutherans there is little difference between the races with respect to maternal ambition for either sex: in both cases, the tendency is for mothers to voice higher ambitions for daughters than for sons. Thus black mothers of daughters score 14.6 compared with 14.1 for mothers of sons, and white mothers' scores are 14.1 and 13.5 respectively.

Among High Protestants maternal ambition for sons is very similar among black (14.3) and white (14.5) mothers, but black High Protestant mothers have higher ambitions for daughters, as a rule (16) than their white co-religionists (15).

Black Catholic mothers average higher ambitions for both sons (15) and daughters (14) than white Catholic mothers, 14 and 12, respectively. Thus, it is evident that the disparity in ambition between black and white Catholic mothers is greater with respect to daughters than to sons.

Among the nondenominational group, white mothers (16) have higher ambitions for their sons as a rule than black mothers (15), whereas the latter exhibit slightly higher ambitions for daughters (17) than do their white counterparts (16). Indeed, their score is virtually the same as that of Jewish mothers of sons (17). Jewish mothers value education for daughters less (16) than nondenominational mothers do in both races.

It is evident from this discussion that there are complex interactions between race, religion, and sex of child in relation to maternal valuations of education. Thus, among blacks, nondenominational and High Protestant mothers have the highest ambitions for daughters, but nondenominational and Catholic mothers are most ambitious for sons. Among whites, nondenominational mothers exhibit the highest ambitions for daughters, whereas Jewish mothers exhibit the highest ambitions for sons (at least in my white sample). If mother's ambition alone determined IQ scores, one would expect to find more pronounced differences in some religious groups than in others. But it will be remembered that rather pronounced sex differences in IQ favoring girls were found only among High Protestants in each race. It turns out that black High Protestant mothers have considerably higher ambitions for daughters (16) than for sons (14); the difference on this score among white High Protestants is smaller, although in the same direction.

Perhaps the most interesting case is that of the Jews. The mothers' ambitions for sons are higher (17) than for daughters (16), but the IQ scores of the two sexes are identical (110). Clearly, something more than maternal ambition is involved in the determination of sex differences on IQ test performance within and between religious groups in each race, as well as between races.

Maternal investment of time and other resources was earlier reported to be significantly higher in daughters than in sons in both races. It is therefore interesting to identify the religious and denominational subgroups in which the overall pattern of sex differences is found and where maternal investment is not conditioned by sex of child.

Among blacks *all* Protestant mothers—Baptist, Methodist, High Protestants—invest more time and other resources in daughters than in sons, the difference being most pronounced among High Protestants (24 vs. 22).[6] Black Catholic mothers average very nearly the same amount of investment in children of each sex (23), sons having a very slight edge. A similar but more pronounced difference favoring sons (24) over daughters (23) is exhibited by nondenominational/nonreligious black mothers. It is noteworthy that these are the only two groups in the black sample where boys also average slightly higher IQ scores than girls.

Among whites, Baptists alone among the Protestant groups exhibit virtually no difference in their investment in boys and girls (21). Methodists/Lutherans and High Protestants invest more in daughters (23) than in sons (21). There are virtually no denominational differences among white Protestants with respect to investment in sons, but with respect to daughters there is a rise as one goes from Baptists (21) to Methodist/ Lutheran (22.8) to High Protestants (23.4).

White Catholic mothers do not appear to favor one sex over the other. They average the lowest investment scores in the white sample with respect to both sons and daughters (both 21).

White nondenominational and Jewish mothers also invest equally in their sons and daughters, but their scores are the highest in the whole sample (24), equaled only by those of black nondenominational mothers of sons. The only other groups that approach the top scores are black and white High Protestant mothers of daughters (24 and 23, respectively), who, it will be recalled, are the same groups in which girls average considerably higher IQ scores than boys.

Black Baptist and other fundamentalist mothers invest less than than any other group in the sample in their children, but the investment in sons is even less (19), as a rule, than in daughters (20). Further, black Baptist mothers of sons also use the most discipline (16) in the entire sample. They use less discipline in relation to daughters (14), a score similar to that of black Methodist mothers of sons and daughters and to black and white Catholic mothers of sons. The highest average discipline score in the white sample, incidentally, is exhibited by white Catholic mothers of sons.

Black nondenominational and High Protestant mothers of daughters average the lowest discipline (11) in the black sample. They tend to use slightly more discipline in relation to sóns, but they discipline boys considerably less than all other religious and denominational groups in the black sample, which in all cases except for Methodists use a good deal more discipline toward boys than toward girls.

White mothers, as a rule, employ less discipline than their black co-religionists in relation to children of both sexes, except for Catholic mothers, who average a similar level of discipline toward sons (14) as black Catholic mothers (13.5), while toward daughters they use more discipline (13) than blacks (12). White Baptist mothers use as much discipline in relation to both sexes (13) as Catholic mothers of daughters. Methodist mothers of sons use somewhat less discipline toward sons (12) than Baptists but more than High Protestant mothers of sons (10). Both these groups use less discipline toward daughters than toward sons; but even with respect to daughters, Methodists average higher scores (10.5) than High Protestants (9). Sex differentiation persists even among white nondenominational mothers, who, though they average the lowest discipline scores in the entire sample, still employ more discipline in relation to sons (9) than to daughters (8). Jewish mothers are the only group in the entire sample who use as little discipline in rearing sons as in rearing daughters (9). Interestingly, they are also the only group in the white sample in which boys' average achievement score (6.8) is slightly higher than that of girls (6.5). In the black sample nondenominational mothers are the only other group exhibiting this pattern: their sons' average score is 6.6, compared with a mean score of 6.1 for daughters.

While sex differences in achievement are small in Jewish and black non-denominational groups, it is worth looking more carefully at these groups because, as I pointed out in Chapter 3, they have the closest similarity in IQ and achievement scores. With the exception of nondenominational white children, they also average the highest scores in the sample on both IQ and achievement tests. In most analyses these three groups of mothers appear most consistently to employ enlightened strategies of socialization. They have high ambitions for their children. In the case of nondenominational mothers, blacks are more ambitious for daughters, as a rule, whereas among their white counterparts there is very little difference in the value played on future educational attainment of boys and girls. Among Jews, mothers have higher ambitions for sons than for their daughters, but they as well as white nondenominational mothers invest resources and time equally in sons and daughters. And black nondenominational mothers, if anything, tend to in-vest slightly more in sons, perhaps in compensation for the greater vulnera-bility of boys to the destructive effects of a caste system which demands and enforces their subordination in a society which traditionally accords superordinate status to males, thus making black males victims of sharper role contradictions than black females. While black nondenominational mothers use more discipline on their children than white nondenominational and Jewish mothers, they use markedly less discipline on their sons than other black mothers of sons and they do not employ significantly more aversive discipline in relation to boys than to girls. Only one other group of black mothers do not differentiate their use of discipline according to sex of child—Methodists—but their mean scores on discipline for both sexes (14) are markedly higher than those found among nondenominational black mothers (12 and 11, respectively, in relation to boys and girls).

All in all, it appears that the markedly higher average IQ and achievement scores found among sons of black nondenominational mothers relative to the sons of black mothers in all other religious groups results from a strategy in which they implement their relatively but not inordinately high ambitions by a heavy investment in their sons and a quite moderate use of aversive discipline.

It is interesting to note that black Catholic mothers of sons average the same score on their valuation of education (15) as nondenominational mothers of sons, but they average lower investment scores (23 vs. 24) and considerably higher discipline scores (13.5 vs. 12.0). It seems likely that this *combination* of differences rather than each taken alone accounts to some extent, if not altogether, for the large difference in the IQ scores (9 points) and achievement scores (2 stanines) of these two groups of black boys.

The markedly higher mean IQ and achievement scores of the daughters compared with the sons of white High Protestant mothers also appear to result from the combination of higher valuations of education, higher investment, and less use of discipline in relation to girls in this religious group. Indeed, white High Protestant mothers use less discipline in relation to girls than any other religious group except white nondenominational mothers of girls; their ambitions for and investment in their daughters are on the average higher than for sons, and they are higher on these variables, as a rule, than any of the other Protestant groups in the white sample. Black High Protestant mothers voice higher ambitions for their daughters (16 vs. 15), they invest more in their daughters (24 vs. 23), but they also discipline them more (11 vs. 9) than their white co-religionists. Black High Protestant girls average virtually as high an IQ score (107) as the daughters of nondenominational black mothers (108), but their mean achievement score is somewhat lower (5.5 vs. 6.1). In both races, High Protestants *girls'* IQ scores exhibit the closest similarity to the scores of children of nondenominational and Jewish mothers, and taken together these groups average the highest scores in the entire sample. In contrast, sons of High Protestant mothers, particularly among blacks but also among whites, are less proficient intellectually than children in the aforementioned groups, very possibly because disparities in maternal ambition, investment in the child, and the use of discipline are greater between High Protestant mothers of sons, on the one hand, and nondenominational and Jewish mothers, on the other, than between mothers of daughters in the two races.

Summary

The previous chapter compared the social sources of variation in three dimensions of socialization among black and white mothers. I reported there that in both races, sex of child is an independent predictor of each socialization dimension.

In this chapter sex of child was shown to condition maternal values and practices to a varying degree in different SES levels and in different religious groups within each race. Such variations in the manner of socializing boys and girls, rather than biological differences, seem to be the source of sex differences in intellectual and scholastic competence.

In both races, maternal ambition is conditioned most by the child's sex at the low-SES level: among whites, mothers exhibit higher ambitions for sons, and among blacks, ambitions are higher for daughters. In both races, mothers invest more in daughters than in sons, but among blacks such sex differences are most pronounced at the middle-SES level and least pronounced at the high-SES level. Among whites such sex differentiation is most pronounced at the middle- and high-SES levels. In both races, aversive discipline is more frequently employed toward sons than daughters. These differences are most pronounced among blacks and most pronounced among whites at the high-SES level.

A higher proportion of black girls than of boys score in the highest third of the IQ continuum only in the middle-SES stratum, the same stratum in which mothers exhibit the most pronounced sex differences with respect to investment in child and use of aversive control. Being the beneficiaries of higher investment and less aversive control, black girls at the middle-SES level score higher than boys on IQ tests.

In the white sample, a higher proportion of girls than of boys score in the upper third of the IQ continuum only in the high-SES group, the same group in which maternal investment is significantly higher and aversive control significantly lower in girls than in boys.

Among blacks, no significant differences are found between boys' and girls' achievement levels in any of the three SES groups. The same is true among whites at the low- and high-SES levels. But at the middle-SES level, a significantly higher proportion of girls than boys average scores in the highest third of the achievement continuum. This finding suggests the presence of a sleeper effect. The advantages middle-SES girls derive from higher maternal investment come to fruition more slowly than in the case of high-SES girls. The white lower-middle-class home does not offer as stimulating a milieu as the upper-middle-class home, but, sustained by higher maternal investment and exposed to a broader range of formal knowledge in school, middle-SES girls appear to "pick up steam" as their years of schooling increase.

The increment in IQ and achievement scores among white middle-SES girls compared with low-SES girls is substantially greater than in the case of boys in the two strata. This appears to be due to the fact that with a rise from the low- to the middle-SES level, the optimal strategy of high investment–low aversive discipline is more readily adopted toward girls than toward boys.

Mother's religious and denominational affiliation also influences strategies of socializing daughters and sons and appear to be a source of observed differences in test scores of boys and girls. Although in most groups, mean IQ differences between the sexes are small, mostly favoring girls, among black and white High Protestants these differences are largest and are as large as or larger than the differences between the races. Among whites, Jewish boys and girls have identical IQ scores, and among blacks, sons of denominational mothers score slightly higher than daughters: their mean score, the highest in the black sample, is identical to scores of Jewish children.

The three groups in which differences between the races virtually disappear are Catholic children of both sexes and nondenominational boys; in all other groups there is a 5- or 6-point difference between black and white children of the same sex within each religious group, except in the case of Baptist girls, where whites' mean score exceeds blacks' by 8 points. In virtually all comparisons, race differences in the case of both sexes are larger among the various Protestant denominations than between non-Protestants.

In general, sex differences are less pronounced in achievement test scores than IQ scores in both races, particularly among blacks, and in all except two groups girls tend to have slightly higher scores than boys; among white Protestants this difference is largest. In contrast to other groups, black nondenominational and white Jewish sons average higher achievement scores than daughters of the same religious background. The only two groups in which the mean achievement scores of the two sexes are identical are black Baptists, who exhibit the lowest scores, and white denominational children, who exhibit the highest scores in the entire sample.

The direction and extent of sex differences in test scores among various religious groups generally correspond to differences in maternal values and socialization strategies with respect to the two sexes. Black High Protestant mothers have considerably higher ambitions for daughters than for sons, and a similar, though less pronounced, difference is found among white High Protestants.

Among blacks, *all* Protestant mothers invest more in daughters than in sons, but the difference is most pronounced among High Protestants. Among whites, there is a rise in investment in the child only with respect to daughters as one goes from Baptist to Methodist to High Protestant. There are virtually no denominational differences on investment scores with respect to sons. By contrast, black nondenominational and Catholic mothers invest more in sons, and these are also the only groups in which boys average higher IQ scores than girls.

White mothers employ less aversive discipline than their black co-religionists in relation to both sexes except in the case of Catholics; toward sons, whites and blacks are very similar, and toward daughters, whites use more discipline than blacks. White Baptist mothers use as much discipline in relation to daughters as to sons, while Methodists and High Protestants use less discipline toward daughters than toward sons. The same pattern of sex differentiation in use of aversive control is found among white nondenominational mothers, although they average the lowest discipline scores in the sample. Jewish mothers are the only group in the entire sample who use as little discipline in relation to sons as to daughters.

It is noteworthy that the three groups in which the highest average IQ scores are found—black and white nondenominational and Jewish children—are the same groups in which mothers most consistently employ enlightened strategies of socialization in relation to both sexes. Jewish mothers are more ambitious for sons than for daughters, but exhibit an egalitarian strategy of socializing the two sexes. The IQ scores of both sexes are identical, but their sons average higher achievement scores than their daughters.

Black nondenominational mothers are more ambitious for daughters than for sons, but they invest more in sons and use only slightly more discipline toward sons than toward daughters. However, they use considerably less discipline than other black mothers. Their distinctive mode of rearing sons probably accounts for the fact that black nondenominational boys average the highest IQ and achievement scores in the black sample and are virtually on a par with Jewish boys in the white sample.

White nondenominational mothers are only slightly more ambitions for sons than for daughters, and, like Jewish mothers, they invest equally highly in the two sexes. Although they use slightly more discipline in relation to sons than to daughters, they are no higher on this score than Jewish mothers. While their daughters average slightly higher IQ scores than sons, both sexes average identical achievement scores, which are the highest in the entire sample.

Without employing multivariate analysis, it is not possible to determine to what extent the variations between religious and Protestant denominational groups in sex-differentiated socialization strategies in both races result from religious factors or from the fact that religious affiliation and SES are confounded in each race. What appears to be a religious source of sex-differentiated child rearing may in actuality be a function of differences in the socioeconomic composition of the religious groups studied. But even if that should prove to be the case, it would not gainsay the findings of this chapter, namely that the extent and nature of sex differentiation in socialization vary not merely by socioeconomic status and religion, but also by denomination among Protestants in both races. Such variables, therefore, deserve far more systematic scrutiny than they have as yet received in the study of sex differences in the development of intellectual competence in childhood and youth and in the comparative study of the achievements of adult men and women in both races.

A discussion of the theoretical implications of the findings in this chapter is reserved for the final chapter. The task of the next chapter is to present the results of the multivariate analyses that test the value of a theoretical model based on both social-structural and socialization variables for the prediction of IQ and achievement test performance of black and white children and of boys and girls in the two races.

Notes

1. It is also worth noting that the difference between white high-SES girls and boys is exactly as large as that between white and black high-SES boys (5). In the low-SES group, white boys' mean IQ score exceeds that of girls by four points (100 vs. 96). That difference is larger than the difference between black and white girls (3). In those two instances the sex difference among whites is as large or larger than the differences between the races.

2. In an earlier phase of analysis when the black and white samples were simply dichotomized (middle class/working class) the same pattern of sex differences was observed in the white working class; using early interaction with child as the variable analyzed (one component of the composite variable, investment in child) and using maternal aspirations as the other variable (one component of valuation of education). The details of that analysis are reported in Blau (1972). Other preliminary analyses (not published) show that white girls' achievement scores consistently varied more with level of maternal aspirations. The greater responsiveness of girls to their mothers' aspirations is not a sign of the "naturally" greater docility of girls but rather results, I strongly suspect, from the tendency of mothers to invest more in positive forms of interaction and to rely less on discipline in rearing daughters than in rearing sons, which yields a higher "return" on their investment.

3. It will be recalled that IQ differences between the sexes were also largest among High Protestants in both races. White girls in this group maintain their early IQ advantage over their male counterparts on achievement tests in later grades, whereas black girls' scores (5.5) are only slightly higher than those of boys (5.2), just as in the case of most of the other religious groups.

4. White Methodist mothers of daughters and of sons score 14.1 and 13.5 respectively; the scores of High Protestant mothers are 15.2 and 14.5 respectively, and those of nondenominational mothers are 16.2 and 15.9 respectively.

5. The findings suggest, further, that variations in findings dealing with the same variables could be expected in other studies where the religious composition of samples differed, and that researchers interested in sex differences in socialization would be well advised to obtain information about parents' religious and denominational affiliation as well as SES and race.

6. Baptist mothers' scores for daughters and sons are 20 and 19, and Methodist mothers score 22 and 21.

CHAPTER 9

Social Antecedents of Intellectual and Scholastic Competence: Race and Sex Comparisons

Previous chapters traced the influence, first, of social and family-structural variables and, next, of three dimensions of maternal values and socialization practices. The explanatory power of the structural model was reported in Chapter 4 and that of the socialization model in Chapter 6.

The first part of the present chapter compares these two sets of predictors and the amount of variance they explain in black and white children's test scores when the two models are combined into what is labeled the full model for purposes of this study.[1]

The second part of the chapter compares the predictive value of the full model in explaining the IQ and achievement test scores of boys and girls in each race and concludes with a comparison of boys' and girls' test scores with race as a variable in the equation. In this way, it is possible to determine the residual differences in test scores between children of the same sex in the two races.

Social-Structural and Socialization Predictors of IQ Scores

The full model, which combines measures of parents' location in the stratification system, mothers' religious affiliation and religiosity, family structure, and extrafamilial roles of mothers with the three dimensions of socialization, accounts for more variance in the IQ scores of children of both races than either the social-structural or the socialization model alone. It accounts for an identical amount of variance in the scores of black and of white children, which in each race amounts to 22 percent. However, as Table 9-1 shows, there are interesting differences of several kinds between the races.

First, five variables explain as much variance in white children's IQ scores as eight variables do in the scores of black children. Second, while in both races socialization processes exert a stronger independent effect than structural factors, the former are stronger predictors of white than of black children's IQ scores. Thus, the value mothers place on education is a considerably stronger predictor of white (beta = .26) than of black scores (beta = .16). Similarly, investment in the child predicts white children's scores (beta = .19) somewhat better than those of black children (beta = .13). Discipline does not enter the equation in either race.

Sex of the child continues to exert a small but significant effect on white children's scores; girls average about 3.5 points higher on IQ tests than boys (beta = .12) after other variables are controlled. But this is not the case among black children. A further difference is that parents' demographic origins exert a small but significant independent effect on white children's IQ scores (beta = .11). White children of northern-born parents reared in larger communities average higher scores than those from southern and/or smaller communities.[2] Neither mothers' religious affiliation nor religiosity exerts any direct effects on white children's IQ scores once other variables of the model are taken into account. It will be recalled that religious affiliation in the structural model did not increase the variance explained in white IQ scores. But religious affiliation *is* a direct source of variation in the maternal values and socialization practices of white mothers. Once these are taken into account, however, religion exerts no further direct effects on white children's performance on IQ tests.

In the case of blacks the situation is quite different. First of all, at no point in the multivariate analysis did parents' demographic origins enter the equation, not even at the first stage of the multivariate analysis. But parents' social-class origin was a significant predictor of black children's scores independently of other measures of parents' origins and of current socioeconomic status and milieu. Religion adds significantly to the variance explained in black children's IQ scores independently of other social-structural variables, and the effect of religious affiliation persists when family structure and extrafamilial roles of mothers are included in the structural model. Significant

TABLE 9-1. Regression: IQ Scores of Black and White Children and Races Combined on Full Model

Standardized Coefficients (F in parentheses)

Variables	Standardized Coefficients		
	Blacks	*Whites*	*Races Combined*
SES	.085	—	.097
	(2.78)		(6.43)*
Demographic origin	—	.105	—
		(6.80)*	
Origin family size	—	—	—
Number of children	−.089	—	−.058
	(4.33)*		(4.13)*
Marital status	—	—	.040
			(2.27)
Organizational membership	—	—	—
Years employed	.076	−.079	—
	(3.65)	(4.09)*	
Valuation of education	.155	.258	.182
	(11.35)*	(29.00)*	(31.24)*
Investment in child	.132	.194	.149
	(7.92)*	(16.19)*	(19.86)*
Discipline	—	—	—
Religiosity	−.074	—	−.058
	(3.87)*		(4.63)*
Fundamentalist	−.089	—	−.069
	(4.30)*		(4.54)*
High Protestant	—	—	—
Catholic	—	—	—
Jewish	—	—	—
Nondenominational	.073	—	.048
	(3.60)		(3.14)
Sex of child	—	.120	.050
		(8.89)*	(3.83)
Race	—	—	.152
			(23.57)*
Exposure to whites [a]	—	—	—
Intercept	81.92571	58.94615	66.90764
R^2 =	22%	22%	30%
N =	579	523	1102

[a] not included in white or combined races analyses
*$p < .05$

religious effects are also observed on the socialization practices of blacks as well as whites independently of other structural variables.[3]

In the full model, mother's religious affiliation and religiosity continue to exert small but significant independent effects on black children's IQ scores even when all other variables are taken into account. Thus, children of

Baptist and other fundamentalist mothers average lower scores than other black children (beta = −.09), and those of nondenominational and nonreligious mothers average higher scores (beta = .07). And, independently of religious affiliation, children of more religious mothers average lower scores (beta = −.07) than those of less religious ones.

In short, mother's religious affiliation has both indirect *and* direct effects on black children's intellectual development even when other variables with which religious affiliation is confounded are taken into account. The evidence indicates consistently that black Baptist and other fundamentalist mothers are more inclined to employ socialization strategies that inhibit the development of intellectual competence. Even when this is taken into account, their children average lower scores than other black children as well as white children. Conversely, the children of nondenominational black mothers, who employ the most enlightened strategies of socialization, average higher scores than other black children even when all other variables in the equation are controlled. But the nondenominational group constitutes a very small proportion of black mothers, while Baptist and other fundamentalists constitute the large majority, and therein, as we shall see, lies an important source of the disparity in the test performance of black and white children.

Two further findings deserve mention. The duration of mother's employment since the birth of the child appears to have opposite effects on the IQ scores of children in the two races: a small but significant negative effect on white children (beta = −.08) and a positive one on black children (beta = .08), which only approaches significance. These differences were observed early in the analysis, but it is of some importance that they persist after all the other variables are in the equation. It was reported in Chapter 7 that white mothers with longer tenure in the labor force since their children's birth tend to place a lower value on education and to invest less time and other resources in their children than white mothers who were full-time homemakers. But even when these socialization variables are taken into account, extended work tenure persists as a negative predictor of white IQ scores.[4]

In the black sample, mother's tenure in the labor force proved not to be an independent predictor of mother's values or practices once all the social-structural variables were controlled,[5] but when socialization variables are also taken into account, black children of working mothers average slightly higher IQ scores than children of mothers who have not worked over the children's lifetime.

The number of children in the family is a significant independent predictor of black children's IQ scores (beta = −.09) but not of white children's scores. That is not to say that large families do not have any detrimental effects on white children's intellectual development, for that is not true. It was shown in Chapter 7 that larger families depress maternal valuation of education and investment of time and other resources in children in both races. Once these two variables are taken into account, there are no further effects on the IQ scores of white children. But in the case of black children, the detrimental effect of larger families on IQ test performance persists even after these effects on socialization are taken into account. In short, large families not only exert negative effects on the intellectual development of children indirectly, through the negative effects they have on maternal ambitions and investment of time and resources, but also directly depress black children's scores.

A similar pattern of differences between the races can be observed with respect to SES. Socioeconomic status exerts no direct effects on white children's scores once the other variables in the equation are taken into account. It does, to be sure, exert very strong effects, indeed the strongest ones compared with other variables considered, on mother's valuation of education, investment in the child, and use of aversive discipline, and its effects on each of the socialization dimensions are stronger among white than among black mothers relative to other variables in the equation. However, variations in child rearing explain most of the observed relationship between parents' socioeconomic status and white children's IQ scores.

In the case of black children, it requires that the combination of religious affiliation, variation in family size, and mother's work-force participation plus variations in socialization be taken into account before the effect of SES on IQ becomes negligible.

With black and white children's scores combined, SES continues to exert a significant effect (beta = .10) on IQ independently of all other variables in the equation, albeit a weaker one than mother's valuation of education (beta = .18), investment in the child (beta = .15), or race (beta = .15). Religion also continues to exert a significant independent effect: children of fundamentalist mothers average lower scores. While children of nondenominational mothers still tend to score higher than other children, this variable by itself does not significantly increase the variance explained after socialization variables are added to the equation.

Among the family variables, family size continues to exert a negative effect (beta = −.06). While marital status enters the equation, it does not increase significantly the variance explained in IQ scores. With all the variables in the equation, girls still average scores about 1.5 points higher than boys.

With the full model, the race difference in children's scores is very much reduced. The actual mean difference in IQ between black and white children in the sample, the reader will recall, is 10 points. But with all the variables, including sex of child, in the equation, the net difference is reduced to 3.96 points.[6]

The fact that the net race difference is reduced when sex of child is in the equation indicates that complex interactions serve to magnify the residual "race" effect. Further evidence that these multiple interactions between race, sex, and other variables operate to inflate the magnitude of IQ difference between the races was presented in Chapter 4, in which the IQs of girls and boys were separately regressed on structural variables. The residual race difference amounted to 2.9 IQ points among boys and 2.7 among girls.

Moreover, there is important evidence that an interaction exists between religious affiliation and race on IQ scores. When IQ is regressed on the full model for each religious group separately with the races combined, race does not even enter the equation of High Protestant and nondenominational children. That is, in these two groups race is not a predictor of children's IQ scores once other variables in the model are controlled.[7] Among the three remaining religious groups, a race "effect" is observed of varying magnitude. Among children of Baptist and fundamentalist mothers, black children net a score 6.7 points (beta = .19) below that of whites; among Catholics, black children's net score is 5.2 points below whites' (beta = .20); and among Methodists, black children's net IQ score is 4.9 points below that of whites (beta = .18).[8]

Predictors of Achievement Test Performance

The full model (with IQ scores included in the equation) increases the variance explained in black children's achievement scores by only 1 percent and in white children's scores by 4 percent (Table A-23, page 249).

IQ scores are somewhat stronger independent predictors of black children's achievement scores (beta = .47) than of white children's (beta = .41). SES is also a stronger predictor of black scores (beta = .19) than of the scores of white children (beta = .11). Mother's valuation of education, in contrast, is the strongest predictor of white children's scores (beta = .20), but once IQ is taken into account, mother's valuation of education does not even enter the equation for blacks. The same pattern of difference between the races is observed with respect to the effect of mother's investment in the child. Without IQ in the equation it is a stronger predictor of white achievement scores (beta = .18) than of black ones (beta = .09); with IQ in the equation, its effect is weakened but still significant among whites (beta = .10), but it does not enter the equation for blacks. In short, while valuation of education and investment of resources in the child promote early intellectual competence in both races, these variables continue to affect the scholastic proficiency of white children as they progress through their school career, whereas in the case of black children they do not. The greater reliance of black mothers on aversive modes of controlling their children during later childhood may well undercut the otherwise positive effects of valuing education and investment in their children.

Indeed, although aversive discipline has negative effects on achievement in both races, it is a significant independent predictor only of black children's scores (beta $= -.11$) whether or not IQ is a variable in the equation. While discipline enters the white equation, its independent effect is weak (beta $= -.06$) and does not significantly increase the amount of variance explained in white scores.

Black children of nondenominational mothers average higher achievement scores than other black children with other variables in the equation controlled. Even when their initial advantage on the IQ test is taken into account, they sustain significantly higher achievement scores (beta $= .08$) than other black children. High Protestant black children also tend to sustain higher scores than other black children, but with IQ added to the equation a high Protestant background makes no further contribution to the scholastic proficiency of black children. Thus, their initially higher IQ score entirely accounts for their higher achievement scores.

Mother's religiosity exerts a weak but significant negative effect on the achievement of white children even with other variables including IQ in the equation (beta $= -.09$). With the full model, IQ included, Jewish children net significantly lower achievement scores than other white children (beta $= -.10$).[9]

A reversal in direction is observed with respect to the effect of parents' demographic origins on white children's achievement scores. Although white children of northern-born parents reared in larger communities display a small net advantage in IQ scores, once IQ is controlled their achievement scores are no higher than those of other white children; if anything, their scores are slightly, though not significantly, lower, an indication that their early advantage on IQ test performance is not sustained in their performance or achievement tests three or four years later.

White girls sustain a slight advantage in achievement relative to white boys (beta $= .06$) net of other variables in the equation, but when IQ is added to the other variables in the full model, sex of child no longer enters the equation. That is to say, whatever superiority white girls show in achievement scores relative to boys is merely a function of their higher IQ scores.

With the two races combined and with race and IQ added as variables to the full model, IQ remains the strongest predictor of children's achievement scores (beta $= .41$); race (beta $= .22$) and socioeconomic status (beta $= .15$) are weaker predictors; and next in order of importance are mother's valuation of education (beta $= .10$) and discipline (beta $= -.08$). The remaining predictors, each of which slightly but significantly increases the variance explained, are mother's religiosity (beta $= -.04$), Jewish background (beta $= -.05$), and nondenominational background (beta $= .04$).

Without IQ in the equation, the net advantage of white children over black children in average achievement is about one stanine, compared with a zero-order difference of two stanines. In short, the full model serves to reduce the disparity in achievement scores between the two races by about half of that actually observed. With IQ added to the equation, the disparity is further reduced to a little over three-quarters of a stanine (B = .79). Thus, a very considerable amount of the difference in black and white achievement scores can be accounted for by social influences, more widespread in black families than in white ones, that inhibit the intellectual development of children prior to school entry and continue to exert negative effects on scholastic aptitude over the span of later childhood. Socioeconomic status of parents exerts a stronger and more enduring direct effect on scholastic ability than it does on IQ test performance. That is, parents' socioeconomic attributes, independently of their effects on measured modes of socializing children, facilitate or handicap children's scholastic performance. The concrete help, support, and culturally enriching experiences that well-educated parents are able to provide facilitate their children's mastery of the content offered by the school, which sustains their motivation to learn. Children whose parents lack the formal knowledge and skills that compose the school curriculum cannot look to them for help. Given these inequalities in resources, in the case of whites, mother's valuation of education nevertheless continues to exert a significant net effect on children's scholastic aptitude even after its more powerful effects on IQ are taken into account. That it does not do so in the case of blacks is due, I believe, to the larger families of black mothers and to their heavier reliance on aversive forms of control, which, other studies also show (Furstenberg, 1971), serve only to undercut children's identification with parents and their goals, particularly those that require sustained work and effort from the child. A strategy that combines a high valuation of education with high investment of resources and relatively low reliance on aversive forms of control is characteristic of only one subgroup in the black sample, nondenominational and nonreligious mothers, and it is their children who sustain the highest achievement scores in the black sample. Furthermore, this is the only group in the black sample in which boys are somewhat more successful academically than girls.

Social Sources of Sex Variations in IQ Scores

In chapters 7 and 8, it was shown that race, socioeconomic status, and religious affiliation of mothers influence, on the one hand, how boys and girls are reared and, on the other, variations in the intellectual and scholastic abilities of each sex. Having established in some detail the nature and extent of these differences, a comparison is now in order of the amount of variance the full model explains in the scores of boys and girls in each race.

The full model accounts for somewhat more variance in the IQ scores of black girls (26 percent) and white boys (25 percent) than of either black boys or white girls (20 percent and 21 percent respectively). Further evidence is that mother's valuation of education and investment in the child are the two variables that most consistently predict IQ scores, although they do so to varying degrees in the four groups (Table A-24, page 250).[10] Thus, mother's valuation of education exerts the strongest independent effect on black boys' and white girls' scores (beta = .28 and .30, respectively); its effect on white boys' scores is somewhat weaker (beta = .20), while its effect on black girls' scores is very weak (beta = .09) and does not increase significantly the variance explained in their scores. It is of some interest, incidentally, that mother's valuation of education carries more independent weight in the two groups that are less favored foci of maternal ambition in the two races—that is, black boys and white girls. The independent effect of maternal investment in child, in contrast, is rather similar in three groups—black and white girls (beta = .19 and .15 respectively) and white boys (beta = .21) but it does not enter the equation in the case of black boys.

With respect to social-structural variables, two variables are significant predictors of boys' scores in both races: mother's religiosity exerts a negative effect of similar magnitude on IQ scores of black and white boys (beta = −.14); and in both races sons of nondenominational mothers average higher mean scores than sons from other religious backgrounds, although this effect is stronger in the case of black (beta = .15) than of white boys (beta = .09). A fundamentalist background exerts an independent negative effect only on black girls' IQ scores (beta = .15). It does not enter the equation of black boys nor those of white children.

Mother's tenure in the labor force since the child's birth appears to exert opposite effects on the IQ scores of boys in the two races, positive in the case of blacks (beta = .17) and negative in the case of whites (beta = −.12). An analysis of covariance reveals a complex interaction between race, years mothers worked, and father absence in their effect on boys' IQ scores. Among blacks, maternal employment unequivocally benefits sons' IQ test performance, regardless of whether their fathers are present or absent from the home.[11] Among whites the effect of maternal employment is contingent on mother's marital status. In white father-present families in which mothers serve as full-time homemakers, sons' average IQ score is 108, which is slightly but not significantly higher than that of sons of working mothers in father-absent homes (106).[12] Sons of working mothers in father-present homes have slightly lower IQ scores (103). Sons of full-time homemakers in father-absent familes average the lowest scores (96). But there are far fewer such cases (2 percent) in the white sample than in the black sample (12 percent). In sum, the difference between the races in the effect of maternal employment on sons' IQ scores is more apparent than real. The two highest-scoring groups of sons among whites are those of married full-time homemakers and working mothers without spouses. Sons of married working mothers score slightly lower and sons of full-time homemakers without husbands are markedly lower.[13] What is noteworthy from the standpoint of social policy is that in both races mother's labor-force participation in father-absent families appears to benefit sons' performance on IQ tests. However, the proportion of children being reared in father-absent families is considerably higher in the black (29 percent) than in the white sample (8 percent).

Father presence is the only family structure variable that exerts a significant independent effect on white girls' IQ scores (beta = .11). White girls' IQ test performance seem to benefit from the presence of a father regardless of mother's employment history.[14] Among black girls, family size exerts an independent negative effect on IQ scores (beta = −.13).

Parents' demographic origins constitute a significant predictor of white boys' IQ scores (beta = .12) and also enter the equation for white girls without increasing significantly the variance explained in their scores. Socioeconomic status enters the equation only in the case of black girls, but even then its contribution to the variance explained is not significant once other variables in the equation are controlled.

Predictors of Achievement Test Scores of Black and White Boys and Girls

In order to distinguish variables that predict achievement of boys and girls directly from those that do so indirectly, through their influence on IQ scores, IQ scores have been included as a variable in the prediction equation for the four sex-color groups. With IQ entered as a variable, the variance explained in each of the groups rises considerably (Table A-25, page 251). Thus, four variables explain 24 percent of the variance in black boys' achievement scores, but with IQ scores in the equation that figure rises to 44 percent. Seven variables account for 31 percent of the variance in black girls' scores; with IQ in the equation that figure rises to 45 percent. Six variables account for 34 percent of the variance in white boys' achievement scores; with IQ added to the equation 44 percent of the variance is accounted for. Finally, four variables account for 30 percent of the variance in white girls' achievement scores, and the inclusion of IQ increases the variance explained to 44 percent.

For all four groups, of course, IQ constitutes the strongest single predictor of achievement, but it is a considerably stronger predictor of black boys' achievement scores (beta = .50) than of white boys' (beta = .38). Indeed, independently of IQ scores, only two variables, socioeconomic status (beta = .18) and mother's use of aversive discipline (beta = −.16), increase by a significant amount the variance explained in black boys' achievement scores (Table A-25, page 251). Mother's valuation of education no longer enters the equation, which indicates that it exerts no further direct effect on black boys' achievement, once its effect on IQ is taken into account. Sons of black nondenominational mothers continue to sustain higher scores than black boys from other religious backgrounds, but the effect of religious background is considerably reduced when IQ is a variable in the equation, which indicates again that the superior achievement of this group relative to other black boys is largely a function of their earlier intellectual competence, although even net of IQ they sustain a slight advantage in achievement test performance. Although the effects of variations in socioeconomic status on achievement test scores are somewhat reduced when IQ is in the equation, it is clear that this variable is more directly a source of variation in black boys' achievement than in their IQ scores. This is even more true with respect to the effects of aversive discipline, for with IQ in the equation its negative effect becomes stronger rather than weaker, an indication again that whatever their sons' IQ score may have been early in their school careers, the generally heavy reliance of black mothers on aversive controls in relation to sons is counterproductive, for it undermines both the will and the ability to learn formal skills and knowledge.

Performance on IQ tests early in the school career is, as already indicated, a weaker predictor of white boys' achievement scores than of those of black boys or girls. The effect of socioeconomic status, however, is the same (beta = .18) for white as for black boys, and in both races sons of nondenominational mothers average higher scores net of IQ test performance and their generally higher SES than boys from other religious backgrounds. Two additional variables continue to exert significant independent effects on white boys' achievement scores. Mother's religiosity exerts a negative effect (beta = −.17), and mother's valuation of education a positive effect (beta = .18) of similar magnitude.

There is very little difference in the weight of IQ as a predictor of black (beta = .44) and white (beta = .42) girls' achievement scores. With IQ in the equation, socioeconomic status continues to exert the strongest effect on black girls' achievement scores (beta = .21) but does not even enter the equation of white girls. Mother's valuation of education continues to be the strongest predictor of their achievement (beta = .30), second only to IQ scores. In the case of black girls, mother's valuation of education net of IQ and socioeconomic status exerts only a small effect on their achievement scores (beta = .10), equal in magnitude but opposite in direction to the effect of a fundamentalist background (beta = −.10). The positive effect of presence of a father in the home (beta = .08) and the negative effect of aversive discipline (beta = −.07) on black girls' achievement persist but they are attenuated and neither alone adds significantly to the variance explained when IQ is in the equation.

In the case of white girls alone, investment in the child continues to exert a small independent effect (beta = .11) on achievement scores, although with IQ in the equation it no longer increases significantly the variance explained. Interestingly, with IQ in the equation, mother's years of labor-force participation appears to exert a weak positive independent effect on white girls' achievement (beta = .07), which does not increase significantly the variance explained in their scores. Nevertheless, this finding would seem to offer some support for the hypotheses advanced by other investigators (Hoffman et al., 1974) that mothers committed to a career may provide a role model for daughters which in later childhood might find expression in a heightened motivation to do well academically.[15] Analysis of the sexes separately reveals that a Jewish background is a negative predictor of girls' achievement scores (beta = −.13) but not of boys' when all variables in the model are controlled.[16]

What is evident from the comparative analysis of the four sex-race groups is that not a single variable in the model in the present study carries the same weight as predictors of either IQ or achievement test performance in all four groups. With respect to the prediction of IQ, only one variable, mother's valuation of education, enters all four equations. Mother's investment in child enters the equation in three of the groups. But even these two variables, particularly the first, vary considerably in their net weight, and the variation is not merely by race or by sex but by both race *and* sex. Thus, for example, mother's valuation of education is the strongest single predictor of white girls' and black boys' IQ scores and among the weakest predictors of black girls' IQ scores; the strongest predictor of *their* scores is mother's investment in the child. For white boys, mother's valuation of education *and* investment in the son are of equal importance as predictors of IQ. But in the case of black boys the latter variable does not even enter the equation. To cite only one more instance of the variability of the independent predictive value of variables across race and sex groups, let us take IQ as a predictor of achievement test performance. While it is the strongest single predictor of achievement in all four groups, it is strongest as a predictor of black boys' achievement and weakest as a predictor of white boys' achievement, whereas it carries about equal weight as a predictor of black and white girls' achievement scores.

There are, however, also some interesting uniformities according to sex across races, and according to race across the sexes. Thus, a nondenominational background benefits the intellectual and scholastic competence of boys in both races, while mother's religiosity depresses IQ scores of boys in both races, but independently of IQ its effects persist only on white boys' achievement. Family composition seems to affect girls' scores more than those of boys. Thus, the presence of a father in the home has a positive effect on black girls' achievement scores and on white girls' IQ scores. Family size exerts a negative effect on black girls' IQ scores but does not enter the equation of white girls.

Mother's duration of employment since the study child's birth affects the IQ scores of boys in both races in what appears to be opposite ways, being a positive predictor of black boys' scores and a negative one of white boys' scores. But as already noted, further analysis revealed that white sons of working mothers in father-absent homes do not average significantly lower scores than sons of full-time homemakers in father-present homes. But father absence is far rarer among families in the white than in the black sample. Mother's years of work also emerges as a positive, although weak, predictor of white girls' achievement scores.

A few uniformities across sex lines within each race are also found. Mother's use of aversive discipline, which is generally more widespread and more pronounced among blacks than among whites, is a negative predictor of achievement scores of both sexes among black children, albeit a stronger one in the case of boys than of girls independently of other variables. Variations in SES also affect achievement scores of both sexes of black children to about the same degree and do so more than in the case of white children, particularly compared with white girls. The IQ scores of both sexes among white children are affected by parents' demographic origins, but they significantly increase the variance explained only in boys' scores, whereas they do not enter the prediction equations of either sex among blacks.

Given the nature of the issues being addressed in the present study, it is necessary to present two further sets of multivariate analyses comparing the predictors of boys' and girls' IQ and achievement scores with race entered as a variable in the full model because this helps to further clarify how the three dimensions of socialization mediate the effects of structural variables on test scores of each sex.

Predictors of Boys' and Girls' IQ Scores with Race in the Equation

The full model explains more of the variance in IQ scores in each sex than the one based on social and family structural variables alone—28 percent of the variance in boys' scores and 33 percent in girls' scores—which represents an improvement of about 6 percent over the structural model in the prediction of boys' scores and 4 percent in girls' scores (Table A-26, page 252). With the inclusion of the three socialization dimensions, three structural variables that contributed a significant amount to the explanation of the variance in boys' IQ scores no longer even enter the equation—socioeconomic status, family size, and Jewish religious background. Thus it is their effects on the socialization beliefs and practices of mothers that entirely explain the contribution of these particular structural variables to the variance in boys' scores. Evidently, mothers' valuation of education and the extent of their investment of time and resources are more strongly conditioned by socioeconomic factors in the case of male children, and the negative effect of family size on boys also apparently is accounted for entirely by its negative effect on maternal ambition and investment in sons. Finally, the superiority exhibited by Jewish boys net of other variables in the structural model does not persist in the full model, which indicates that their mothers' higher valuations of education and higher investment in them account for their higher IQ scores relative to boys from other religious backgrounds. But these same attributes, also characteristic of nondenominational mothers, do not fully explain their sons' intellectual superiority relative to boys from other religious backgrounds. For though the independent effect of a nondenominational background on IQ scores is reduced when socialization variables are controlled, the sons of nondenominational mothers continue to average higher scores than boys from other backgrounds (beta = .10). This fact, coupled with the finding that the negative effect of mother's religiosity is not diminished but is even slightly strengthened when socialization variables are controlled (beta = −.14), suggests that a secular, nontraditional, nonauthoritarian world view that stresses the importance of rational forces and of self-direction is particularly conducive to the early intellectual development of boys and also serves to sustain their motivation and ability to excel academically during the period of later childhood, when peer pressures are particularly strong on males to direct energy to pursuits that signify masculinity, such as the development of athletic prowess, which in American society confers greater prestige in preadult stages of life than excelling intellectually (Coleman, 1959 and Turner, 1964).[17]

In contrast to boys, the effects of socioeconomic status and of family composition on girls' IQ scores are partly but not wholly mediated by socialization variables. Although the effect of socioeconomic status is considerably attenuated when variations in socialization are controlled for, it continues to exert a significant independent effect on girls' IQ scores, and its weight is only slightly less strong than the contributions of mother's valuation of education and investment of time and resources. Similarly, the negative effects of a fundamentalist background and of large family size are only very slightly attenuated by taking into account socialization factors, and each continues to make a significant contribution to the variance explained in girls' scores. The effect of a paternal presence in the home, which was already very weak but significant in the structural model, is further weakened when socialization variables are taken into account, and its net contribution only approaches significance (beta = .06), a further indication that as between the two, the presence of many siblings and the attendant responsibilities that fall more heavily on daughters than on sons have a more detrimental effect than father absence on the early intellectual development of girls.

One further point of particular interest is the comparison of the magnitude of the "race effect" among each sex. With socialization variables in the model, the difference in the mean IQ scores of black and white boys increases by about one point and those of girls by about 1.3 points, compared with the differences between the races observed in the structural model. This I take as further confirmation of the presence of complex interaction effects on IQ that occur between race, religion, SES, and socialization variables. Without the presence of interaction terms in the equation, these register as race effects in the analyses of the scores of children of each sex.[18]

Predictors of Boys' and Girls' Achievement Scores with Race in the Equation

The full model increases the variance explained in boys' achievement scores only 1 percent (56 percent vs. 55 percent explained by the structural model). Similarly, the full model increases the variance explained in girls' achievement scores only by 2 percent (58 percent vs. 56 percent) when IQ scores are added to the equation.[19] But as in the case of IQ scores, the full model provides confirmation and explanation of the mediating processes by which socioeconomic status, in particular, influences scholastic ability of boys and girls (Table A-27, page 253).

Two of the three socialization variables, valuation of education and discipline constitute significant predictors of the achievement scores of both sexes, but the positive effect of mother's values is stronger on girls' achievement (beta = .14) than on boys' (beta = .08), whereas the negative effect of aversive discipline is slightly stronger on boys' scores (beta = −.10) than on girls' (beta = −.07). Mother's investment in child persists in exerting a weak effect on girls' scores (beta = .05) but is not a predictor of boys' scores independently of the other variables in the equation.

Taking socialization variables into account reduces the net effects of IQ on girls' scores (beta = .40 vs. .45) slightly more than on boys' scores (beta = .41 vs. .43), but it remains the strongest predictor of achievement scores among both sexes. The presence of the socialization variables in the equation reduces the independent effect of socioeconomic status on achievement scores more than the effect of IQ among both sexes (from beta = .23 to .15 among boys and from beta = .27 to .15 among girls). The positive effect of a nondenominational background (beta = .08) and the negative effect of mother's religiosity on boys scores (beta = −.09) persist virtually unchanged in the full model as compared with the structural model, but the effect of mother's organizational memberships is reduced (beta = .06) so that it ceases to make a significant contribution to the variance explained in boys' scores. Thus, it is evident that it is the effect of mother's organizational participation in promoting more enlightened modes of socializing sons that largely explains its positive effect on boys' achievement.[20] The effects of socioeconomic status, however, are both indirect, through its effects on socialization values and practices, and direct on achievement scores independently of other variables in the equation among both sexes (beta = .15). The weight that race exerts on boys' achievement scores is virtually unaffected by the addition of socialization variables to the equation (beta = .16 vs.

.17), but in the case of girls its weight as a predictor increases from beta = .22 to .27. The residual difference between black and white boys' mean achievement scores is a little less than two-thirds of a stanine whether the structural model or the full model is used with IQ scores in the equation. The corresponding difference between black and white girls' scores is about four-fifths of a stanine with the structural model but almost one stanine with the full model. The increment of difference between the races that occurs in girls' but not in boys' scores when socialization variables are added to the prediction equation suggests that the locus of interactions between race and structural and socialization variables in their achievement scores is mainly among girls. To put this more simply, the effects of structural variables on achievement are conditioned by racial variations in socialization more in the case of girls than of boys.

Summary

The explanatory power of the social-structural model was reported in Chapter 4 and that of the socialization model in Chapter 6. It was shown that social-structural variables explain more variance in the IQ scores of black children and socialization variables explain more variance in white children's scores. With the structural model, the residual mean IQ difference between black and white children becomes smaller than with the socialization model, and that difference becomes even smaller when boys and girls are analyzed separately.

The manner and extent to which social structural variables influence black and white mothers' socialization strategies were compared in Chapter 7. Sex of child proved to be a significant predictor of black and white mothers' valuation of education, investment in the child, and use of aversive control, and therefore Chapter 8 compared the nature and extent of differences in the socialization of black and white boys and girls at various socioeconomic levels and in various religious groups. The evidence suggests that such differences are a significant source of sex differences in intellectual and scholastic competence observed in different socioeconomic and religious contexts.

The first part of the present chapter, which combined social-structural and socialization variables, provided evidence that the full model has more predictive and explanatory power than either the structural or socialization models and that it accounts for an identical amount of variance in the IQ scores of black and white children.

However, interesting race differences of several kinds were reported. First, five variables explain as much variance in white children's scores as eight variables do in the scores of black children. Second, in both races, socialization processes exert stronger direct effects than structural factors, but they are stronger predictors of white than of black children's IQ scores.

White girls' IQ score advantage over white boys persists when all other variables are controlled, but this is not the case among black children. White children of northern-born parents reared in larger communities average higher scores than those from southern and/or small communities, and children of nonworking mothers average higher scores than those of working mothers. Neither SES, mother's religious affiliation, nor religiosity exert any direct effects on white children's IQ scores, with the full model. These variables, to be sure, exert strong direct effects on maternal values and practices, and such variations in child rearing account for observed differences in the intellectual competence of white children from different socioeconomic and religious backgrounds.

In the case of blacks, the situation is quite different. With the full model, family size and a fundamentalist background persist as negative predictors of black children's IQ scores. Children of nondenominational mothers and those of mothers with longer labor-force participation average higher IQ scores than other black children. Once all these variables plus maternal ambition and investment in the child are taken into account, the relationship of socioeconomic status to black children's IQ scores becomes negligible and does not increase significantly the variance explained in black children's scores.

However, with black and white children combined, SES continues to exert a significant effect on IQ scores, albeit a weaker one than mother's valuation of education, investment in the child, or race. Family size persists as a negative predictor of IQ scores, and children of fundamentalist mothers and of more religious mothers average lower scores, while those of nondenominational mothers average higher scores than other children.

With the full model the residual race difference in IQ scores, though slightly higher than with the structural model, is considerably lower than with the socialization model. Important evidence of two kinds indicate that complex interactions operate to inflate the magnitude of IQ difference between the races. First, when the sexes were analyzed separately with the social-structural model, only trivial race differences remained, amounting to less than 3 IQ points among each sex, which is less than the zero-order differences of 4 points between white girls and boys or the residual difference of 3.5 IQ points between them that remains with the full model.

Second, important evidence that an interaction exists between race, religious affiliation, and IQ is forthcoming when IQ is regressed on the full model for each religious group separately with the races combined. In two groups—High Protestant and nondenominational children—race does not even enter the equation; that is, race is not a predictor of IQ once all other variables are controlled. In the three remaining religious groups, a residual race difference of varying magnitude is observed which, in each case, is lower than the zero-order race difference in black and white children's IQ scores.

A comparative analysis of the four sex-race groups reveals that not a single variable in the full model carries the same weight as predictors of either IQ or achievement scores. The two variables that most consistently predict IQ scores are mother's valuation of education and investment in the child, although they do so to varying degrees in the four sex-race groups. The full model accounts for somewhat more variance in the IQ scores of black girls and white boys than of either black boys or white girls. Two social structural variables are significant predictors of boys' IQ scores in both races: mother's religiosity exerts a negative effect and nondenominational background a positive one. Parents' demographic origins is a predictor only of white boys' scores. Mother's tenure in the labor force since the child's birth is a positive predictor of black boys' scores. In the case of white boys, an interaction is observed between mother's work-force tenure and marital status. Sons of full-time homemakers in father-present homes average slightly higher IQ scores than those of working mothers in father-absent homes. Sons of working mothers in father-present homes score somewhat lower, and those of full-time homemakers in father-absent homes average the lowest scores, just as is the case among blacks. However, there are far fewer such cases in the white than in the black sample.

Black girls are the only group in which socioeconomic status persists as a predictor of IQ scores with the full model, but its effect is weak and nonsignificant. A fundamentalist background and family size are negative predictors of black girls' scores. White girls in father-present families average higher IQ scores than those in father-absent homes. Mother's valuation of education is the strongest single predictor of white girls' and black boys' IQ scores and a weak one of black girls' scores. In the case of white boys, mother's values and investment in the child carry equal weight. Maternal investment in the child is the strongest predictor of black girls' scores, but does not enter the equation of black boys.

Aversive control is a weak negative predictor of black girls' IQ and achievement scores. It is a stronger predictor of black boys' achievement scores and carries nearly as much weight as SES, but it is not a predictor of white children's achievement scores. Mother's valuation of education is a predictor of black girls' and white children's achievement scores, but its effect is strongest on white girls' scores. Mother's investment in the child persists as a weak predictor of white girls' achievement scores, but does not enter the equations of the other three groups. Sons of nondenominational mothers in both races average higher scores than other boys and sons of white, more religious mothers average lower scores than other white boys. Daughters of black fundamentalist mothers and white Jewish mothers average lower achievement scores than their race peers when other variables are controlled.

SES is a predictor of black children's and of white boys' achievement scores, but not of white girls' scores. IQ scores are the strongest predictor of achievement scores in all groups, but its weight is strongest in the case of black boys and weakest in the case of white boys.

Two further sets of multivariate analyses, comparing the predictors of boys' and girls' IQ and achievement scores with race as a variable in the full model, help to clarify further how socialization processes mediate the effects of social structural variables on test scores of each sex.

The full model explains more of the variance in IQ scores in each sex than the structural model. Three structural variables that contribute significantly to the variance explained in boys' scores no longer enter the equation with the full model—socioeconomic status, family size, and a Jewish background. Thus, it is their effects on mother's socialization beliefs and practices that entirely explain the contribution of these particular variables to the variance in boys' scores. Mother's valuation of education and the extent of investment in the child are more strongly conditioned by socioeconomic factors in the case of male children. The negative effect of family size also is fully accounted for by its negative effect on maternal ambition and investment in the child, and these two variables also account for Jewish boys' intellectual superiority.

The fact that the intellectual superiority of sons of nondenominational mothers persists and that the negative effect of mother's religiosity is not diminished with the full model suggests that a secular, nonauthoritarian world view that stresses rationality and self-direction is particularly conducive to the early intellectual development of boys and also serves to sustain their academic motivation and ability in later childhood. Mother's valuation of education is the strongest predictor of boys' scores, but maternal investment also makes a significant contribution as strong or stronger than structural variables.

In the case of girls, the significant effects of socioeconomic status, although attenuated, persist as do also the negative effects of a fundamentalist background and of a large family. The positive effect of father presence is also attenuated and only approaches significance with the full model. But mother's valuation of education exerts a stronger effect than structural variables on girls' than on boys' IQ scores. Maternal investment is as strong a predictor as mother's values of boys' scores.

All my findings serve to confirm the more general proposition that observed disparities in the measured intelligence of black and white children of each sex are not due to inherent race differences, but are the result of social factors and of complex interactions between them.

My analysis has shown that such differences are not uniform, but highly variable, that only trivial IQ differences remain when the sexes are analyzed separately with only structural variables controlled; and that among children in two religious groups race differences in IQ disappear altogether when structural and socialization factors are controlled. Thus, one locus of interactions is between race, sex of child, and IQ scores. A second locus of interaction is between race, social-structural variables, and socialization processes, and a third locus of such interactions is between race, religion, social-structural variables, and socialization variables. These results testify to the complexities involved in making valid comparisons of the measured intelligence of children in two such differently situated groups as blacks and whites have been and continue to be in American society.

This chapter completes the task of reporting the empirical findings of my study. The final chapter discusses in greater detail the theoretical implications of my findings and sets forth some more general propositions about the relationships of sex, social structure, modernization, and childhood socialization processes to the development of intellectual competence and concludes with a brief afterword on some social policy implications of my findings.

Notes

1. That is not to suggest that my theoretical model is exhaustive. The effects, for example, of the racial, socioeconomic, and religious composition of neighborhoods in which children are reared and of their peers, and variations among schools they attend and among their teachers may well also be sources of variation in the test scores of children within each race as well as between the races.

2. This finding with respect to children's IQ scores is consistent with the findings of Blau and Duncan (1967) that men who grew up in larger communities attain higher occupational status than those with more rural origins.

3. Black mothers' valuation of education was the only socialization dimension on which religious affiliation exerted no significant independent effects.

4. That the effects of mother's work tenure on IQ scores are sex-specific will be shown and explained presently.

5. However, mother's exposure to whites, which is quite strongly associated with length of employment ($r = .34$), was found to exert a positive effect on investment in the child, net of other social structural variables.

6. Without sex of child in the equation the variance explained in IQ scores for the whole sample is virtually the same as when sex is included. However, the coefficient for race rises from beta = .15 to beta = .18 ($F = 5.17$), and there is a small rise in the weights of investment in child and valuation of education and a small decrease in the betas of SES and family size. The reason that the net difference between the races is larger is due to the fact that there is a significant interaction between race and sex (stepdown $F = 4.56$) on IQ, such that white girls have significantly higher scores than white boys even with other variables in the equation, whereas this is not the case among blacks. There is also a significant interaction between sex of child and race on valuation of education ($F = 23.23$); white mothers value education more for boys; among blacks, the opposite is true. There is also a significant interaction between race and sex in relation to mother's religiosity ($F = 4.45$) such that religiosity is higher among mothers of white boys than of white girls whereas among blacks there is only a slight difference: girls' mothers exhibit slightly higher scores on religiosity.

7. The five variables that are significant predictors of High Protestant children's IQ scores are years mother worked (beta = $-.27$), investment in child (beta = .21), sex of child (beta = .16), socioeconomic status (beta = .15), and aversive disci-

pline (beta = −.10). The foregoing set of variables accounts for 29 percent of the variance in High Protestant children's IQ scores. Only two variables prove to be significant predictors of nondenominational children's IQ scores: father presence in home (beta = .21) and investment in child (beta = .18), which together account for 8 percent of the variance in their IQ scores.

8. Other significant predictors of fundamentalist children's IQ scores, besides race, are mother's valuation of education (beta = .18), number of children in family (beta = −.13), socioeconomic status (beta = .09), and mother's organizational memberships (beta = .08), which account for 16 percent of the variance in their scores. Twenty-five percent of the variance in Methodist/Lutheran children's scores is explained by three variables besides race: investment in child (beta = .26), mother's valuation of education (beta = .24), and socioeconomic status (beta = .11). Four variables besides race account for 21 percent of the variance in Catholic children's IQ scores: mother's religiosity (beta = −.24), investment in child (beta = .20), mother's valuation of education (beta = .17), and parents' demographic origins (beta = .17). Three variables account for 21 percent of the variance in Jewish children's IQ scores: investment in child (beta = .28), mother's valuation of education (beta = .21), and mother's religiosity (beta = −.21). It is noteworthy that investment in child proves to be a significant predictor of children's scores in five out of the six religious groups and that valuation of education is a significant predictor in four of the six groups.

9. This surprising finding will be specified when the predictors of achievement are compared for boys and girls and will be explained in a broader theoretical context in Chapter 10.

10. This finding is of a similar order to one reported earlier that these two socialization dimensions are most consistently significant predictors of IQ scores of children of different religious backgrounds.

11. This is so for various reasons. Black men as a rule have lower educational and occupational attainment and lower incomes than white men. There is a weaker association between black mothers marital status and years worked (−.1) than white mothers' (−.2). There is a much stronger negative correlation between years mothers worked and family size among blacks (−.3) than among whites (−.07). Furthermore, there is a stronger association between years mother worked and her educational attainment (.3) and other SES measures (.2) among black than among white mothers (less than .1). Finally, the zero-order correlation between years mothers worked and black children's IQ scores is .20 compared with −.06 among whites.

12. Since neither mother's marital status nor work tenure is predictive of sons' achievement scores, it can reasonably be concluded that whatever early advantage on IQ tests white sons of married full-time homemakers exhibit has no significant long-term consequences.

13. Indeed, the magnitude of difference in IQ scores of sons of full-time homemakers and of working mothers in father-absent-homes (10 points) is identical to the zero-order difference in IQ scores of black and white children in my sample.

14. Thus, white daughters of full-time homemakers in father-present families score 109 and in father-absent familes 105; the mean scores of daughters of mothers who worked less than five years in father-present and father-absent families are

110 and 105, respectively, and the mean scores of daughters of mothers who worked 5 or more years are 108 and 102, respectively.

15. It is possible that if I had a direct measure of mother's commitment to a career and it was combined with length of labor-force participation, it would prove to be a stronger predictor of girls' achievement than length of employment alone.

16. A rather lengthly explanation of this finding is reserved for the concluding chapter, in which some broader theoretical propositions derived from my empirical findings are discussed.

17. The social pressures on girls as they approach adolescence, traditionally at least, have been to subordinate intellectual interests and abilities in favor of developing "feminine" attributes to enhance their attractiveness to the opposite sex and to follow the dictum that girls must not outshine boys intellectually.

18. An analysis of variance, previously alluded to, of race by sex and seven levels of SES revealed the presence of significant interactions between race and SES, for example, on the following variables: Catholics, Jews, demographic origins, mother's years of work since child's birth, family size, mother's organization memberships, investment in child, and approaching significance on the use of discipline. All but the last have significant stepdown F's as well as significant univariate F's. These results are further testimony to the complexities involved in making valid comparisons of the sources of variance in the test performance of black and white children. They further serve to underline the naiveté of Arthur Jensen about the possible environmental as distinct from genetic sources of group differences in IQ scores.

19. When IQ is not added to either equation, the full model increases the amount of variance explained by 5 percent in each sex group. Thus the full model explains 45 percent of the variance in boys achievement scores, as compared with 40 percent by the structural model, and in the case of girls the respective increment is from 43 percent to 48 percent.

20. In Chapter 7, mother's organizational participation was shown to be a significant predictor of black mothers' valuation of education, investment in child, and less reliance on aversive discipline. Whether more enlightened mothers are more apt to belong to organizations or become more enlightened through their participation is a moot question. I would guess that the influence is reciprocal.

Social Structure and Socialization: Sources of Racial and Sexual Differences in Competence

My guiding concern in this study has been to trace the social processes through which enduring structural inequalities in black and white parents' access to a multitude of economic and social resources are reflected in their children's performance on IQ and achievement tests during the elementary school years.

Components of Socioeconomic Status That Predict Test Scores

By decomposing socioeconomic status into four constituent variables—parents' socioeconomic origin status, parents' educational attainment, occupational status of higher-ranking parent, and mother's social milieu—it was possible to demonstrate that these components are considerably more highly correlated with each other among whites, an indication that a greater degree of status consistency exists among them than among blacks. Thus, utilization of either parent's educational attainment or occupational status, the two most commonly employed controls in the comparison of black and white children's test performance, does not achieve the intended purpose of equalizing the social environments of children in the two races. Even black parents with the same educational and occupational status as whites do not have the benefit of the same social milieu (i.e., exposure to mainstream middle-class influences) or the same opportunities for association with whites of similar status. Consequently, the current educational and occupational attainments of black parents do not obliterate altogether the effects of their considerably lower social origins on their children's IQ scores, as they do among whites.

Indeed, the three significant predictors of black children's IQ scores are quite different from the predictors of white children's scores. Mother's social milieu is the strongest, followed by parents' social-class origins and mother's exposure to white friends and/or co-workers. Together these explain 14 percent of the variance in black children's IQ scores. In contrast, the strongest predictor of white children's scores is parents' educational attainment, followed by parents' demographic origins. While occupational status of higher-ranking parent enters the equation, it does not increase significantly the variance explained in white scores, which amounts to 12 percent.

When the IQ scores of black and white children are combined and regressed on the same six measures of parents' origin and current status, with race included as a variable in the regression equation, race proves to be the strongest independent predictor of IQ, followed by mother's social milieu and parents' education. Neither occupational status nor parents' origin family size adds significantly to the variance explained, although each variable enters the equation. These variables account for 23 percent of the variance in IQ scores in the combined sample, and when they are controlled, the zero-order difference in IQ scores between black and white children is reduced by four points, from 10 to 5.9 points.[1]

The components of socioeconomic status that predict scholastic achievement scores of black and white children in the fifth and sixth grades exhibit fewer differences than the predictors of IQ scores.

IQ score, as one would expect, is the strongest predictor of achievement scores and carries virtually the same weight in both races. Parents' educational attainment is a somewhat weaker preditor of black scores than of white scores, but mothers' social milieu exerts virtually the same effect on black and white scores. Parent's occupational status enters the black equation but does not significantly increase the variance explained in black children's achievement scores. Parents' demographic origins have a weak but significant independent effect on white scores.

IQ scores plus the two components of socioeconomic status—parents' education and social milieu—account for a slightly higher proportion of variance in the achievement scores of black children (42 percent) than the same variables plus parents' denographic origins account for in white children's scores (39 percent).

When the achievement scores of black and white children are combined and regressed on the same set of variables but with race included in the equation, IQ remains the strongest predictor, followed by race, parents' education, and social milieu. (Occupational status enters the equation but does not increase significantly the variance explained.) These variables account for 55 percent of the variance in achievement scores of the races combined, and reduce the zero-order difference in achievement scores between the races from two stanines to slightly less than one stanine (.94).

The Religious Factor

The discovery of the importance of the religious factor, particularly the denominational affiliations of Protestant mothers, in accounting for differences in the intellectual and scholastic competence of children in the two races is one of the more important contributions of the present study. Indeed, it serves notice that despite the secular trends that typify urban-industrial societies variations in religious affiliation and religiosity continue to constitute significant parameters of social structure within which basic orientations toward modern modes of thought and knowledge are differentially nurtured and sustained through association with other like-minded people in the family and other primary groups.

This is not to say that religious and denominational affiliations are not strongly influenced by a person's location in the social-stratification system. But within each stratum affiliation with and membership in one religious group as against another also has some independent albeit subtle effects on the ways in which women, and probably also men, conceive of and carry out the parental role. Their goals and strategies, in turn, mediate the effects of race and socioeconomic factors on the early development of intellectual competence and on the subsequent scholastic performance of their children, which condition to some degree educational and occupational decisions in later stages of life.[2]

When mother's religious/denominational affiliation is added to the four measures of past and current socioeconomic status (with exposure to whites in the black equation as well), an interaction between race, mother's religion, and children's IQ scores becomes evident. Among blacks, a Baptist or other fundamentalist affiliation depresses IQ scores; its effect is second only to the positive effect exerted by mother's social milieu. The previously significant effect of mother's exposure to whites is somewhat reduced so that now it only approaches significance, a confirmation that black fundamentalist women are least likely to have white co-workers or friends.[3] A nondenominational or nonreligious background, in contrast, has a weak but significant positive effect on black children's scores, somewhat less than the effect of parents' origin social class, the fifth variable that entered the equation. Adding religious variables to the equation increases the variance accounted for in black children's scores by 2 percentage points, from 14 to 16 percent.

In the case of whites, taking into account mother's religious affiliation does *not* increase the variance explained (12 percent) in children's IQ scores. Although a nondenominational background has a weak positive effect, it does not significantly increase the variance explained by parents' education and demographic origins.[4]

Religiosity, although analytically distinct from religious and denominational affiliation, varies with denominational affiliation in contemporary American society as well as with race. Whatever their religious affiliation, black mothers as a rule register somewhat higher mean religiosity scores than their white counterparts. Significant differences in religiosity between religious groups are found only among white mothers. In both races, Baptist and other fundamentalists are most religious and nondenominational/nonreligious women are least religious.[5] Greater religiosity, of course, signifies greater involvement in one's religious community and a firmer commitment to its norms. Thus a devout Baptist or Catholic might be expected to be more committed to a traditional mode of child rearing—more resistant, for example, to "sparing the rod," particularly in the rearing of sons, than more secularly oriented mothers, and more likely to stress obedience than intellectual curiosity and flexibility in child rearing.

Mother's religiosity exerts an independent though weak effect on IQ and achievement test performance. When IQ scores are regressed on socioeconomic components, religious affiliation, and religiosity, both religious variables enter the equations. The effect of religiosity on IQ scores is weak and does not significantly increase the variance explained net of religious affiliation, but it exerts a small, significant effect on achievement scores and diminishes the negative effect of a fundamentalist background, so that it no longer adds significantly to the variance explained in black children's IQ scores.[6]

Adding religious variables to socioeconomic measures serves to further reduce white children's IQ advantage over black children by two additional points, from 5.9 to 3.9, which is markedly lower than the zero-order difference between the races in my sample of 10 IQ points.

Thus, it is clear that differences in the religious constituency and involvement of the two races are a significant source of the disparity in black and white children's IQ scores independently of socioeconomic differences. Further, the religious factor, though certainly associated with socioeconomic variables in both races, exerts a stronger independent effect on the life chances of black children, at least at this historical juncture, to the extent that early intellectual competence is a determinative factor in children's school performance.

Significance of Structural Differences Between Black and White Social Classes

A very large majority of the black working class maintains its traditional adhererence to the Baptist denomination and other fundamentalist sects. And they remain the modal religious groups even in the black middle class. Historically, fundamentalist creeds in the United States attracted the poorer, less educated segments of society, both black and white. The tradition of a lay ministry with no more formal schooling than the congregants is giving way to a pattern like that practiced in higher Protestant denominations among both races, although this change is probably proceeding more rapidly in white than in black urban communities. With the advent of a more educated ministry and laity, adherence to a literal interpretation of the Bible, to an other-wordly orientation and a hellfire and brimstone eschatology, is gradually giving way to teachings more consonant with modern secular knowledge and thought. But in the past and still at the present time, fundamentalism, particularly black fundamentalism, retains a sectlike character and remains grounded in traditional beliefs far removed from the mainstream culture of an advanced industrial society. Its major strength is centered in rural areas and in the urban ghetto, and its persistence as the major affiliation of black people is fostered not merely by their economic and educational disadvantages but also by the segregated character of religious and social life in the United States and by a sense of estrangement engendered by the continuing discrimination black people experience in the midst of a hostile or at best indifferent white society.

The fact that even in the black middle class over two-fifths of mothers still adhere to Baptist and other fundamentalist Protestant religions suggests that these groups retain importance as a bulwark of black identity and social support, continuing to provide emotional solace and release to their members even when they experience improvement in their material lives. It is not difficult to understand the continuing adherence of blacks to the religious community that has sustained their hope and spirit over the long period of their oppression. But while the sectlike character of Baptist and other fundamentalist sects sustains religiosity and offers emotional support and release, it may also serve to insulate its members from significant aspects of the mainstream secular culture.

The religious factor helps account for a number of similarities observed between the black middle class and the white working class, the most significant one being that children of these groups have identical mean IQ scores (100). While on all indicators of *current* SES black middle-class parents exhibit lower scores than white middle-class parents, their scores are higher than those of white working-class parents. However, with respect to social-class *origins*, the scores of these two groups are virtually the same and substantially lower than the social-class origin scores of white middle-class parents. An important structural difference between the two middle classes, then, is that the overwhelming majority of middle-class blacks are upwardly mobile people with working-class origins who have relatively recently ascended to middle-class status. Just the opposite is true of the white middle class, in which members with middle-class origins constitute the majority relative to the upwardly mobile members of their stratum.

Another structural difference between the two middle classes is their religious composition, which helps further to account for the disparity in IQ scores of black and white children in those strata and for the similarity in scores between black middle-class and white working-class children.

The white middle class is more heterogeneous in its religious composition and has a larger constituency of just those religious groups whose children average higher IQ and achievement scores, mainly High Protestants, Jews, and nondenominational respondents. In the black middle class, largely a "new" middle class, the modal denomintional affiliation continues to be Baptist and other fundamentalist (44 percent). Together with the Catholics (11 percent) those groups constitute a majority of the stratum (55 percent). In the white working class, fundamentalists constitute a smaller proportion (27 percent) and Catholics a larger one (35 percent); together these two groups constitute 62 percent. In these four religious/racial groups there is very little difference in the IQ scores of children; middle-class black Baptists' average score is 97, compared with 99 among white working-class Baptists; black middle-class Catholics' average score is 100, compared with the virtually identical mean score of white working-class Catholic children (101). Thus, in two important respects, class origins of its members and homogeneity of religious composition, the black middle class structurally resembles the white working class more closely than it does the white middle class. Both factors—parents' social class origins and fundamentalism—have negative effects on black children's IQ scores independent of current socioeconomic status. That is, they serve to delay the diffusion of secular knowledge and of socialization stategies that encourage intellectual competence in children in an advanced society.

Because of the persistence of residential, religious, and social segregation of blacks, upward social mobility does not promote the same *rate* of acculturation to mainstream culture—i.e., white middle-class culture, which dominates all major institutions of the society among blacks as among whites. Evidence of this is the positive effect that mother's exposure to whites has on black children's IQ score independently of SES and religious affiliation.[7]

An old middle class—one in which a very substantial proportion of its members were reared in middle-class homes, were socialized in its style of life, and acquired higher education—is, as a rule, most closely in touch with the mainstream culture and with innovative developments in the realms of technology and ideas. It is not simply that established middle-class members have more resources of income, education, and status, but, having them, they can deploy them with greater ease to implement their goals, one of which is to maintain and perpetuate their position in the stratification system from one generation to the next. In an open-class industrial society, new technological advances and the demand for new products expand mobility opportunities for talented and ambitious members of the working class. The newer recruits, through informal association with established members of their destination class, gain exposure to and gradually adopt their style of life, including the better books and journals that serve to disseminate new knowledge and perspectives on such matters as the socialization of children. Through informal channels, newer members acquire knowledge about educational toys, games, books, nursery schools, summer camps, instruction in the arts, and other cultural opportunities, and learn to utilize these ever-increasing opportunities for the intellectual enrichment of their children. That is why parents' social-class origins make no further contribution to the prediction of IQ scores of white children once other structural variables are controlled, the most important of which is parents' education.[8]

In contrast to the situation in white society, the black middle class is very largely a new middle class, and one which contains a relatively smaller proportion of the black population than the white middle class does of the white population. In 1968, when the data were gathered, the very large majority of the black middle class had working-class origins, and only a small minority of its members had been reared and socialized in the middle class. Moreover, even this minority of established middle-class members had grown up in a socially segregated milieu, largely barred from residential and social interaction with middle-class whites. Few members of even the old black middle class had the same access to educational opportunities and generally to the mainstream cosmopolitan culture as their white counterparts. And because they were so small a segment of their class, their influence could not become as readily diffused in their stratum. Indeed, their problem is to preserve values and a style of life that they have won for themselves against the pressure of the multitude of new arrivals to their stratum, who have made material gains but also bring with them a more homogeneous tradition, more southern rural, more fundamentalist, more religious, and in general, more traditional patterns of childbearing and child rearing. These patterns persist to a greater degree even in the face of increments of formal education because fewer opportunities exist within the black community for exposure to a social milieu where parents are conversant with modern theories of child development. The very idea of rearing children "according to the book" other than the Bible is alien to people from a rural folk tradition who had little access to "experts" and the world of written cultural generally. Moreover, many of these recent newcomers to the black middle class feel that since the socialization they received proved not to be an impediment to their economic and social ascent, there is no compelling need to depart from old and tried ways, not recognizing that the world in which their children will have to make their way calls for different qualities and skills than the world they themselves grew up in.

In this structural context, formal education is of course also a modernizing influence, but not to the same degree as in white society. The effects of formal education of parents in the black community are conditioned by great variations in the social milieu in which they are rearing their children, ranging from a very substantial fundamentalist component, even in the middle class, to a small High Protestant and an even smaller nondenominational, nonreligious component, with a still relatively small component of college-educated parents and a substantial component of parents who have not completed high school.[9]

The foregoing discussion serves to explain why parents' social-class origins continue to exert a significant effect on black but not on white children's scores. The effects of gains in parents' educational attainment and occupational attainment on children's scores are optimized in a structural context that offers numerous opportunities to associate with others of different and more advantaged backgrounds than one's own, for these others often serve as the purveyors of cultural patterns not previously encountered by the new middle-class recruit. But the more limited are opportunities for association with purveyors of a rapidly changing mainstream culture, the less pressure there is to forswear traditional ways for more modern ones. Thus, for example, the new recruit to the white middle class may initially have no inclination to seek out expert guidance in childrearing. But if acquaintances, friends, and neighbors, as well as her pediatrician, refer to and discuss Dr. Spock's book, a mother is likely to acquaint herself with its contents, particularly if she is ambitious for her child. If neighbors and friends take their preschool children to the library, to museums, to the theater, she is more likely to follow suit than is the mother rearing a child in a context where the large majority of her associates had the same humble beginnings where such patterns of investment in children were largely absent. In this context, therefore, the higher social origins of parents are a significant differentiating variable in maternal values and behavior (Blau, 1964, 1965; Gordon, M., 1972). The small proportion of black established middle-class members also would have learned in their homes while growing up patterns rather different from those of the new recruits to the stratum and may well influence their friends and neighbors; but since they are a small minority, their *span* of influence is necessarily far more limited than that of their counterparts in a stratum containing a considerably larger segment of established middle-class members.

Still another obvious but nonetheless significant difference in stratification processes as they affect socialization of children in the two races is the fact of segregation itself. Here I am speaking not simply of school segregation but of the residential and social segregation of black parents rearing children who must compete with and will necessarily be judged by norms based on white performance.

Mother's exposure to white friends and co-workers is not a variable in the majority, more advantaged population but is, of course, a variable in the case of blacks, exerting a small but significant effect on black children's IQ independent of other socioeconomic variables. Although with religious affiliation controlled, its effect is diminished, it nevertheless merits discussion.

All other things being equal, children of mothers who grew up with and now have white friends and/or co-workers average higher IQ scores than those whose mothers have no such opportunities. This certainly does not stem from any innate superiority of whites that magically rubs off on those blacks with whom they happen to develop social relationships of a more or less equalitarian character. The evidence suggests that such association benefits black children's test performance not directly but indirectly, through its beneficial effects on reducing family size and increasing black mothers' investment in their children.

Such patterns of behavior as exposure to child-rearing experts, regularly telling stories and reading to children, and teaching them basic verbal and numerical skills in the preschool years were probably not widespread in the lives of black mothers, particularly those who grew up in poor, southern, rural, fundamentalist homes with large families, just as these patterns would have been the exception rather than the rule among white mothers with the same backgrounds. But the proportion of such mothers is very much smaller in my white sample than in the black sample. It must also not be forgotten that southern blacks, particularly if they were poor, were denied access to public libraries and other cultural institutions and that the purchase of books and magazines is generally rare among poor people with limited education.

The expenditure of time and economic resources on such media rises with income and educational level but also is influenced by the social and cultural milieu in which a mother is rearing her child. The popular distinction between low-, middle-, and high-brow cultural consumption patterns is relevant not merely to adults but to their provision of such artifacts to their children. The use of nursery schools, summer camps, and instruction in music or other arts is not simply a function of income or even of parents' education but is conditioned by the customs of neighbors, friends, and relatives. The investment of time and resources by parents in intellectually stimulating activities and artifacts, either for themselves or for their children, but particularly for the children, is very much promoted by informal social mechanisms that operate in the context of informal relations in neighborhoods and other primary social groups. And such patterns at present are more widespread in the white middle class, particularly the white upper middle class, than elsewhere in the society because that is the stratum in which the mainstream culture in an industrial society is largely created and maintained and where high cultural innovations first become diffused. That is why exposure to whites, independently of other social- and family-structural variables, operates to decrease black mothers' fertility and increase their investment of time and other intellectually stimulating resources in their children.

From the foregoing discussion a set of propositions of a more general order can be derived concerning the contingencies that influence the impact of rising educational attainment of parents on measured intelligence of children.

Historically and currently, differential access of groups within a nation (and between nations) to *written* culture and to the social processes by which its products are disseminated conditions the effects of increments in parents' formal education and occupational status on children's performance on written tests. All other things being equal, these two parental variables will explain more of the variance in children's scores in groups more advantaged currently and historically than in less advantaged ones. Further, the effects of parent's social class origins, as distinct from their current class position, will more frequently persist as a predictor of children's scores in structural contexts where a large majority of stratum members have low socioeconomic origins as compared with contexts in which the latter constitute a minority, particularly when other status characteristics—race, religion, ethnicity—operate in addition to occupation, income, and educational attainment as significant barriers to informal association between newcomers and longer-tenured members of the more advantaged class.

The less permeable are the barriers to free association with members of more advantaged classes, the more weight the characteristics of the informal social milieu of parents and children will exert on the *rate* of intellectual development of children independently of formal educational and/or occupational attainments of their parents.

In short, *environments are cumulative* (Myrdal, 1950; Stinchcomb, 1969, Bourdieu and Passeron, 1977; Bourdieu, 1973; Swartz, 1977; Collins, 1977). Thus, an increment in parents' formal education benefits the IQ of the white child more than the black because it is associated with a greater improvement in the social environment of both parents and the child, for several reasons. First, there are many more white than black middle-class people, and their mean level of education is higher; second, many more of the white middle class have longer tenure in the middle class; and third, for those with recent tenure in the white middle class, race constitutes no social impediment to association with acculturated middle-class members, as it does for blacks in a still largely segregated society.[10]

Family Structure and Extrafamilial Roles

Extension of the structural model to include three variables of family structure—number of children, father presence, sex of child—and mother's extrafamilial participation, measured by years mother worked outside the home since child's birth and voluntary association memberships, further increases the variance explained in both IQ and achievement scores of black children, and in IQ scores of white children.

Black mothers have larger families as a rule than white mothers (except at the high-SES level among college graduates), and family size exhibits a stronger negative zero-order association with IQ and achievement scores of black than of white children. A higher proportion of black than of white mothers are rearing children in fatherless homes, and black children from father-absent homes have significantly lower achievement scores than other black children. A higher proportion of black mothers were employed at the time studied and had had longer tenure in the labor force since the birth of the study child than white mothers. Black children of longer-employed mothers have significantly higher IQ and achievement scores than other black children, but no significant differences are observed at the zero-order level among white children. Finally, an increment in IQ and achievement scores is exhibited by black and white children as the number of mother's organizational memberships rises.

When the two measures of family structure and two measures of mother's extrafamilial participation are added to the measures of parents' origin and current socioeconomic status and religious variables, it becomes evident that taking family variables into account increases the variance explained in test scores of children in each race by 2 percent, but that the magnitude of the effects and, in one instance, the direction of the effect differ among black and white children.[11]

Among the family variables, family size exerts the strongest negative effect on black children's scores. Indeed, its weight is virtually the same as that of the composite measure of SES in relation to black scores, but its effect on white scores is considerably weaker and only approaches significance. Presence of a father in the home exerts a weak positive effect on white IQ scores which only approaches significance, but does not enter the black equation. Conversely, mother's organizational memberships exerts a weak positive effect on black IQ scores but does not enter the white equation. Finally, mother's years of tenure in the labor force since birth of the study child exerts a positive (and significant) effect on black children's scores, while it appears to be a negative predictor of white children's scores.

With family variables and mother's organizational memberships added, the structural model explains 18 percent of the variance in black and 14 percent of the variance in white children's scores. When the two samples are combined, the variance in IQ scores explained rises by 2 percentage points to 25 percent and the residual difference between the races is further reduced, albeit slightly, to 3.5 IQ points.

Family structure and mother's extrafamilial participation exert considerably stronger effects on IQ scores than on achievement scores in both races. Indeed, with IQ controlled, none of the above variables even enter the white equation, an indication that whatever effects they exert on white children's achievement test performance, they operate indirectly through their effect on IQ scores. But in the case of black children, the small positive effect of mother's organizational participation persists, and presence of father in the home, which did not enter the black IQ equation, exerts a small positive effect on black children's achievement scores. Each of these variables singly does not significantly increase the variance explained in black achievement scores, but together they raise the variance explained by the structural model to 43 percent and slightly reduce the mean achievement score difference between black and white children to .87 of a stanine. But they do not increase the variance explained by the structural model in the combined sample, which remains 55 percent.[12]

The Significance of Sex of Child

White girls' mean IQ score (109) is significantly higher than that of white boys (105).[13] Among black children, girls' mean score (97) is virtually no higher than that of boys (96). In short, there is a significant interaction between race and sex on IQ scores. When sex of the child is added to the structural model, it turns out to be a significant predictor of white children's IQ scores but not of black children's scores. The net advantage of white girls over white boys amounts to 3.3 IQ points (compared with a zero-order difference of 4 points), an indication that about one point of the IQ difference between the sexes among whites is accounted for by *social-structural* factors, leaving a residual difference between them of about three points.[14]

Further, it is important to note that the race-sex interaction on IQ scores has the effect of increasing the difference in IQ scores between the races. This becomes evident when girls and boys are analyzed separately. The mean difference between black and white girls, which at the zero order level amounts to 12 points, is reduced, net of the other structural variables, to 2.7 IQ points, and the zero order difference between black and white boys of 9 points is reduced to 2.9 IQ points. That is, the mean score difference between the races becomes one point less when the sexes are analyzed separately than when sex is included as a variable in the structural model. Thus, within each sex the residual mean race difference is less than the residual difference of 3.3 points between white girls and boys. It is also of importance to note that social-structural variables account for more of the race disparity in the scores of girls than of boys. Indeed, the structural model accounts for 29 percent of the variance in girls' IQ scores as compared with 22 percent in boys' scores. The early advantage that white girls exhibit on IQ test performance relative to black girls is more a function of differences in socioeconomic, religious, and family factors between the races than in the case of white and black boys, which suggests that as black Americans move toward parity with whites, these gains will be reflected sooner in IQ score gains of black daughters than of black sons. This conclusion is consistent with empirical evidence of various kinds, e. g., that black women as a rule have higher educational and occupational attainment than their male counterparts and that they appear to have made more educational gains during the 1960s and 1970s than black men (U.S. Bureau of the Census, 1977).

Finally, a number of differences are discovered in the nature and/or magnitude of predictors of girls' and boys' IQ scores. Socioeconomic status is a considerably stronger predictor of girls' than of boys' scores. Girls from Baptist or other fundamentalist backgrounds score significantly lower on IQ tests than those from other religious backgrounds. Mother's religiosity is a negative predictor of boys' IQ scores, and boys from a nondenominational/nonreligious background or a Jewish background net higher IQ scores than other boys. Girls from a High Protestant background net somewhat, but not significantly, higher scores than girls from other religious backgrounds. Family size depresses girls' IQ scores somewhat more than it does those of boys, and presence of father in the home benefits girls but exerts no independent effect on boys' scores.

In sum, the foregoing results provide what I believe to be convincing evidence that no single measure of environment is sufficiently comprehensive to encompass the range of differences between the situations of blacks and whites in American society that have resulted from the discrimination and segregation imposed by the superordinate race on the subordinate one. Environments are cumulative, and the advantages afforded one group are cumulative just as are the deficits imposed upon the other. The analysis has detailed the nature and relative contribution of each of the *social-structural* sources to the IQ gap. With these variables controlled, only a trivial residual mean score difference is left between the races. Even the latter, as I will report presently, is obliterated among selected subgroups when the structural model is extended to include socialization variables.

The foregoing analysis also raises certain new and important questions about the sources of early sex differences in IQ test performance which have been reported repeatedly in the literature but for which no satisfactory explanation has as yet been forthcoming. One common explanation offered is that girls mature earlier than boys, and the implication generally is that this is an inherent sex difference. If that were indeed true, one would expect girls in *both* races to average significantly higher scores than boys, but that is not the case. The locus of girls' superiority on IQ test performance seems to be primarily among Protestants, most markedly among High Protestant children in both races.[15] Jewish boys and girls have *identical* mean IQ scores (110); white Catholic girls and boys have virtually identical mean scores (103 and 102, respectively); and nondenominational girls (113) register only a 2-point advantage over boys from the same background. Among blacks, Catholic *boys'* scores are one point higher (101) than girls'; among children from a nondenominational/nonreligious background, boys' mean score (110) is 2 points higher than girls'. Such group variability constitutes evidence against the existence of inherent differences in the intellectual development of male and female children and suggests instead that *social* factors, specifically differences in the modes of socializing boys and girls, most marked among High Protestants, are the source of sex differences in IQ test performance in those groups where they are found.

Social Structure and Socialization

It has been shown that race, socioeconomic status, religious and denominational affiliation, and sex, which constitute analytically distinct but concretely related bases of stratification in American society, each exert some independent influence on children's intellectual ability and scholastic performance.

Three dimensions of socialization were found to *mediate* the effects of these social structures on the development of intellectual and scholastic competence among children—mother's valuation of education, investment in the child, and belief in and use of aversive discipline. Analysis of these dimensions of socialization enlarges our understanding of how structural factors influence social processes within families so that formal schooling significantly enhances the mobility chances of some but not of other children growing up in disadvantaged families.[16]

A major proposition for which the present study provides evidence is that children's school test performance can be fruitfully conceived of as a return arising from a process of *social exchange* between children and their principal and earliest socializer, usually the mother. This enduring process, which starts as a child's birth and continues throughout childhood and youth, has significant consequences not merely for the future educational and occupational achievements of a person but also for his or her efficacy as a parent.[17] Mothers who place a higher value on educational and occupational attainment and thereby make more demands on their children in the intellectual realm also give them more material and nonmaterial resources. The mother who invests more of the resources at her disposal—time, effort, knowledge, money—to provide experiences that promote growth of her child's verbal capacities and sense of self-efficacy becomes an important source of gratification. The child is thereby put under an obligation to reciprocate or to repay that investment while at the same time his or her capacity to do so is being progressively enhanced as he or she moves from the home into the school. Such exchanges are not calculated or even necessarily conscious, but it is a matter of common observation that whenever individuals are the beneficiaries of gratifying experiences from another, they are more inclined to invest more time and expend more effort in activities valued by that significant other (Homans, 1962; Blau, 1964). Conversely, when they frequently are the objects of unpleasant or demeaning experiences from another, they are not under the same obligation to voluntarily exert effort to comply with the other's wishes or expectations. Instead, if they have any choice, they will seek to withhold compliance, to distance themselves from the other, and to search for significant others who *do* afford them gratifications for the performance of valued activites.

Mothers and probably also other socializers who place a high value on educational performance and who implement their ambition by investing in rewarding and stimulating interaction with the child will, all other things being equal, receive a higher return on their investment (as measured by children's school test scores) than those who invest less. But the return on a mother's positive forms of investment is also conditioned by the extent to which she relies on aversive forms of control. The more she resorts to such means, the less will be the return she commands from the child, at least in terms of school performance and probably also in other activities she values. Thus, a mother who values education more and invests in more positive transactions with her child but who also subjects the child frequently to aversive forms of control engages in a counterproductive strategy, one that minimizes rather than maximizes the return from her investment. Indeed, chances are that the return on maternal investment will be higher even for those mothers who do not place as great a value on education if they are also sparing in their use of aversive discipline, although perhaps not as high as in the case of mothers who both value education highly *and* employ the optimal strategy to implement their goals.

The three socialization dimensions—mother's valuation of education, extent of investment in the child in early and later childhood, and variations in the use of aversive discipline—are interrelated in both races.[18]

The ambitions of black mothers for their children's future attainments as a rule exceed those of their white counterparts, everything being equal. When differences between the races in all social-structural variables are taken into account, it is found that blacks do *not* invest less of the resources at their disposal than white mothers. But their reliance on aversive forms of control, repeatedly observed throughout the analysis, is significantly greater than that of their white counterparts even when the full battery of structural differences between them are controlled.

The *incidence* of optimal as opposed to counterproductive strategies of socializing children, even among mothers who place a high value on educational attainment, as well as among those who are less ambitious for their children, is considerably higher among white than among black mothers.[19]

Thus, while mother's values exert an independent effect on children's IQ and achievement scores in both races, they constitute a stronger predictor of white than of black children's scores.

The regression of each dimension of socialization on the set of structural variables within each race and with the races combined makes it possible to specify more precisely the processes through which social structures differentiate maternal values and socialization strategies within each race, to determine to what extent they are similar or different, and to assess the effect of race on socialization processes when many of the important differences in the structural attributes of black and white families are taken into account.

Structural factors condition diffusion of maternal values and strategies that influence the development of children's intellectual competence in much the same way, with a few exceptions, in the two races. The *direction* of the effects of structural factors as a rule are the same but the *magnitude* of their effects are often different.

Parents' socioeconomic status exerts the strongest independent effect of all structural variables on each of the three dimensions of socialization in both races. That is, the value placed on educational attainment and investment in the child rises and the belief in and use of aversive controls decreases with rising SES. But, in respect to each dimension of socialization, SES is a stronger predictor of white than of black mothers' values and behavior.[20]

Religious affiliation exerts an independent effect on white mothers' valuations of education but none on black mothers. White Jewish and nondenominational/nonreligious women stress educational attainment more than other mothers, white and black. The religious factor, however, *is* an independent predictor of maternal behavior in both races. Among blacks, fundamentalist mothers invest less time and other resources in children and Catholics invest more than do black women of other religious backgrounds; the same is true when the races are combined. Among whites, Catholic mothers invest *less* while Jewish and nondenominational mothers invest *more* in their children than mothers of other religious groups. Jewish and nondenominational mothers also maintain their advantage when the races are combined. Religion is also an independent predictor of the use of aversive discipline in both races. Among blacks, three religious groups—High Protestants, Catholics, and the nondenominational—tend to use *less* discipline than other mothers, while among whites, fundamentalist and Catholic mothers use more discipline than other mothers. When the races are combined, religious effects are strengthened: High Protestant, Jewish, and nondenominational mothers use less discipline than women from other backgrounds, and, independently of the above, highly religious mothers generally tend to rely more on aversive controls than less religious ones.

Family structure variables exert stronger effects on black than on white mothers' valuations of education. Family size, in particular, depresses maternal ambition more among blacks than among whites. Presence of a father in the home exerts a weak positive effect on black mothers' values but exerts no independent effect on white mothers' values.[21] Mother's years of employment since the child's birth appears to exert a weak negative effect on white mothers' values, while organizational memberships exerts a positive one. Mother's organizational memberships is also a positive predictor of black mothers' values, but years of work exerts no independent effect on black mothers' ambitions for their children.

The extent of mother's investment in the child is also more strongly depressed by increasing family size among black than white mothers. With the races combined, the effects of family size are second only to that of SES as an influence on maternal investment. The beneficial effects of organizational participation on investment in child are considerably stronger in the case of black than of white mothers. Association with white friends and co-workers also promotes maternal investment in their children among black mothers when other structural variables are controlled.[22] Both of these findings serve to emphasize the considerably greater significance that isolation from the mainstream culture has for delaying the diffusion among blacks of socialization patterns that promote children's intellectual and scholastic competence. Finally, among whites but not among blacks, more extended maternal employment appears to exert a weak negative effect on investment in the child.

Family structure variables do not exert any independent effects on the use of aversive controls among black mothers,[23] but white mothers in father-absent homes use more discipline than those in homes with a father present.

Sex of child conditions maternal valuations and socialization strategies in both races. In general, black mothers espouse higher ambitions for daughters than for sons, with the sole exception of Catholics, who tend to espouse higher ambitions for sons. With all structural variables taken into account, black mothers value education more for daughters than for sons.

The general tendency among white mothers is to espouse higher ambitions for sons relative to daughters, but they exhibited considerably less homogeneity in 1968 than black mothers. Three religious groups—Baptists/other fundamentalists, Catholics, and Jews—exhibit higher ambitions for sons, whereas Methodists, High Protestants, and nondenominational mothers tend to stress, albeit weakly, more education for daughters. With other structural variables taken into account, white mothers net a higher valuation of education for sons than for daughters.[24]

Sex of child also conditions maternal strategies of socialization, and the direction of the effect is the same in both races: mothers invest more time and other resources in daughters and use more aversive discipline in relation to sons. The sex effect, independently of other structural variables, is of about the same magnitude with respect to investment in children in the two races, but it carries considerably more weight among blacks than among whites as a differentiating variable in the use of discipline. Indeed, next to SES, sex of child is the strongest single predictor of how extensively black mothers rely on aversive forms of control as a means of socializing their children.[25]

With structural variables controlled, the direction of the effect of race is reversed on two of the socialization dimensions: black mothers, were all other things equal, would exhibit a higher valuation of education than white mothers and they would invest more time and other resources in their children than their white counterparts. But the tendency of black mothers to rely more on aversive forms of control persists and can be taken as evidence that the experience of slavery followed by a repressive system of caste supported by the threat of violence has left its bitter mark on black culture, particularly with respect to the socialization of males. Reliance on aversive forms of control, which may well have been necessary for survival under conditions of subjugation, is dysfunctional for performance of tasks that require the exercise of autonomous intelligence. I would go further and advance the hypothesis that heavy use of aversive forms of control in socializing black males, particularly, is a significant source of the greater proneness of black than of white males to crimes of violence, the principal victims of which are black people themselves.

Socialization Predictors of Black and White Test Scores

Regression of IQ and achievement scores on the three socialization dimensions allows a test of three propositions: (1) the likelihood that mothers can command conformity to their values is conditioned by the extent of their positive investments in their child; (2) the return gained from resources invested is conditioned by variations in modes of control; (3) in social contexts where aversive modes of control are less prevalent, as among whites, the socialization component will have *more* predictive value than in contexts where aversive controls are more prevalent, as among blacks.[26]

The results of the analysis lend support to these hypotheses. The socialization model accounts for 19 percent of the variance in white IQ scores and 16 percent in black IQ scores. Further, while mother's valuation of education and investment in child are predictors of IQ scores in both races, each exerts a slightly stronger effect on white than on black scores because discipline, a predictor only of black children's scores, serves to weaken the effects of higher maternal ambition and investment in children. With the races combined, discipline adds significantly to the variance explained (28 percent) in the whole sample, but the magnitude of the race difference is also considerably increased (beta = 5.9) as compared with that observed with the structural model (beta = 3.5).[27]

In sum, more of the within-group variance in black children's scores is explained by the structural model, whereas more of the within-group variance in white children's scores is explained by the socialization model because among white mothers a closer articulation exists between structural gains and maternal ambitions, and between maternal ambitions and effective implementing strategies. In consequence, a gain in socioeconomic status is translated *sooner* into an increment of gain in children's test scores, thereby widening the gap between white and black children *when only socialization measures are taken into account*. It is important to stress, however, that that increment of difference in performance arises not from inherent differences between the races but from *social* factors, past and present, of a cumulative nature. If that were not the case, we should find no variations in mean differences in the test performance of children in the two races according to the theoretical model used. Testing alternative social models recognizes the analytical distinction between structure and process and thus makes a contribution to the substantive understanding of the *sources* of variation in intellectual and scholastic competence both within and between two groups that, because of their vast differences in historical and continuing experiences, exhibit markedly different structural properties. These differences make for differences in the rate of change in those processes of socialization relevant for the development of intellectual competence in childhood.

Independent Effects of Social Structure and Socialization on Test Performance

The unification of the social-structural and socialization models into a "full" model serves to explain an identical amount of variance in IQ scores of black and white children (22 percent), which in each case represents a higher figure than is explained by either of the partial models. At the same time, with the full model the net mean difference in black-white scores is 2 IQ points less than with the socialization model (3.9 vs. 5.9) and about a half point more than with the structural model (3.5). The increment of variance explained in black scores is only 4 percent more with the full model than with the structural model, compared with an increment of 7 percent in white scores.[28] Further evidence of the greater significance of structural factors as sources of variance among black children's scores is provided by a comparison of the predictors of IQ in the two groups.

While in both races mother's valuation of education and investment in children are the strongest predictors of IQ scores, the weight exerted by each dimension is stronger on white than on black scores.[29] Only three structural variables enter the white equation when socialization dimensions are controlled: girls score higher than boys; children of native-born parents from larger communites score higher; and children whose mothers had not worked since their birth score higher. It is noteworthy that with socialization variables taken into account, neither socioeconomic status nor religious variables enter the white equation. But the importance of the religious factor persists as a predictor of black children's scores. Family size persists as a negative predictor and mother's years in the labor force as a positive one. Although the effect of socioeconomic status is considerably weakened when socialization dimensions are taken into account, it persists as a predictor of black scores. I interpret this as further evidence that the cumulative character of structural deficits makes socioeconomic status a more significant direct source of within-group variance in the development of children's intellectual competence in black than in white families.

With the races combined, the net effect of socioeconomic status on IQ scores becomes somewhat stronger than on black scores alone, the negative effects of a fundamentalist background and mother's religiosity and the positive one of a nondenominational background each become weaker, as does also the negative effect of family size. But father presence, which did not enter either the black or white equation, does enter the equation when the races are combined. Its effect, however, while positive, does not significantly increase the variance explained. Mother's valuation of education and investment in child each carry more independent weight than any other variable as a source of variance in the whole sample, just as they do in each race.[30] Finally, net of all the aforementioned factors, girls average scores about 1.5 points higher than boys in the combined sample, considerably less than the differential in the white sample alone. In sum, each of the social factors that inhibit the development of intellectual competence in childhood is both more prevalent among black families than among white ones, and each independently serves to widen the gap in test performance between the races.

The fact that instead of diminishing the residual mean difference between the races, the inclusion of socialization variables in the model slightly increases it relative to the structural model is further evidence that complex interaction effects between race, religion, social structure, sex of child, and socialization variables serve to exaggerate observed differences in IQ test performance between the races. The plausibility of this interpretation is strengthened by two important sets of findings.

First, regression of IQ scores of children in *each religious group* on the full model reveals that the mean difference between black and white children of the same religious background is not uniform but highly variable. Indeed, among two groups—High Protestants and nondenominational/nonreligious children—the race difference in IQ scores disappears altogether. That is, once the variables in the full model are controlled for, race no longer enters the equation, an indication that social differences entirely account for differences in IQ scores of black and white children in these groups. Among the remaining religious groups, the largest residual race differences occur among Baptists and other fundamentalists (6.7 points); among Catholics, white children's mean score is 5.2 points higher than that of black children, and among Methodists the difference is 4.9 points. Moreover, the two variables that predict IQ most consistently are investment in child, which is a predictor of scores in all but one religious group, and mother's valuation of education, which is a predictor in all but two religious groups. Clearly, the primary locus of the cumulative deficits of black people is among Baptist and other fundamentalist blacks.

The second set of findings providing evidence that observed differences in IQ test performance are exaggerated by complex interaction effects of race, sex of child, and social-structural and religious variables is forthcoming when the IQ scores of the two sexes are analyzed separately, using the full model.

Structural and Socialization Predictors of Boys' and Girls' Test Performance

The full model increases the variance explained in girls' IQ scores less (4 percent) than in boys' scores (6 percent) but explains more of the variance in girls' (33 percent) than in boys' scores (28 percent). But among each sex the full model compared with the structural model also serves to increase the residual score difference between the races—among girls by an additional 1.3 IQ points and among boys by an additional point. Thus, it appears that the source of the significant race-by-sex interaction actually observed on IQ scores arises from the stronger interaction that occurs between structural and socialization factors among girls than among boys.[31] That is, variations in social structure condition the socialization of girls more than that of boys at present, and a shift toward a more effective strategy of socialization (that is, one that promotes earlier intellectual development) with gains in socioeconomic status becomes diffused more rapidly with respect to the rearing of daughters than of sons. When, however, there are marked differences between two groups in the prevalence of middle-class status attainment and the length of tenure in the middle class and significant barriers to association between new and longer established members, as is the case with white and black families in American society, then changes in the socialization of girls proceed more rapidly in the more advantaged than in the less advantaged group; this results in a greater gap in the rate of intellectual development of girls than of boys. But the difference between girls also can be expected to diminish more rapidly as the two groups move toward parity in socioeconomic status and family size.

These propositions find support when the IQ scores of each sex are separately regressed on the full model. With socialization variables controlled, socioeconomic status, which in the structural model has a considerably stronger independent effect on girls' than on boys' scores, no longer enters the boys' equation. But among girls its effect, though substantially diminished, persists as a significant predictor, as do the negative effects of a fundamentalist background and family size. The positive effect of father presence on girls' scores is somewhat attenuated and no longer significantly increases the variance explained. Among boys, inclusion of socialization variables does not attenuate the weak and nonsignificant effect of demographic origins; it very slightly reduces the positive significant effects of a nondenominational background and strengthens the negative effect of mother's religiosity.

In contrast to girls, none of the family structure variables enter the boys' equation. Mother's valuation of education is the strongest predictor of boys' scores relative to other variables in the equation, and also relative to the weight it exerts on girls' scores. Investment in the child exerts a slightly weaker independent effect on the variance in boys' scores than on girls' scores. Aversive discipline also exerts a weak though not significant negative effect on girls' scores, whereas it does not enter the boys' equation. Finally, with the full model, the residual difference between the races among each sex is virtually of the same magnitude (Among girls beta = 4.0; among boys beta = 3.9).

With the full model the net race difference in achievement scores among boys is slightly reduced to three-fifths of a stanine compared with the structural model, but in the case of girls it *increases* to about a stanine, an indication that the locus of the interactions between race, structural, and socialization variables on achievement test performance is also among girls. Moreover, with socialization variables added to the equation, the weight of IQ scores and socioeconomic status as predictors of achievement scores becomes virtually the same in the two sexes,[32] though in both sexes IQ, of course, continues to exert a more powerful effect than SES. But the weight of SES, which was stronger on girls' than on boys' scores with the structural model, is reduced *more* by inclusion of socialization variables in the case of girls than of boys, an indication that variations in socialization mediate the effect of socioeconomic status on girls' scores somewhat more than on boys' IQ scores. The religious factor, in contrast, continues to carry more weight in the determination of boys' scores and remains virtually unaffected by the inclusion of socialization variables in the regression equation. But when socialization variables as well as structural variables are controlled, the small deficit in achievement scores exhibited by Jewish girls relative to other girls rises slightly.

The positive effect of mother's organizational memberships on boys' scores is weakened when socialization variables are taken into account, an indication that it is mainly through the benign effects on socialization practices that mothers' organizational participation promotes scholastic competence in their sons.

Finally, while socialization variables exert independent effects on achievement scores of both sexes, the effects of mother's valuation of education is stronger on girls' than on boys' scores, whereas discipline exerts a stronger negative effect on boys' than on girls' scores. Investment in child exerts a weak nonsignificant effect on girls' achievement scores but does not even enter the boys' equation, which is further confirmation that the returns on maternal investments are conditioned by variations in the use of aversive control: where reliance on this type of discipline is high, as it is in relation to boys compared to girls, the effects of mother's positive investment in child are neutralized.

The full model, relative to the structural model, increases the variance explained in the achievement of both sexes, although the increment is slightly greater in girls' scores (from 56 percent to 58 percent) than in boys' scores (from 55 percent to 56 percent).

The foregoing discussion has identified multiple interactions between race and sex, structural variables, and socialization variables that contribute to the explanation of variations in children's IQ and achievement test performance. In order to "tease out" the sources of interactions, it has been necessary first to combine the races and then to compare the residual race difference within each sex to establish that the disparity in scores between black and white children is by no means uniform but instead varies in magnitude because of differences in the socialization of male and female children within each race and because of differences in the extent to which socialization factors mediate the effects of social-structural factors on the development of school competence among each race and each sex.

Determinants of Competence in Four Race-Sex Groups

Dichotomization either by race or by sex of child serves to advance our understanding of how each conditions the relations among social structure, socialization, and competence but does not allow precise identification of the variables that predict competence in each of the four race-sex groups or an estimate of the variance explained by the full model within each group.

The full model explains more variance in the IQ scores of black girls (26 percent) and white boys (25 percent) and less in the IQ scores of black boys (20 percent) and white girls (21 percent). Moreover, the type and number of variables that enter each equation and the magnitude of their effects differ from group to group.

Mother's valuation of education is the only variable that predicts IQ scores in all four groups, but it is the strongest predictor of white girls' and black boys' scores, a somewhat weaker predictor of white boys' scores, and a still weaker predictor of black girls' scores. In short, mother's achievement values exerts the strongest effects on the development of intellectual competence in each race on that sex for which more modest ambitions prevail; in the case of blacks, boys, and in the case of whites, girls. Investment in child exerts slightly more pronounced effects on the IQ scores of black girls and white boys than on those of white girls, but it is not a predictor of black boys' IQ scores. Discipline does not significantly increase the amount of variance explained in IQ scores of black girls.

Black girls are the only group in which SES persists as an independent predictor of IQ scores and also the only one in which a fundamentalist background and family size are predictors of IQ scores. Father presence, in contrast, is the only variable of family structure that serves as a significant predictor of white girls' scores. Mother's tenure in the labor force is a predictor of boys' scores in both races, positive on black boys' scores and negative on those of white boys.[33] Finally, boys from nondenominational backgrounds net higher IQ scores in both races, but their advantage relative to boys from other religious backgrounds is greater among blacks than among whites. However, the detrimental effect of mother's religiosity on boys' IQ scores is the same in both races. Parents' demographic origins appears in the equations of both sexes among white children, but it significantly increases the variance explained only in boys' scores.

The variance in *achievement* scores explained by the full model is greatest in white boys' scores (34 percent), somewhat less in white and black girls' scores (31 percent and 30 percent, respectively) and least in black boys' scores (24 percent). With IQ added to the equation, the amount of variance the full model explains in achievement scores becomes virtually the same in all four groups.[34] IQ score is a markedly stronger predictor of achievement scores of black boys (beta = .50) than of white boys (beta = .38) or of black (beta = .44) or white girls (beta = .42). Independently of IQ scores, socioeconomic status and a nondenominational background are positive predictors and aversive discipline is a negative predictor of black boys' achievement scores. What is notable is the power of both IQ and aversive discipline as predictors of black boys' IQ achievement scores relative to other groups. It is evident that the variation in black boys' scores more than in any other group is conditioned by preschool experiences in the home and that once this critical period passes, other social influences, very possibly those of peers, are stronger determinants of their scholastic achievement than of any other group of children. Being the object of more aversive discipline than any other group serves only to undermine at a too-early age a mother's capability of promoting conformity to her values.

Socioeconomic status is the second strongest predictor of black girls' achievement scores (after IQ scores), and the negative effect of a fundamentalist background, already noted in relation to IQ scores, persists in relation to achievement test scores independently of its effect on IQ. Black girls from father-present homes tend to score higher than those from father-absent homes, as do also daughters of mothers who place a higher value on education and who use less discipline, but none of these three predictors singly increases the variance explained in black girls' scores.

White girls are the only group in which socioeconomic status does not enter the equation and also the one in which mother's valuation of education constitutes the strongest single predictor of achievement scores. Indeed, its effect on achievement scores is as strong as on IQ scores and persists even when IQ is taken into account. The effect of investment in child, although weaker, also persists on achievement scores only in this group. Years of mother's labor-force participation also exerts a weak positive effect on white girls' achievement scores, the only group in which this particular variable predicts achievement scores. Jewish girls net lower achievement scores relative to other white girls once the effects of other variables that enter the white girls' equation are taken into account.

The IQ scores, as already reported, exert less weight on white boys as a predictor of achievement scores than on any other group in the sample but, of course, remain a stronger predictor than any other single variable in the equation. Net of IQ, socioeconomic status and mother's valuation of education each exert a positive effect of the same magnitude, while mother's religiosity exerts an effect virtually as strong but negative. Thus, religiosity not only depresses white boys' IQ scores but persists and even has a slightly stronger negative effect on their achievement scores, whereas among black boys the negative effects of mother's religiosity, confined to their IQ test performance, is replaced by the negative effects of discipline, which varies less with mother's religiosity among black than among white mothers of sons. Finally, white like black sons of nondenominational mothers net higher achievement scores than boys from other religious backgrounds. Thus they tend to sustain the superiority in achievement tests that they exhibit earlier in their school career on IQ test performance, though their advantage is not as great relative to other white boys as is that of black sons of nondenominational mothers relative to other black boys.

Certain of these findings require further comment and interpretation— for example, the opposite effects that mother's years of work appears to exert on black and white boys' IQ scores.

When mother's years of work and marital status are simultaneously controlled, it becomes evident that white mother's abstention from labor-force participation benefits the IQ scores only of boys in father-present families. In father-absent families, in contrast, white boys' IQ scores rise with mother's years of labor-force participation. Indeed, white boys in father-absent homes with working mothers average only slightly lower IQ scores (2 points). Thus the two groups with the highest scores among white boys are those of nonworking mothers in father-present families and those of working mothers in father-absent families. The lowest scoring white boys are those of nonworking mothers in father-absent families, just as is the case in the black sample. Further, it appears that during the specific era covered by the study, married white mothers who chose to work for an extended period of their child's life were significantly less ambitious for their sons and invested less time in sons than other mothers only among white High Protestants, the specific locus of the employment-marital status interaction on IQ and the sole white group in which mother's work tenure is a predictor of sons' IQ. The fact that a full-time maternal presence benefits specifically sons in father-present High Protestant homes may well reflect something about the quality of relationships between fathers and sons in this group during that era. For example, they may well have provided instrumental leadership and left to their wives the task of providing expressive input and support, a division of labor that Talcott Parsons and his colleagues (1955) believe promotes optimal articulation between the family and an urban-industrial economy. If such a division of labor does prevail between parents, then the white male child with a full-time mother appears to exhibit some advantage in *early* intellectual development over white males whose mothers are employed outside the home in contexts where optimal socialization strategies are more prevalent. But it is questionable whether any extended benefits are conferred upon white males by such an arrangement, since, first, early IQ scores are less predictive of later scholastic achievement of white boys than of any other group and, second, length of mother's labor-force tenure is not a predictor of male achievement test performance. But it *is* a weak predictor of *higher* achievement for white girls when structural and socialization variables are controlled and a much stronger positive predictor of black boys' IQ scores.

Indeed, in contexts where a division of labor between mothers and fathers exists, the benefits of father presence for *sons* becomes somewhat equivocal. If full-time mothering of sons is required as an antidote to a critical or distant father, the father's presence in the home may represent a mixed blessing. At least, this is my interpretation of the findings, since sons of white mothers *without husbands* show an increment in IQ scores with years of maternal employment just as do black boys, who more frequently grow up in father-absent homes. Mothers without husbands, if they work, are more constrained to develop a career orientation. Such an orientation *traditionally* has been discouraged for women but strongly encouraged for men. But expanding opportunities for women to pursue careers coupled with rising divorce rates among whites has resulted since 1968 in growing repudiation of the ideology that child rearing is the mother's sole responsibility and gainful employment the primary and sole responsibility of the father. An alternative ideology that requires a more egalitarian *sharing* between the sexes of child-rearing and breadwinning responsibilities has spread in the seventies among younger, better-educated mothers, the very group that two decades earlier had embraced the feminine mystique. Thus, the selective process that operated then may now be reversed in such a way that it is precisely the better-educated mothers with husbands willing to share child-rearing responsibilities who are choosing to remain in the labor force. Under such conditions, the direction of effect of mother's labor-force tenure on boys' IQ scores could be expected to be the same as found in the present study for black boys. Indeed the results of a very recent study provide evidence that the total investment of time in the child by all persons is greater in the families of working mothers than in those of nonworking mothers (Lindert, 1978).

It is noteworthy that the presence or absence of a father in the home, a variable that does not enter boys' equations, is a positive predictor of white girls' IQ scores and of black girls' achievement scores. Moreover, simultaneous control of mother's work-force tenure and marital status reveals that the mean IQ scores of white girls with fathers present is higher than the scores of those being reared without fathers in the home, regardless of mother's work history. In short, father presence unequivocally benefits girls' early intellectual development, but its effects on boys are more variable and ambiguous. While the present study does not have the data to permit further explanation of the reasons for these differences, the results of other investigators' research suggest that just as white mothers invest more in daughters than in sons, so also do fathers, and that they are less inclined to invoke authoritarian modes of control in relation to daughters than to sons (Lynn, 1974; Baumrind, 1971).[35]

Such evidence suggests that because fathers tend to use more positive forms of control and less aversive discipline in relation to daughters than to sons, father absence often represents a relatively greater deprivation for girls than for boys. Indeed, it is very possible that a theoretical model that includes measures of paternal as well as maternal socialization strategies could fully account for the early IQ advantage exhibited by white girls relative to white boys and might also serve to reduce even further the residual difference between the races.

Mobility Processes and Sex Bias in Socialization

Occasionally a finding emerges in the course of data analysis that goes so counter to expectation that it becomes a challenge precisely to the extent that it appears to defy explanation. The finding that though Jewish girls' mean achievement score places them in third rank among girls in the sample, independently of other variables in the full regression equation, a Jewish background emerges as a significant *negative* predictor of achievement relative to other girls in the sample surprised and puzzled me. The search for an explanation proved to be fruitful not merely for understanding that specific finding but for yielding some more general propositions about the connection between sex bias and social-mobility processes.

With respect to sons, Jewish mothers' mean score on valuation of education is considerably higher than that of any other group of mothers of sons in the entire sample. With respect to daughters, Jewish mothers exhibit more moderate ambitions. To be sure, their mean valuation of education for daughters is also quite high, but it is more modest than the ambitions black and white nondenominational mothers and black High Protestant mothers express for their daughters, and only very slightly higher than those of white High Protestant mothers. Moreover, while in all the aforementioned groups in 1968, maternal ambitions for daughters are as high as or higher than for sons, the *reverse* is true for Jewish mothers; the prevalent pattern of ambition among them favors sons over daughters, a pattern which is also characteristic among white fundamentalist and Catholic mothers in both races, groups of predominantly lower socioeconomic status than Jews. In short, Jewish mothers have the dubious distinction of being the only high-status, secularly oriented group in which the traditional sex bias of valuing education more for males than for females persists in an era when similarly advantaged mothers exhibit a shift in the direction of rectifying that ancient pattern of injustice.

It has already been shown that maternal valuation of education is by far the single strongest predictor of white girls' IQ scores and that this variable exerts a stronger effect on white girls' than on white boys' scores. Thus, the *relative* deprivation that the traditional pattern of higher maternal ambition for boys imposes on girls is generally greater, but it is especially likely to produce strains for girls in a social context where educational and occupational achievement in general are highly valued but where mothers (and probably also fathers) encourage exceptionally high attainments for males only, and where this sex bias is already evident in later childhood. Jewish daughters are disadvantaged in this respect not merely relative to their brothers. They are additionally disadvantaged by the fact that the direction of bias among the Jews is currently a deviant pattern within higher-status groups, of which Jews by now have become a part. In short, Jewish girls are deprived not merely relative to Jewish boys but also relative to the girls from high Protestant and nondenominational backgrounds who are most likely to be their classmates and friends in elementary and high school. Jewish girls receive less encouragement to strive for high attainments via their own efforts than their brothers and than their sex and class peers.[36]

But while Jewish mothers exhibit a marked sex bias in their ambitions, they are the most egalitarian religious group in their strategies of socializing sons and daughters. Moreover, the Jews are the only group in the entire sample in which boys and girls average *identical* IQ scores (110): in all other white groups, girls average higher IQ scores than boys. The same pattern pertains to achievement scores with one exception; namely, among nondenominational whites, where the mean scores of the two sexes, the highest in the entire sample, are identical (7.4). Thus, in contrast to their values, Jewish mothers exhibit no sex bias in their socialization behavior; they average virtually identical scores on investment of time and other resources and in use of aversive controls with daughters and with sons. However, *relative to other groups* Jewish mothers use the least discipline toward their sons, no more than nondenominational mothers do; but they use *more* discipline toward daughters. In short, among Jews, boys and girls are the beneficiaries of the same optimal strategy, but relative to others of the same sex they are not. Jewish boys are the most advantaged relative to boys from other religious backgrounds (Blau, 1977). They are the beneficiaries of the highest encouragement for achievement, the same high investment, and lower use of aversive controls than sons of white denominational mothers. Jewish girls, however, receive less maternal encouragement for achievement and more discipline than daughters of nondenominational mothers. Each factor is a deterrent to high achievement. Thus, Jewish girls are disadvantaged relative to *two* sets of peers—Jewish boys *and* High Protestant and nondenominational *girls*, the two groups most like the Jews in socioeconomic status. White High Protestant and nondenominational daughters, in contrast, receive as much or more encouragement to strive for high educational and occupational attainment and less aversive discipline than sons.

In sum, Jewish mothers, like white fundamentalist and Catholic mothers, provide their daughters with *less* encouragement for high achievement than they do their sons, and it is precisely such encouragement that was shown to be the strongest predictor of girls' achievement test performance.

When the case of the Jews is viewed in a broader sociohistorical context, propositions at a higher level of generality can be derived concerning the social structural sources of sex inequality in achievement and its relationship to social mobility processes in modern and developing societies.

William Goode (1963) has written that one of the changes promoted by modernization processes is a trend toward greater equality between the sexes. The evidence of the present analysis suggests that while over the long term his generalization holds, in the initial phases of modernization, when education becomes a route to upward occupational mobility, inequalities between the sexes in access to educational opportunities become *more* pronounced and a bias favoring males as a rule (but not in all cases) is exhibited in the extent to which encouragement and support for high educational attainment is offered by parents in the formative stages of their children's lives.

The magnitude and direction of association between sex of child and mother's valuation of education constitutes one index of the prevalance of sex bias within a group. Typically, as societies move away from an agricultural economy toward urbanization and industrialization, emphasis on education as a means of upward mobility increases, but this value typically diffuses in stages through a society among the more advantaged classes involved in trade, commerce, and industry earlier than among unskilled, peripheral groups; among city-dwellers earlier than among rural people; among people who engage more in extrafamilial roles earlier than among those who do so less; among religious subgroups with a literary tradition and an educated clergy earlier than among those with a folk tradition; and earlier among less devout than among more devout co-religionists.

Characteristically, when education becomes perceived by a group as an accessible route to upward mobility, a bias favoring more education for males is likely to become most pronounced. When resources are scarce and choices have to be made, families as a rule will offer more encouragement and support to the sex perceived as having the best chance of gaining entry into higher occupational positions and thereby achieving the highest returns of income and social status.

In virtually all societies, women traditionally have been barred from the more remunerative, more powerful, and more prestigeful occupations and allowed mainly into occupations in which, for whatever reason, male candidates were scarce. Even in such occupations, income differentials favoring males have been typical. If, in addition to sex bias, prejudice based on race, ethnicity, or religion is extant in the society, it would be expected that sex bias would be more pronounced in groups that have been targets of such discrimination than in groups not subject to discrimination and that the sex perceived to have the better chance of occupational success will receive more encouragement and support for higher education. However, as achievement of high occupational goals within a group becomes more prevalent, sex bias in parents' valuation of education diminishes and may even become reversed, particularly in an era in which occupational opportunities increase for the traditionally less favored sex, as has been the case in the American economy in the seventies.

In short, variations in the direction and extent of sex bias with respect to valuations of education exhibited by mothers are found between religious groups within each race. Among whites, three groups favor *sons*, to varying degrees: Catholics exhibit the strongest bias ($r = -.33$), followed by Jews ($r = -.23$) and fundamentalists ($r = -.18$). A weak tendency to favor *girls* is observed among High Protestants ($r = .12$), Methodists ($r = .06$), and nondenominational/nonreligious mothers ($r = .08$).

I would suggest that three social factors operate to promote a bias favoring males: (1) a historical patriarchical tradition, (2) prevalence of working-class origins, and (3) minority-group status.

White Catholics, fundamentalists, and Jews have in common a patriarchical religious tradition; among white Catholics and fundamentalists, working-class origins are prevalent, but this is far less true of the Jews in my sample.

Both Jews and Catholics constitute minorities in American society, but

Jews were the first ethnic minority to seek higher education on a *large* scale, and they therefore bore most heavily the brunt of prejudice which existed until very recently in many colleges and universities and in the higher occupations (Baltzell, 1964) and which is still visible in the corporate sector. It is therefore not surprising that Jews of the generation represented in my sample should in 1968 still continue to exhibit a sex bias which has abated among white High Protestants during the present era.[37] Nor is it surprising, when viewed in theoretical perspective, that sex bias is even more widespread among Catholics. Because of their minority status, the greater prevalence of working-class origins, and the lower prevalence of college graduates among them relative to most Protestants and Jews, white Catholics could be expected to exhibit the strongest bias in favor of sons. By now predominantly middle-class, the Jews exhibit less sex bias than Catholics, but their uneasiness about discrimination remains a factor in the persistence of a bias in favor of sons, which is not exhibited by Protestants with middle-class origins who have not had to cope with discrimination. The same direction of bias but of lesser magnitude is exhibited by white Baptists and other fundamentalists who are substantially of working-class origin, like white Catholics. Unlike the Catholics, they do not occupy the status of a religious minority. However, Baptists have more recent rural origins and in that respect they are also a minority relative to other whites of their generation, though they are not, to be sure, a discriminated-against religious minority.

The historical experience of blacks has been quite different from that of *any* group of whites. Discrimination and exclusion from white institutions of higher learning and higher occupations, regardless of religion or class, has been a pervasive feature of American black history, and though considerably attenuated in this decade, the attainment of higher education continues to be more problematic for blacks generally than for any group of whites. Lower-working-class and more recent rural origins predominate in all religious groups of blacks in the age group of black mothers represented in my sample. Finally, unlike whites, American blacks have no patriarchical tradition owing to the fact that black males were even more assiduously oppressed than females and the penalties for any indication of "uppityness" were even more severe for them than for black females in the post-Reconstruction South. Consequently, a bias favoring more education for females became established in the Negro community which, though realistic in the context of a caste system, still operates to discourage black males from the educational route even after the legal bulwark of that system was largely destroyed during the decase of the sixties. The considerable incidence of black female-headed households and the marked advantages education affords women in such a position (Blau et al., 1978) probably contribute to the persistence of such a bias.

Since none of the factors that might account for variations in the direction or magnitude of sex bias among whites is applicable to blacks, one would not expect nor does one find a pattern of variation among them comparable to that found among the whites. Instead, a rather marked bias in favor of feamles is found among High Protestants (r = .35) and nondenominational mothers (r = .33), the two groups with the highest socioeconomic status and the highest mean valuation of education in the black sample in 1968. In both these groups, unlike their white counterparts, the mean education attained by wives is higher than that of their husbands, which added to their own success would tend to strengthen the belief that encouragement and support of sons continues to entail greater risks than investing ambition in daughters. And indeed in the late sixties when the sample was interviewed, black females were making greater educational and occupational gains than black males, as they still are tody. However, the considerable gains also exhibited by black men currently may well serve to attenuate such a bias among present and future cohorts of mothers.

Black Catholic mothers are the only group in the black sample that exhibit the same pattern of bias favoring males (r = −.26) as is observed among white Catholics, Jews, and fundamentalists. They are also the only group in the black sample in which husbands' mean educational attainment is slightly higher than that of their wives (a pattern that is typical among whites). They are predonimantly of middle SES. Indeed, Catholics are the only black religious group that averages a sohewhat higher SES score than their white co-religionists, despite the fact that their socioeconomic *origins* are lower. They also constitute a far smaller minority amid the overwhelming majority commitment of blacks to Protestantism than do their white co-religionists. Thus, in a number of their characteristics, black Catholics in our sample are atypical relative to other black religious groups and more similar to whites, which may well account for their adoption of a pattern of sex bias which is deviant in the black context but not in the context of white minorities struggling to achieve or maintain their newly won middle-class status. It is of some interest that when the IQ scores of children from each religious group are separately regressed on the full model, only two variables enter the black Catholic equation—mother's exposure to whites (beta = .50) and mother's religiosity (beta = −.45). Since this is the only group in which mother's exposure to whites even enters the prediction equation, it suggests that black Catholic mothers, being a deviant minority, if they have opportunities for association with whites are more prone to adopt the latter as their reference group, and by adopting the values and strategies of white associates thereby enhance the early intellectual development of their sons, in particular, who average higher IQ scores than any other group of black boys, except those from a nondenominational background.

The relation of maternal values to sex of child constitutes one measure of differential socialization of the sexes. The magnitude and direction of association between maternal investment in child and in the use of discipline constitute two additional measures of the prevalence of sex bias in different religious groups which also make for sex differences in early intellectual development.

A strategy of low investment and high discipline undifferentiated according to sex of child is traditional in all groups in which members of low socioeconomic status and rural origins predominate who do not place much value on educational attainment. As gains in resources begin to occur, sex differentiation of values develops according to the principles elucidated in the foregoing discussion so that increments in maternal ambition are greater first for the sex perceived as having the best mobility chances. Educational values, as a rule, influence investments of time and other resources, regardless of sex of child earlier than they influence modes of controlling children. And effective strategies of socializing girls diffuse more readily than in relation to sons.

Among white Protestants, fundamentalists, who are predominantly of low and middle socioeconomic status and more frequently of a rural background, exhibit the lowest valuation of education and are inclined to hold higher ambitions for boys. But they exhibit virtually no differences in strategies of socializing daughters and sons, which in both cases is one of low investment and high discipline. High Protestants, in contrast, who are predominantly of higher status, tend to encourage daughters more and exhibit the largest disparity in their socialization of the two sexes. Investment in daughters is higher than in sons. Indeed, their mean investment in sons is no greater than that of fundamentalist or Methodist mothers, but these two groups exhibit a linear rise in investment in daughters and a more marked decrement in the use of aversive discipline in relation to daughters than in relation to sons. Nondenominational mothers exhibit substantially increased investment in their *sons*, thereby largely obliterating the difference between the sexes on this score, but the decline in the use of discipline relative to either group is also more marked toward daughters than toward sons. As a result, the disparity between the sexes on this score becomes more pronounced in this group (r = .23) than in any other group in the white sample.

White Catholics value education more for sons, but invest no more in them than in daughters. They invest slightly less in both sexes than fundamentalists, though the latter group contains a larger component of low-SES members. White Catholic mothers use *more* discipline toward sons than any other white religious group, but in relation to daughters they are on a par with fundamentalists. The disparity between the sexes, however, is no greater on this score among Catholics than among Methodists and High Protestants.

A different historical tradition prevailed among Jews than among Christians. For centuries, Jews lived as a despised and separate minority in Christian countries, denied the right to own land when land was the major source of wealth and confined to the realms of skilled trades, commerce, and finance. Those who prospered gained status. But learning and piety have had a special significance for Jews in preserving their identity as a people in a Christian world. Thus religious learning, which was the prerogative of males primarily, also became an avenue of economic and social mobility. A youth who was a talented religious scholar, whatever his social origins, enhanced a family's status, even the status of the well-to-do or wealthy. For poor Jews (and most Eastern European Jews were poor) an important avenue of upward mobility for males was religious learning. Because intellectuality was valued and its exercise confined to males, males became the earliest beneficiaries of a strategy which combined high investment and a low use of aversive control. While there is no systematic empirical data on this aspect of Jewish maternal behavior, there is a considerable amount of literature to support the proposition that, unlike Christians, Jewish mothers traditionally invested more and used less aversive controls in relation to sons than to daughters, but like Christians, valued education more for sons than for daughters. As long as economic resources were scarce, and a choice had to be made, an optimal strategy of socialization was exercised more often in relation to males than females. But as Jews utilized the far greater opportunities for upward mobility available in America, they extended toward daughters a strategy that had earlier been more prevalent in relation to males, although they still retain their traditional bias favoring more education for males than for females. Thus, only among the Jews has an optimal strategy become diffused later in relation to females than to males, the reverse of the process currently among white Christians. Both Protestants and Catholics move toward effective strategies of socialization earlier in relation to daughters than in relation to sons, which may be a significant source of the advantage white girls exhibit on IQ test performance relative to white boys within every religious group except the Jews, where, it will be recalled, boys' and girls' mean IQ scores are identical. With respect to *achievement* scores, the same pattern of sex differences is observed except in two groups: Jewish boys exhibit slightly higher scores than Jewish girls, while nondenominational boys and girls have identical scores.

Among blacks, mothers in all Protestant denominations, but High Protestants more markedly, invest more in daughters than in sons, and all except Methodists discipline sons more than daughters. Black Catholic mothers, however, invest as much in sons as in daughters, but, like Protestants, discipline them more than daughters.

Black nondenominational mothers are the only group in the entire sample, black or white, that tend to invest more in sons than in daughters and hardly discipline sons any more than daughters. Indeed, they use considerably less discipline toward sons than any other group of black mothers, which may account for the fact that their sons' mean IQ and achievement scores are the highest in the black sample and that their sons' advantage relative to other black children persists even when all the variables in the full model are controlled.

It can hardly be due to chance that only two groups of boys in the entire sample—black nondenominational and white Jewish sons—exhibit IQ and achievement scores as high or higher than the scores of girls of their own religious background and that they are located precisely in the same groups where mothers exhibit an *egalitarian* socialization strategy of high investment and low use of aversive control in both races in relation to both sexes. Instead, the juxtaposition of these two findings can be taken as evidence for the proposition that no *inherent* differences exist between the rate of intellectual development of black and white boys and girls either in early or later childhood and that differentials in tested abilities, where they have been observed, have *social* sources in these stages of life, just as differential achievements between the races and sexes do in later stages of life. That is not to say that the *nature* of the social factors that account for disparities in achievements between males and females in each race in later stages of life is the same as in earlier stages. While I would expect parental values and childhood socialization to be components of a theoretical model that seeks to account for race and sex differences in educational attainments, differences in opportunities and social expectations operating in youth and adulthood of an age cohort could be expected to exert more *direct* effects on educational and occupational attainments of each sex in adulthood.

Afterword

My sample of children aged nine to twelve in 1968 by now are in their early twenties. In the current decade, educational and occupational opportunities for blacks have expanded very considerably, aided by affirmative action programs, and this has had the effect of raising hopes and expectations among *all* black youth. Those who acquired the education and experiential skills required for entry into middle-class occupations have fared at least as well as white youth (Wilson, 1978). At the same time, the position of black youth lacking such skills has become worse in an increasingly bifurcated labor market characterized by an expanding middle-class occupational sector and a shrinking sector of marginal low-skill, low-paying jobs. Their high expectations coupled with the realization that in contrast to educated blacks they are barred from the middle-class job sector has produced widespread alienation and demoralization among poorly educated youth which finds expression in an alarming rise in unemployment and crime rates over the past ten years.

Over twenty years ago, Robert Merton, in a brilliant theoretical essay, "Social Structure and Anomie" (1957), foretold what lay in store for American society in the seventies. In a society that prescribes success goals universally, but in which pronounced inequalities exist in access to the prescribed means for their achievement, rising rates of illegitimate or disapproved modes of response are predictable. That disproportionate numbers of black youth would rather forgo employment in low-status jobs and depend on welfare for a livelihood exemplifies *retreatism*. Resort to criminal activity as a source of economic gain exemplifies *innovation*. A significant rise in such forms of deviant behavior signifies a decline in the strength of societal norms to control behavior which, in turn, serves to further increase their incidence, a process that can eventually erode the social order and bring about anomie. Such a strain toward normlessness imposes heavy costs not merely on the unsuccessful, but on all members of the community.

Unless *effective* programs are instituted by policymakers to remove or at least alleviate the cognitive deficits that are disproportionately high among poor minority children and youth, the prospects are not good for arresting or reversing the spread of alienation and demoralization among the black underclass.

This book has presented in considerable detail evidence that their cognitive deficits are not inherent but result from identifiable environmental deficits of a cumulative and complex nature that are associated with poverty, but which constitute independent impediments to the intellectual development of minority children.

Poor black ghetto children with several closely spaced siblings reared by poorly educated mothers without work experience, organizational ties, or exposure to white friends and co-workers are most at risk of entering school with severe cognitive deficits. In both races, sons of nonworking mothers in father-absent homes average the lowest IQ scores, but the incidence of such families is far higher among blacks than among whites.

National data reveal that in 1977, one out of every three black families, compared with one out of nine white families, was headed by a woman and that 29 percent of all never-married black female household heads were unemployed, compared with 9 percent of their white counterparts. Black female household heads have substantially less education and larger families than their white counterparts, and an increased number of dependents is directly associated with the incidence of poverty in such families: two out of three households headed by women with four or more children have incomes below the poverty level. One of the most important factors contributing to the markedly lower income of female-headed families is the absence of wage earners: one out of four such families had no wage earner, compared with only one out of ten husband-wife families (Blau et al., 1978).

The absence of a wage earner rather than father absence per se deprives children in female-headed families of opportunities to acquire the most elementary formal and experiential knowledge about the world of gainful employment. Mothers and children in such families are most removed from modernizing social and cultural processes that take place in the mainstream society. Such families are usually on AFDC.

The deficiencies of children growing up in such families serve to highlight the shortcomings of the AFDC Program, which was designed over forty years ago to provide subsistence to father-absent families and remains the closest approximation to a family policy yet devised by the United States.

AFDC is not a substitute for a comprehensive family policy. From its inception, it was too narrowly conceived and was predicated on certain assumptions that for several reasons have had dysfunctional consequences for black families in particular.

Finding employment traditionally has been more problematic for black men than for black women, who were usually able to at least find work as domestics in middle-class homes. Unemployment rates among black males have always exceeded those among white males, and when black males were employed, their incomes were lower. Consequently, their role as breadwinner has been more problematical for black than for white men, and black women have traditionally been in the labor force in far greater numbers than white women, regardless of their marital status.

By making father absence a condition for mothers and their offspring to receive a meager but relatively secure stipend, AFDC served to further weaken the already tenuous position of black men in family life and it served also to undermine their sense of responsibility as socializing agents for the children they fathered.

Another invidious effect of AFDC has been to encourage among poor blacks a pattern that had been normative primarily in the white middle class in which the father served as sole breadwinner and head of the family while mothers stayed out of the labor force to bear and rear children, thereby making mothers as well as children economic dependents of men. This pattern strengthened marital ties in the white middle class and the authority of males as long as educational and occupational opportunities for men far exceeded those of women. This pattern also became widespread in the white working class after unionization of industry led to higher wages and greater job security among blue-collar workers.

Because white mothers were usually married and *not* gainfully employed, the conclusion seemed to follow that it was also in the best interest of children in father-absent families to have a full-time mother. This has been largely an article of faith, *not* a conclusion based on systematic empirical evidence. Nevertheless, it was this assumption that underlay the original eligibility requirement that AFDC mothers *not* be gainfully employed. This has produced a curious anomaly. Among the black middle class, mothers, as a rule, are gainfully employed whether or not they are married, following a pattern traditional among blacks, and black working mothers bear fewer children than nonworking mothers. But among poor black father-absent families, it has become normative for mothers not to work, and it is precisely in this group that the pattern of large families still persists.

Thus, many of the pathological conditions found among AFDC families can be traced to the program itself. Indeed, AFDC is part of the problem of black ghetto family life and therefore should be dismantled and replaced by a comprehensive family program more in keeping with the facts of life in contemporary America.

An income maintenance program for *all* families below or at the poverty line obviously needs to be one cornerstone of an effective family policy: adequate food, housing, medical care, and family planning are basic prerequisites of a program that aims to strengthen the capacity of parents to effectively prepare their children for adulthood in a complex, changing society.

A second cornerstone of a coherent family policy should be to create mechanisms and incentives for poorly educated teenagers and youth to further their education and vocational training, to postpone parenthood, and to limit the number of children they bear, because large families are the strongest negative family predictor of poor children's IQ scores. By upgrading educational and occupational skills and limiting the dependency ratio in poor families, chances can be extended for poor minority parents to upgrade their occupational options and to escape welfare dependency or low-paying, dead-end jobs. Neither age, sex, marital status, nor work status should constitute a barrier to subsidies and counseling under such a program. Instead of penalizing poor families with a wage earner, incentives should be created for both mothers and fathers to work, and supplemental grants and services should be made available to low income families to encourage and support their efforts to become and remain self-sufficient.

A third essential cornerstone of a comprehensive family policy should be the establishment of a quality day-care and cognitively oriented preschool education program on a sliding scale fee basis for children of working mothers and of mothers seeking further education and/or vocational training. Particular incentives and support should be provided to poor minority parents to utilize such programs for their children while they upgrade their own education and vocational skills in preparation for entering the labor force.

Evidence is accumulating that quality public day-care and preshcool cognitively oriented education programs can and do promote intellectual development among poor minority children. For example, several studies (Abt Associates, 1979) of public day-care programs for infants and toddlers, six weeks to three years of age, reveal that the quality of day care is strongly related to group size and caregiver/child ratios. The recommendation that a 1:5 ratio be made a standard and that group size ceilings should be enforced in public day-care programs is consistent with my findings concerning the detrimental effects of large families on the early cognitive development of children. Findings with respect to preschool children are similar: "Across all study sites, smaller groups are consistently associated with better care, more socially active children and higher gains on two developmental tests." Another important finding of that study was that caregivers with education or training relevant to young children "deliver better care with somewhat superior developmental effects for children."

Some rigorously designed longitudinal studies of the effects of cognitively oriented preschool education on high risk, poor children provide solid evidence of positive and sustained gains in school achievement and grade placement among them five years after entry into elementary school and markedly superior achievement compared with similar children who did not attend preschool (Weikart et al., 1978a; Weikart et al., 1978b).

Other longitudinal studies also report significant long-term positive effects on the school performance of children who had been enrolled in experimental infant and preschool programs which had deliberate cognitive curricula (Lazar et al., 1977).

Such preschool interventions need to be augmented in the primary school grades with a program to select and train master teachers and volunteer personnel in schools to work intensively with poor minority and white children who continue to exhibit deficits in basic language, verbal, and numerical concepts and skills.

The results of an intriguing and innovative study based on longitudinal data (Pederson, Faucher, Eaton, 1978) suggest that highly dedicated and competent first-grade teachers can have dramatic and enduring effects in raising the competence and self-esteem of poor minority children and thus can promote higher educational attainment and occupational outcomes in adulthood.[38]

I am well aware that implementation of the foregoing proposals would entail the expenditure of considerable public funds. At the same time it should be evident to policymakers and informed citizens generally that *prevention* of school failure would be far less costly over the long run than continued investment in programs that have proven at best to be ineffective and at worst counterproductive.

A recent innovative quantitative benefit cost study of the social rate of return on public funds invested in one highly successful preschool project shows that the costs were more than compensated by the accrued benefits the project yielded for children, their families, and the larger community (Weber et al., 1978). Other investigations on a broader scale of the economics of human capital investments reveal the tremendous monetary and human costs that presently burden communities with large enclaves of poor minorities (Lindert, 1978). These costs will surely rise in the future unless the society embarks on a massive program of amelioration and prevention of school failure, which is one root cause currently of the disproportionately high rates of unemployment, criminal activity, and imprisonment among poor black youth. Nothing less than a massive effort to establish and implement a comprehensive family policy will suffice to eradicate the pervasive legacy of discrimination and segregation that lingers on in the lives of poor blacks.

It is all too evident to anyone who has given any serious thought to the problem that the negative effects of that legacy are not confined to poor blacks, but are also increasingly endangering the quality of life of all citizens—black and white.

If a concern for justice does not move the polity to take action soon, then self-interest will surely sooner or later require it.

Notes

1. White exposure, though not included in the analysis of the combined sample, is, of course, confounded with race and thereby serves to exaggerate the residual difference between the mean scores of the two races.

2. Such decisions may well exert some influence on religious and denominational intergenerational continuity and change. That is, the children in my sample who attain higher educational and occupational status will be more likely to shift their denominational affiliation from, for example, Baptist or other fundamentalist affiliations to High Protestant than those with more limited educational and occupational attainments.

3. The zero-order association between a fundamentalist affiliation and white exposure is −.28, in contrast to the association between the latter and other affiliations, which is weakly positive.

4. Throughout the analysis of IQ scores, parents' demographic origins remain a positive predictor in the white equation but never enter the black one. Among whites, fundamentalism shows the strongest negative association with northern origin and size of origin community (−.23). The strongest positive association with the latter two variables is a Jewish affiliation (.29).

5. Interestingly, Jewish women have mean religiosity scores identical to white nondenominational women.

6. At a later point, it will be shown that the adverse effects of mother's religiosity are sex-specific, that is, that they operate in relation to boys in both races and that a fundamentalist background exerts a significant adverse effect on black girls' scores only.

7. The analysis pinpoints two specific effects of exposure to whites that explain how it benefits intellectual development of black children: it has significant net effects on reducing the number of children black mothers bear and on raising the investment of time, attention, and other rewarding resources in the child. These two variables in the equation neutralize the effect of white exposure. That is to say, once these effects are specified and included in the full equation, white exposure has no further direct effect on IQ scores.

8. This variable is also more strongly associated on the zero-order level with social milieu among whites than among blacks. Parents' educational attainment is the single strongest SES predictor of white children's IQ score.

9. Social milieu is the strongest net predictor of black children's IQ, followed by parents' origin SES and extent of mother's exposure to white friends and coworkers. With these variables controlled, parents' education does not add significantly to the variance explained in black children's scores in contrast to white children's.

10. A simple confirmation of the above proposition is the following: the variance explained in white children's IQ score solely by parents' education is 10 percent; the same variable explains 8 percent of the variance in black scores. The addition of two variables, parents' occupational status and demographic origins, adds 2 percent to the variance explained in white scores. The addition of three different variables—mother's milieu, parents' SES origins, and mother's exposure to whites—adds 6 percent to the variance explained in black children's scores. When religion is added to the equation, parents' education no longer enters. Nevertheless, the variance explained in black scores rises another 2 percent to 16 percent, but in the case of whites there is no improvement at all. Further, when the races are combined and with SES components only in the equation, the mean difference in IQ between black and white children declines from 10 to 5.9 points; when the religious variables are added, that difference declines to 3.9, but the variance explained (23 percent) in the combined sample is not increased.

11. With the addition of more variables it became necessary to combine the measures of parents' origin social class, their educational attainment, the occupational status of the parent with the higher score, and mother's social milieu into a single composite measure of socioeconomic status.

12. In both races SES exerts stronger effects on achievement test performance of children in the fifth and sixth grade than on IQ scores administered in the second grade, even with family variables included in the equation. Indeed, the weight of SES as a predictor of achievement scores is second only to that of IQ in each race. But with the races combined, its weight as a predictor only exceeds that of race very slightly. The net advantage that children from a nondenominational/ nonreligious background exhibited on IQ test performance is maintained on achievement scores in both races. Mother's religiosity exerts a weak negative net effect on white scores and on scores in the combined sample even with family variables controlled.

13. Numerous studies, based mostly on white samples, quite consistently report that girls average higher IQ scores than boys in later childhood (Maccoby and Jacklin, 1974).

14. With sex of child as a variable included in the structural model, the proportion of the variance explained in white scores rises from 14 percent to 15 percent.

15. Thus, white High Protestant girls' mean score (112) is 7 points higher than their male peers. Black High Protestant girls' mean score (107) is 8 points higher than their male peers and 2 points higher than that of white Protestant boys.

16. This is not to deny that children from advantaged homes, as a rule, perform better on IQ and achievement tests, but to identify the socialization strategies that are *direct sources* of their competence, just as they are of those economically disadvantaged children who also perform well on school tests. Counterproductive socialization strategies, which are far more prevalent among disadvantaged families, impede the development of intellectual competence in ways that will be presently explained.

17. Americans are prone to emphasize the pecuniary rewards of higher education and to neglect the very significant contribution that it makes to effective performance of the parental role and thereby to the development of greater intellectual, and probably also emotional, competence in successive generations of

societal members. Moreover, recent evidence strongly suggests that educational attainment may be the strongest demographic predictor of attitudes and behaviors that make for successful aging (Blau, Rogers, Oser, Stephens, 1978).

18. The zero-order association between maternal valuation of education and investment in the study child is .50 among blacks and .55 among whites, that between mother's valuation of education and discipline is −.37 among blacks and −.42 among whites, and that between maternal investment and discipline is −.36 and −.37 among blacks and whites, respectively.

19. Thus, 49 percent of white mothers but only 18 percent of black mothers who score in the top third of the valuation of education continuum employ an optimal strategy of high-investment and low use of aversive control. Among those who score in the lowest third of the valuation of education distribution a counter-productive strategy of low investment-high discipline is exhibited by 46% of the black mothers compared to only 18% of the white mothers.

20. The beta weights of SES on valuation among black and white mothers, respectively are .37 and .47; on investment in child .27 and .33 and on use of aversive forms of discipline −.32 and −.44.

21. The reason for this difference between the races very possibly is that the effects on mother's values of father presence is not uniform across all religious groups among whites.

22. White exposure is also a predictor of black mothers' values, but its net effect is weak and does not increase significantly the variance explained in maternal values as it does in the case of maternal investment.

23. While *current* family structure variables do not register any independent effects, it is interesting to note that mean size of parents' *family of origin* has a weak nonsignificant effect in promoting reliance on aversive control among black mothers, which becomes significant when the races are combined.

24. Since the direction of the sex effect is different in the two races, sex of child does not enter the equation at all when the races are combined.

25. Structural variables account for a considerable amount of variance in maternal values and socialization strategies in both races, but with the exception of investment in child in which the variance explained is identical in each race (37 percent), structural variables explain more of the variance in white mothers' valuation of education (37 percent) than in that of black mothers (32 percent); the differences with respect to the use of discipline are even more pronounced, 34 percent in the case of white mothers compared with 22 percent in the case of black mothers.

26. The last proposition has some bearing on a finding from an early study of modes of supervision in formal organizations that shows that productivity of workers is enhanced more by supervision that relies on statistical records than on close personal surveillance of workers (Peter Blau, 1955).

27. The same pattern of differences is observed with respect to achievement scores, except that with IQ scores in the equation, the socialization model explains the identical amount of variance in the two races (41 percent). The reason for this is that IQ scores' net effect on achievement scores is somewhat stronger in the case

of black than of white children. The negative effect of discipline is stronger on black than on white children's scores, the effects of maternal values are markedly weaker, and the net effect of investment in the child is virtually the same in the two races. Further, when all the above variables are controlled, black boys' scores slightly exceed those of black girls (beta = −.06), an indication that the slight actual advantage of black girls over boys arises from socialization factors.

With the races combined, the mean achievement score difference between the races is slightly greater (beta = .93 of a stanine) compared to the residual differences observed with the structural model (beta = .87), but the proportion of variance explained by the socialization and the structural models in the whole sample is identical (55 percent).

28. Conversely, the increment of variance explained by the full model over the socialization model is 6 percent in black scores and only 3 percent in white scores.

29. The betas for valuation of education are .26 and .16, respectively, for whites and blacks, and the weight of investment in child is .19 and .13, respectively, for whites and blacks.

30. But these effects are somewhat stronger with the races combined than the effect of each is in the black or white group alone.

31. The actual zero-order IQ difference of 12 points between black and white girls is larger than the 9-point difference between boys in the two races, but net of structural factors the difference between girls in the two races becomes some-what *smaller* relative to that between boys (2.7 and 2.9 points, respectively). The structural model thus explains considerably more of the variance in the scores of black and white girls combined (29 percent) than of their male counterparts (22 percent).

32. Among boys, the beta for IQ is .41, compared with .40 among girls, and the beta for SES is .15 among both sexes.

33. These opposite effects, it will be shown presently, are more apparent than real.

34. Forty-four percent in all groups except black girls, in which 45 percent of the variance is accounted for by the full model

35. Furthermore, a more *consistent* association between paternal behavior and achievement motivation of girls than of boys has been reported (Katkowsky, Preston, Crandall, 1964; Bing, 1963), and in a study of seventh-grade children, girls report receiving more love, affection, and nurturance from both parents, whereas boys report more negative, controlling treatment from both parents (Droppleman and Shaeffer, 1963).

36. Jewish daughters instead customarily are encouraged to marry the successful sons of other Jewish parents (Blau, 1977). A 1975 study of the Jewish community in Houston, Texas, found that while Jewish women had higher educational attainment than other white women, their labor-force participation *and* their family size were lower (Schulman et al., 1976).

37. It hardly needs to be pointed out that High Protestant males have traditionally been the most favored and successful in the occupational structure.

38. A further bit of evidence of the critical difference a highly dedicated first-grade teacher can make in a minority child's life comes from a Mexican-American teacher who won the Teacher of the Year Award in the Houston Public Schools. He recounts that on coming to the first grade without a knowledge of English, one private session with his teacher who cared enough to insist that he master a handful of words inspired him not only to become fluent in English, but also to use it to teach others how to speak his native tongue. Now, along with the daily Spanish instruction he gives, he also tries to teach his students "a little bit about life and not to settle for being average" (*Houston Chronicle*, June 11, 1978).

Appendix

TABLE A-1. Regression of Black and White IQ Scores on Components of SES and Parents' Origins

Variable	Blacks			
	B	*Beta*	*Standard Error*	*F*
Social milieu	2.520	0.213	0.595	17.97*
Parents' class origins	0.107	0.107	0.045	5.75*
Mothers' white exposure	1.152	0.091	0.526	5.80*
Parents' education	0.751	0.082	0.464	2.62
Intercept	77.87655		R = 14%	N = 579

Variable	Whites			
	B	*Beta*	*Standard Error*	*F*
Parents' education	2.089	0.207	0.596	12.29*
Parents' demographic origins	1.072	0.120	0.383	7.83*
Parents' occupational status	0.063	0.103	0.036	3.10
Intercept	85.16580		R^2 = 12%	N = 523

TABLE A-2. Regression of Achievement Scores on Components of SES and Parents' Origins, by Race

	Blacks			
Variable	B	Beta	Standard Error	F
IQ score	0.065	0.494	0.005	211.24*
Education	0.166	0.138	0.052	10.30*
Social milieu	0.207	0.133	0.065	10.13*
Occupational status	0.004	0.058	0.003	2.07
Intercept	−3.49892		$R^2 = 42\%$	

	Whites			
Variable	B	Beta	Standard Error	F
IQ score	0.062	0.478	0.005	171.57*
Parents' education	0.239	0.182	0.073	10.79*
Social milieu	0.205	0.136	0.082	6.28*
Parents' demographic origins	−0.082	−0.070	0.042	3.86*
Intercept	−2.06634		$R^2 = 39\%$	N = 523

TABLE A-3. Mean Achievement Scores by Race, Class, and Religion

	Black		White	
Religion and Denomination	Middle Class	Working Class	Middle Class	Working Class
Baptist and other	4.4	3.8	6.2	5.4
fundamentalist	(117)	(250)	(32)	(32)
Methodist, Lutheran	5.0	4.3	6.7	4.9
	(71)	(41)	(59)	(26)
High Protestant	5.9	3.9	6.8	5.2
	(31)	(11)	(80)	(11)
Catholic	4.9	4.4	5.9	5.6
	(29)	(8)	(53)	(42)
Jewish	—	—	6.7	4.7
			(104)	(5)
Nondenominational	6.5	0	7.4	7.3
nonreligious	(16)	(1)	(63)	(4)
F =	11.72***	.36	5.01***	1.85

TABLE A-4. Regression of Black and White Children's IQ Scores on Religion, SES, Parents' Origins, and Exposure to Whites

	Blacks			
Variable	B	Beta	Standard Error	F
Milieu	2.387	0.201	0.547	19.01*
Fundamentalist	−3.158	−0.122	1.122	7.93*
Origin SES	0.107	0.107	0.043	6.18*
Nondenominational	5.935	0.080	2.939	4.08*
White exposure	0.999	0.079	0.523	3.66
Intercept	84.43838		R^2 = 16%	N = 579

	Whites			
Variable	B	Beta	Standard Error	F
Parents' education	1.962	0.195	0.600	10.68*
Demographic origins	1.084	0.121	0.382	8.03*
Social-class origin	0.059	0.097	0.036	2.75
Nondenominational/ nonreligious	2.944	0.068	1.840	2.56
Intercept	85.69401		R^2 = 12%	N = 523

TABLE A-5. Regression: IQ Scores of Blacks, Whites, and Races Combined on Structural Model

Standardized Regression Coefficients (F's in Parentheses)

Independent Variables	Blacks	Whites	Races Combined
SES	.164 (10.21)*	.207 (19.60)*	.231 (37.11)*
Parents' demographic origins	—	.131 (9.19)*	—
Parents' origin family size	—	—	—
White exposure [a]	—	—	—
Fundamentalist	−.106 (5.97)*	—	−.080 (5.67)*
High Protestant	—	.067 (2.38)	—
Catholic	—	—	—
Nondenominational	.083 (4.45)*	.107 (5.04)*	.068 (5.93)*
Jewish	—	—	—
Religiosity	−.076 (3.76)	—	−.056 (3.98)*
Number of children	−.147 (12.13)*	−.085 (4.04)*	−.116 (16.64)*
Marital status	—	.078 (3.44)	.052 (3.54)
Years employed	.081 (3.94)*	−.115 (7.55)*	—
Organizational membership	.075 (2.99)	—	.051 (2.93)
Race	—	—	.123 (13.43)*
Sex of child	—	.115 (7.83)*	—
Intercept	98.09945	80.14178	89.85632
R^2 =	18%	15%	25%
N =	579	523	1102

*$p < .05$
[a] not included for whites and races combined

TABLE A-6. Correlations among Maternal Values, Measures of Investment in Children, and Test Scores—Blacks and Whites

	1		2		3		4		5		6		7		8	
	W	B	W	B	W	B	W	B	W	B	W	B	W	B	W	B
1. Aspirations																
2. Educational expectations	.60	.48														
3. Early interaction	.26	.29	.28	.34												
4. Read Child-rearing experts	.31	.13	.38	.18	.20	.26										
5. Early mastery	.22	.26	.26	.40	.20	.24	.13	.20								
6. Cultural enrichment	.39	.23	.41	.37	.21	.30	.40	.34	.17	.23						
7. IQ score	.36	.27	.35	.33	.22	.23	.30	.17	.22	.31	.28	.27				
8. Achievement score	.38	.26	.42	.37	.22	.22	.34	.18	.25	.32	.31	.26	.56	.60		

TABLE A-7. White and Black Correlations Among Components of Aversive Control and Children's IQ and Achievement Scores

	1		2		3		4		5		6		7		8		9		10
	W	B	W	B	W	B	W	B	W	B	W	B	W	B	W	B	W	B	
1. Authoritarianism																			
2. Fatalism	.56	.49																	
3. Suppression of Autonomy	.46	.36	.41	.36															
4. Coercive Discipline	.33	.22	.30	.15	.31	.19													
5. Husband's use of physical punishment late childh'd	.26	.07	.18	.02	.26	.13	.43	.23											
6. Husband's use of physical punishment early childh'd	.15	.05	.11	.02	.11	.13	.39	.29	.47	.43									
7. Disparagement	.18	.07	.15	.04	.21	.07	.27	.33	.20	.10	.22	.13							
8. Proscriptiveness	.22	.12	.19	.24	.15	.08	.02	.04	.04	.09	-.07	.02	.09	-.03					
9. IQ	-.22	-.19	-.18	-.21	-.16	-.19	-.12	-.15	-.08	-.11	-.09	.03	-.18	-.02	-.11	-.14			
10. ACH	-.30	-.32	-.29	-.27	-.17	-.26	-.23	-.18	-.15	-.08	-.05	.04	-.29	-.07	-.08	-.18	.56	.60	

TABLE A-8. Mother's Valuation of Education by Race, Religion, and SES

Religion	Race	SES					
		Low	N	Middle	N	High	N
Baptist/other	B	12.2	(235)	13.9	(117)	16.6	(15)
fundamentalist	W	11.2	(30)	12.3	(19)	15.6	(15)
Methodist/Lutheran	B	12.5	(32)	14.4	(53)	16.4	(27)
	W	10.8	(13)	12.7	(33)	15.7	(39)
High Protestant	B	14.0	(11)	15.1	(15)	16.3	(16)
	W	12.4	(7)	14.1	(19)	15.4	(65)
Catholic	B	13.2	(5)	14.2	(27)	16.8	(5)
	W	11.3	(30)	13.4	(48)	14.5	(17)
Nondenominational/	B	—	(1)	14.8	(7)	16.5	(9)
nonreligious	W	—	(1)	14.2	(10)	16.5	(56)
Jewish	B	—	(0)	—	(0)	—	(0)
	W	—	(0)	15.8	(18)	16.2	(91)

TABLE A-9. Maternal Investment in Child by Race, Religion, and SES

Religion	Race	SES					
		Low	N	Middle	N	High	N
Baptist/other	B	19.2	(235)	20.8	(117)	23.7	(15)
fundamentalist	W	20.3	(30)	20.9	(19)	23.5	(15)
Methodist/Lutheran	B	20.6	(32)	21.3	(53)	24.1	(27)
	W	20.1	(13)	21.8	(33)	22.5	(39)
High Protestant	B	21.3	(11)	23.2	(15)	24.1	(16)
	W	19.8	(7)	21.0	(19)	23.2	(65)
Catholic	B	20.9	(5)	22.8	(27)	24.2	(5)
	W	19.9	(30)	20.5	(48)	22.1	(17)
Nondenominational/	B		(1)	21.7	(7)	25.0	(9)
nonreligious	W		(1)	23.1	(10)	24.4	(56)
Jewish	B	—	(0)	—	(0)	—	(0)
	W	—	(0)	23.2	(18)	24.2	(91)

TABLE A-10. Use of Aversive Discipline by Race, Religion, and SES

Religion	Race	SES					
		Low	N	Middle	N	High	N
Baptist/other	B	15.5	(235)	14.1	(117)	12.7	(15)
fundamentalist	W	14.1	(30)	13.2	(19)	9.2	(15)
Methodist/Lutheran	B	15.3	(32)	14.1	(53)	10.8	(27)
	W	13.9	(13)	11.9	(33)	9.5	(39)
High Protestant	B	14.8	(11)	12.1	(15)	9.5	(16)
	W	10.8	(7)	11.4	(19)	8.7	(65)
Catholic	B	15.4	(5)	12.3	(27)	12.0	(5)
	W	15.7	(30)	12.9	(48)	11.2	(17)
Nondenominational/	B	—	(1)	12.7	(7)	10.3	(9)
nonreligious	W	—	(1)	8.6	(10)	7.9	(56)
Jewish	B	—	(0)	—	(0)	—	(0)
	W	—	(0)	9.8	(18)	8.7	(91)

TABLE A-11. Mean Number of Children by Mother's Race, Religion, and SES

Religion	Race	SES					
		Low	N	Middle	N	High	N
Baptist/other	B	5.1	(235)	4.1	(117)	3.0	(15)
fundamentalist	W	4.3	(30)	3.5	(19)	3.3	(15)
Methodist/Lutheran	B	5.2	(32)	3.5	(53)	2.5	(27)
	W	3.5	(13)	3.2	(33)	3.6	(39)
High Protestant	B	4.7	(11)	3.5	(15)	2.1	(16)
	W	4.4	(7)	3.6	(19)	3.3	(65)
Catholic	B	4.8	(5)	3.8	(27)	3.4	(5)
	W	4.2	(30)	3.4	(48)	3.2	(17)
Nondenominational/	B	—	(1)	2.4	(7)	3.0	(9)
nonreligious	W	—	(1)	2.5	(10)	3.0	(56)
Jewish	B	—	(0)	—	(0)	—	(0)
	W	—	(0)	3.2	(18)	2.6	(91)

TABLE A-12. Mean Years Mother Worked by Race, Religion, and SES

Religion	Race	SES					
		Low	N	Middle	N	High	N
Baptist/other	B	3.7	(235)	4.6	(117)	6.3	(15)
fundamentalist	W	1.8	(30)	3.8	(19)	2.6	(15)
Methodist/Lutheran	B	3.8	(32)	4.6	(53)	6.6	(27)
	W	1.3	(13)	3.3	(33)	2.4	(39)
High Protestant	B	3.1	(11)	4.4	(15)	7.4	(16)
	W	3.6	(7)	3.4	(19)	2.3	(65)
Catholic	B	3.6	(5)	5.7	(27)	7.8	(5)
	W	1.2	(30)	3.2	(48)	1.5	(17)
Nondenominational/	B	—	(1)	2.4	(7)	7.8	(9)
nonreligious	W	—	(1)	4.1	(10)	2.4	(56)
Jewish	B	—	(0)	—	(0)	—	(0)
	W	—	(0)	2.2	(18)	1.9	(1)

TABLE A-13. **Regression: Mother's Valuation of Education on Structural Model**

Standardized Regression Coefficients (F's in Parentheses)

Independent Variables	Blacks	Whites	Races Combined
SES	.371	.468	.469
	(76.20)*	(129.24)*	(195.08)*
Demographic origin	—	—	—
Origin family size	—	—	—
White exposure[a]	.057	—	—
	(2.31)		
Fundamentalist	—	—	—
High Protestant	—	—	—
Catholic	—	—	—
Nondenominational	—	.088	.061
		(5.37)*	(5.20)*
Jewish	—	.100	.070
		(6.74)*	(6.56)*
Religiosity	—	—	—
Number of children	−.176	−.115	−.152
	(21.99)*	(9.72)*	(32.95)*
Marital status	.056	—	.040
	(2.53)		(2.39)
Years employed	—	−.077	—
		(4.69)*	
Organizational membership	.104	.088	.109
	(6.93)*	(5.32)*	(15.70)*
Sex of child	.129	−.098	—
	(13.87)*	(7.81)*	
Race	—	—	−.170
			(34.62)*
Intercept	7.78735	10.45422	10.87294
R^2 =	32%	37%	34%
N =	579	523	1102

*p < .05
[a] not included for whites or races combined

TABLE A-14. **Regression: Mother's Investment in Child on Structural Model**

Standardized Regression Coefficients (F's in Parentheses)

Independent Variable	Blacks	Whites	Races Combined
SES	.267	.330	.340
	(37.07)*	(60.36)*	(101.04)*
Demographic origin	—	—	—
Origin family size	—	—	—
White exposure[a]	.074	—	—
	(4.11)*		
Fundamentalist	−.078	—	−.079
	(3.80)		(6.80)*
High Protestant	—	—	—
Catholic	.078	−.087	—
	(4.78)*	(5.13)*	
Nondenominational	—	.159	.094
		(16.96)*	(13.19)*
Jewish	—	.169	.088
		(18.51)*	(11.20)*
Religiosity	—	—	—
Number of children	−.209	−.146	−.203
	(33.40)*	(15.73)*	(62.26)*
Marital status	—	—	.042
			(2.89)
Years employed	—	−.086	—
		(5.87)*	
Organizational membership	.205	.096	.154
	(29.54)*	(6.32)*	(33.96)*
Sex of child	.095	.119	.101
	(8.17)*	(11.37)*	(18.21)*
Race	—	—	−.076
			(6.83)*
Intercept	16.41261	18.54196	18.00998
$R^2 =$	37%	37%	39%
N =	579	523	1102

*p < .05
[a] not included for whites or races combined

TABLE A-15. Regression: Mother's Discipline on Structural Model

Standardized Regression Coefficients (F's in Parentheses)

Independent Variables	Blacks	Whites	Races Combined
SES	−.315	−.440	−.436
	(49.14)*	(109.16)*	(186.77)*
Demographic origin	—	—	—
Origin family size	.066	—	.054
	(2.99)		(4.27)*
White exposure[a]	—	—	—
Fundamentalist	—	.089	—
		(5.03)*	
High Protestant	−.076	—	−.083
	(3.77)		(10.16)*
Catholic	−.073	.180	—
	(3.70)	(19.88)*	
Nondenominational	−.055	—	−.093
	(2.07)		(12.30)*
Jewish	—	—	−.093
			(11.35)*
Religiosity	—	.073	.044
		(3.91)*	(3.00)
Number of children	—	—	—
Marital status	—	−.072	−.042
		(4.00)*	(2.88)
Years employed	—	—	—
Organizational membership	−.080	—	—
	(3.60)		
Sex of child	−.169	−.084	−.114
	(20.57)*	(5.50)*	(23.18)*
Race	—	—	−.068
			(5.96)*
Intercept	20.49362	18.59993	20.57580
$R^2 =$	22%	34%	39%
$N =$	579	523	1102

*p .05
[a] not included for whites or races combined

TABLE A-16. Valuation of Education by SES and Sex of Child among Blacks and Whites (Percentages)

	Socioeconomic Status					
	Low		Medium		High	
SEX	M	F	M	F	M	F
Blacks						
Value						
Low	72 (94)	56 (86)	36 (37)	24 (28)	14 (15)	3 (1)
Middle	23 (30)	28 (44)	37 (38)	41 (47)	23 (8)	28 (11)
High	5 (7)	16 (25)	27 (28)	35 (41)	63 (22)	69 (27)
N	131	155	103	116	35	39
	$\chi^2 = 11.19^{**}$		$\chi^2 = 3.89$		$\chi^2 = 3.44$	
Whites						
Value						
Low	60 (24)	81 (33)	36 (24)	49 (39)	13 (17)	13 (21)
Middle	28 (11)	17 (7)	34 (23)	31 (25)	26 (35)	29 (46)
High	13 (15)	2 (1)	30 (20)	20 (16)	62 (84)	58 (92)
N	40	41	67	80	136	159
	$\chi^2 = 4.97$		$\chi^2 = 2.97$		$\chi^2 = 0.49$	

TABLE A-17. Investment in Child by SES and Sex of Child among Blacks and Whites (Percentages)

		Socioeconomic Status					
	Low		*Middle*		*High*		
SEX	M	F	M	F	M	F	

Blacks

Investment

	M	F	M	F	M	F
Low	63 (83)	56 (87)	42 (43)	26 (30)	6 (2)	— (0)
Middle	30 (39)	31 (48)	39 (40)	37 (43)	29 (10)	31 (12)
High	7 (9)	13 (20)	19 (20)	37 (43)	66 (23)	69 (27)
N	131	155	103	116	35	39
	$\chi^2 = 3.21$		$\chi^2 = 10.08**$		$\chi^2 = 2.29$	

Whites

Investment

	M	F	M	F	M	F
Low	48 (19)	49 (20)	43 (29)	23 (18)	15 (21)	8 (12)
Middle	48 (19)	42 (17)	39 (26)	46 (37)	29 (40)	23 (37)
High	5 (2)	10 (4)	18 (12)	31 (25)	55 (75)	69 (110)
N	40	41	67	80	136	159
	$\chi^2 = 0.79$		$\chi^2 = 8.00**$		$\chi^2 = 7.45**$	

TABLE A-18. Use of Discipline by SES and Sex of Child among Blacks and Whites
(Percentages)

	SES					
	Low		Medium		High	
SEX	M	F	M	F	M	F
Blacks						
Use of Discipline						
Low	4 (5)	10 (15)	10 (10)	23 (27)	43 (15)	51 (20)
Middle	25 (33)	38 (60)	33 (34)	46 (53)	51 (18)	28 (11)
High	71 (93)	52 (80)	57 (59)	31 (36)	6 (2)	21 (8)
N	131	155	103	116	35	39
	$\chi^2 = 11.89^{**}$		$\chi^2 = 16.82^{**}$		$\chi^2 = 5.80$	
Whites						
Use of Discipline						
Low	23 (9)	15 (6)	31 (21)	35 (28)	63 (85)	79 (126)
Middle	35 (14)	37 (15)	40 (27)	46 (37)	28 (38)	18 (29)
High	43 (17)	49 (20)	28 (19)	19 (15)	10 (13)	3 (4)
N	40	41	67	80	136	159
	$\chi^2 = 0.87$		$\chi^2 = 1.90$		$\chi^2 = 12.22^{**}$	

TABLE A-19. IQ Level by SES and Sex of Child among Blacks and Whites

(Percentages)

		SES					
		Low		Medium		High	
SEX		M	F	M	F	M	F
Blacks							
IQ Level							
Low		57 (74)	59 (91)	39 (40)	39 (45)	14 (5)	23 (9)
Middle		31 (40)	27 (42)	39 (40)	24 (28)	54 (19)	39 (15)
High		13 (17)	14 (22)	22 (23)	37 (43)	31 (11)	39 (15)
N		131	155	103	116	35	39
		$\chi^2 = 0.43$		$\chi^2 = 7.73*$		$\chi^2 = 2.02$	
Whites							
IQ Level							
Low		48 (19)	56 (23)	31 (21)	18 (14)	13 (17)	6 (9)
Middle		28 (11)	20 (8)	37 (18)	39 (31)	40 (55)	33 (53)
High		25 (10)	24 (10)	42 (28)	44 (35)	47 (64)	61 (97)
N		40	41	67	80	136	159
		$\chi^2 = 0.84$		$\chi^2 = 4.51$		$\chi^2 = 7.52*$	

TABLE A-20. Achievement Level by SES and Sex of Child among Blacks and Whites (Percentages)

| | | SES | | | | | |
| | Low | | Medium | | High | | |
SEX OF CHILD	M	F	M	F	M	F
Blacks						
Achievement Level						
Low	68 (89)	67 (103)	44 (45)	40 (46)	26 (9)	13 (5)
Middle	24 (31)	28 (44)	44 (45)	41 (47)	37 (13)	49 (18)
High	8 (11)	5 (8)	13 (13)	20 (23)	37 (13)	39 (15)
N	131	155	103	116	35	39
	$\chi^2 = 1.75$		$\chi^2 = 2.07$		$\chi^2 = 2.20$	
Whites						
Achievement Level						
Low	25 (10)	32 (13)	25 (17)	11 (9)	13 (17)	10 (16)
Middle	45 (18)	39 (16)	46 (31)	38 (30)	24 (32)	17 (27)
High	30 (12)	29 (12)	28 (19)	51 (41)	64 (87)	73 (116)
N	40	41	67	80	136	159
	$\chi^2 = 0.50$		$\chi^2 = 9.47^{**}$		$\chi^2 = 2.82$	

TABLE A-21. Mean IQ by Race, Religion, and Sex of Child

Religion	Sex	Race			
		Black	(N)	White	(N)
Baptist/other	Boys	94	(167)	100	(26)
fundamentalist	Girls	95	(200)	103	(38)
Methodist/Lutheran	Boys	98	(50)	103	(44)
	Girls	101	(62)	107	(41)
High Protestant	Boys	99	(20)	105	(38)
	Girls	107	(22)	112	(53)
Catholics	Boys	101	(21)	102	(46)
	Girls	100	(16)	103	(49)
Nondenominational/	Boys	110	(8)	111	(29)
nonreligious	Girls	108	(9)	113	(33)
Jewish	Boys	—		110	(54)
	Girls	—		110	(55)

TABLE A-22. Mean Achievement by Race, Religion, and Sex of Child

Religion	Sex	Race			
		Black	(N)	White	(N)
Baptist/other	Boys	4.0	(167)	5.4	(26)
fundamentalist	Girls	4.0	(200)	6.1	(38)
Methodist/Lutheran	Boys	4.5	(50)	5.8	(44)
	Girls	4.9	(62)	6.5	(41)
High Protestant	Boys	5.2	(20)	6.2	(38)
	Girls	5.5	(22)	6.9	(53)
Catholics	Boys	4.6	(21)	5.6	(46)
	Girls	4.9	(16)	5.8	(49)
Nondenominational/	Boys	6.6	(8)	7.4	(29)
nonreligious	Girls	6.1	(9)	7.4	(28)
Jewish	Boys	—		6.8	(54)
	Girls	—		6.5	(55)

TABLE A-23. **Regression: Achievement Scores of Black and White Children and Races Combined on Full Model with IQ in the Equation**

Coefficients for Achievement Score (F's in Parentheses)

Variables	Blacks	Whites	Races Combined
IQ	.472	.412	.406
	(194.26)*	(122.50)*	(297.22)*
SES	.193	.110	.153
	(24.10)*	(5.52)*	(24.55)*
Demographic origin	—	−.069	—
		(3.64)	
Origin family size	—	—	—
Number of children	—	—	—
Marital status	.056	—	—
	(3.11)		
Organizational membership	.052	—	—
	(2.05)		
Years employed	—	—	—
Valuation of education	—	.198	.104
		(19.75)*	(15.84)*
Investment in child	—	.098	.049
		(5.19)*	(3.56)
Discipline	−.109	−.061	−.082
	(9.85)*	(2.29)	(10.50)*
Religiosity	—	−.092	−.042
		(7.19)*	(3.84)*
Fundamentalist	—	—	—
High Protestant	—	—	—
Catholic	—	—	—
Jewish	—	−.098	−.046
		(7.38)*	(4.16)*
Nondenominational	.077	—	.044
	(5.62)*		(4.21)*
Sex of child	—	—	—
Race	—	—	.216
			(82.56)*
Exposure to whites[a]	—	—	—
Intercept	−2.49463	−1.66230	−3.30837
R² =	44%	43%	57%
N =	579	523	1102

*p < .05
[a] not included in white or combined-races analyses

T A B L E A - 2 4 .   Regressions: IQ Scores of Black and White Boys and Girls on Full Model

Standardized Coefficients (F's in Parentheses)

Variables	Blacks		Whites	
	Boys	*Girls*	*Boys*	*Girls*
SES	—	.112	—	—
		(2.73)		
Demographic origin	—	—	.120	.096
			(4.18)*	(2.97)
Family origin size	—	—	—	—
White exposure[a]	—	—	—	—
Fundamentalist	—	−.149	—	—
		(7.38)*		
High Protestant	—	—	—	—
Catholic	—	—	—	—
Nondenominational	.151	—	.092	—
	(7.38)*		(2.45)	
Jewish	—	—	—	—
Religiosity	−.136	—	−.140	—
	(6.03)*		(5.92)*	
Number of children	—	−.134	—	—
		(5.59)*		
Marital status	—	—	—	.107
				(3.96)*
Years worked	.170	—	−.116	—
	(8.43)*		(4.00)*	
Mother's organizations	—	—	—	—
Valuation of education	.279	.090	.197	.300
	(22.62)*	(2.20)	(8.32)*	(19.84)*
Investment in child	—	.188	.206	.151
		(9.08)*	(8.58)	(5.12)
Discipline	—	−.079	—	—
		(2.08)		
Race	—	—	—	—
Intercept	87.69899	81.55071	74.44768	55.79968
R^2 =	20%	26%	25%	21%
N =	269	310	243	280

*p < .05
[a] not included in white sample

TABLE A-25. Regressions: Achievement Scores of Black and White Boys and Girls on Full Model with IQ in Equation

Coefficients for Achievement Scores (F's in Parentheses)

	Blacks		Whites	
Variables	*Boys*	*Girls*	*Boys*	*Girls*
IQ	.495	.441	.381	.418
	(102.79)*	(82.53)*	(50.03)*	(68.84)*
SES	.175	.212	.177	—
	(10.26)*	(13.97)*	(9.14)*	
Demographic orgins	—	—	—	—
Family origin size	—	—	—	—
White exposure[a]	—	−.080	—	—
		(2.97)		
Fundamentalist	—	−.099	—	—
		(4.22)*		
High Protestant	—	—	—	—
Catholic	—	—	—	—
Nondenominational	.081	—	.093	—
	(2.87)		(3.35)	
Jewish	—	—	—	−.126
				(7.17)*
Religiosity	—	—	−.173	—
			(11.73)*	
Number of children	—	—	—	—
Marital status	—	.076	—	—
		(3.17)		
Years worked	—	—	—	.065
				(2.00)
Mother's organizations	—	—	—	—
Valuation of education	—	.095	.176	.303
		(3.41)	(8.80)*	(26.87)*
Investment in child	—	—	—	.107
				(3.49)
Discipline	−.155	−.074	—	—
	(8.90)*	(2.49)*		
Race	—	—	—	—
Intercept	−1.92417	−2.30615	−8.1154	−3.00731
R^2 =	44%	45%	44%	44%
N =	269	310	243	280

*$p < .05$
[a] not included in white sample

T A B L E   A - 2 6 .   Regression: IQ Scores of Boys and Girls on Full Model with Race in the Equation

Standardized Coefficients (F's in Parentheses)

Variables	Boys	Girls
SES	—	.126
		(5.34)*
Demographic origins	.069	—
	(2.57)	
Origin family size	—	—
White exposure	—	—
Fundamentalist	—	−.094
		(4.87)*
High Protestant	—	—
Catholic	—	—
Nondenominational	.099	—
	(6.40)*	
Jewish	—	—
Religiosity	−.136	—
	(12.17)*	
Number of children	—	−.086
		(5.18)*
Marital status	—	.062
		(3.14)
Years employed	—	—
Mother's organizations	—	—
Valuation of education	.257	.148
	(30.34)*	(11.38)*
Investment in child	.131	.148
	(7.53)*	(10.93)*
Discipline	—	−.071
		(3.65)
Race	.150	.153
	(13.14)*	(12.54)*
Intercept	74.09802	68.46512
R² =	28%	33%
N =	512	590

*p < .05

**TABLE A-27. Regression:
Achievement Scores of Boys and Girls on
Full Model with Race and IQ in Equation**

Standardized Coefficients (F's in Parentheses)

Variables	Boys	Girls
IQ	.406	.401
	(139.13)*	(153.09)*
SES	.147	.152
	(10.92)*	(13.08)*
Demographic origins	—	—
Origin family size	—	—
White exposure	—	—
Fundamentalist	—	—
High Protestant	—	—
Catholic	—	—
Nondenominational	.082	—
	(6.80)*	
Jewish	—	−.073
		(6.46)*
Religiosity	−.090	—
	(8.15)*	
Number of children	—	—
Marital status	—	—
Years employed	—	—
Mother's organizations	.057	—
	(2.99)	
Valuation of education	.083	.135
	(4.77)*	(14.97)*
Investment in child	—	.050
		(2.05)
Discipline	−.101	−.068
	(7.23)*	(3.91)*
Race	.164	.269
	(23.21)*	(66.95)*
Intercept	−1.95950	−4.11179
R^2 =	56%	58%
N =	512	590

*$p < .05$

References

ABT ASSOCIATES
  1979 Final Report of the National Day Care Study. *Children at the Center*. Executive Summary. Prepared for the Day Care Division. Office of Human Development Services. U.S. DHEW.

ADORNO, T. W.; FRENKEL-BRUNSWICK, ELSA; LEVINSON, DANIEL; and SANFORD, NEVITT R.
  1950 *The Authoritarian Personality*. New York: Harper.

AICHORN, AUGUST
  1955 *Wayward Youth*. New York: Meridian Books.

ALMOND, GABRIEL A, and VERBA, SIDNEY
  1963 *The Civic Culture: Political Attitudes and Democracy in Five Nations*. Princeton: Princeton University Press.

APPELBAUM, RICHARD
  1971 "Race, class and maternal child rearing: A study of differential behavior in a metropolitan setting." Doctoral dissertation. University of Chicago.

BABBIE, EARL R.
  1964 "The religious factor—looking forward." *Review of Religious Research*, 7:42–53.

BALDWIN, A. L.; KALHORN, J.; and BREESE, F. H.

1949 "The appraisal of parental behavior." *Psychological Monographs*, 63:299.

1945 "Patterns of parent behavior." *Psychological Monographs*, 57:268.

BALTZELL, E. DIGBY

1964 The Protestant Establishment: Aristocracy and Caste in America, New York: Vintage Books-Random House.

BANDURA, ALBERT, and WALTERS, R. H.

1959 *Adolescent Aggression: A Study of the Influence of Child-Training Practice and Family Interrelationships.* New York: Ronald Press.

BANE, MARY JO, and JENCKS, CHRISTOPHER

1976 "Five myths about your I.Q." In N.J. Block and Gerald Dworkin (eds.), *The I.Q. Controversy.* New York: Pantheon, pp. 325–338.

BARRINGER, LELAND

1972 "Maternal child rearing attitudes and practices and children's scholastic achievement." Doctoral dissertation, University of Chicago.

BATTLE, ESTHER S., and ROTTER, JULIAN B.

1963 "Children's feelings of personal control as related to social class and ethnic class." *Journal of Personality*, 31:482–490.

BAUMRIND, DIANA

1978 "Parental disciplinary patterns and social competence in children." *Youth and Society*, 9:239–276.

1971 "Current patterns of parental authority." *Developmental Psychology Monographs*, 4:1–103.

BEAR, ROBERTA M.; HESS, ROBERT D.; and SHIPMAN, VIRGINIA C.

1966 "Social class differences in maternal attitudes toward school consequences for cognitive development in the young child." Paper presented at the American Educational Research Association Meeting, Chicago.

BECKER, WESLEY C.

1977 "Teaching reading and language to the disadvantaged—What have we learned from field research?" *Harvard Educational Review*, 47:518–543.

BERELSON, BERNARD R.; LAZARSFELD, PAUL: and McPHEE, WILLIAM

1954 *Voting: A Study of Opinion Formulation in a Presidential Campaign.* Chicago: University of Chicago Press.

BERG, IVAR E.

1970 *Education and Jobs: The Great Training Robbery.* New York: Praeger.

BERNSTEIN, BASIL A.

1977 *Class, Codes and Control, Vol. 3: Towards a Theory of Educational Transmissions* (rev. ed.). London: Routledge and Kegan Paul.

1970 "Sociolinguistic approach to socialization with some reference to educability." In Frederick Williams (ed.), *Language and Poverty.* Chicago: Markham Press, pp. 25–61.

1964 "Family role systems, communication, and socialization." Paper presented at the Conference on Development of Cross-National Research on the Education of Children and Adolescents. University of Chicago, February.

1961   "Social class and linguistic development: A theory of social learning." In A. H. Halsey, J. Floud, and C. A. Anderson (eds.), *Education, Economy and Society.* Glencoe, Ill.: Free Press, pp. 288–314.

BING, ELIZABETH

   1963   "Effect of childrearing practices on development of differential cognitive abilities." *Child Development,* 34:631–648.

BLAU, PETER M.

   1964   *Exchange and Power in Social Life.* New York: John Wiley and Sons.

   1955   *The Dynamics of Bureaucracy.* Chicago: University of Chicago Press.

BLAU, PETER, and DUNCAN, OTIS D.

   1967   *The American Occupational Structure.* New York: John Wiley and Sons.

BLAU, ZENA SMITH

   1977   "The Jewish prince: Some continuities in traditional and contemporary Jewish life." *Contemporary Jewry,* 3:54–71.

   1974a   "Strategies of socialization and the quality of life in modern society." American Medical Association, *The Quality of Life, Vol. 1: The Early Years.* Acton, Mass.: Publishing Sciences Group.

   1974b   "The strategy of the Jewish mother." In Marshall Sklare (ed.), *The Jew in American Society.* New York: Behrman House.

   1972   "Maternal aspirations, socialization and achievement of boys and girls in the white working class." *Journal of Youth and Adolescence.* 1:35–57.

   1967   "In defense of the Jewish mother." *Midstream,* 13:42–49.

   1965   "Class structure, mobility and change in child rearing." *Sociometry,* 28:210–219.

   1964   "Exposure to child rearing experts: A structural interpretation of class-color differences." *American Journal of Sociology,* 64:597–608.

BLAU, ZENA SMITH; GORDON M. J.; APPELBAUM, R.; GREEN, L.; and KAYE, M

   1971   "Social mobility, maternal practices and scholastic achievement of Negro and white children." Social and Rehabilitation Service, Social Security Administration. HEW Grant no. 10-P-56018/5-4.

BLAU, ZENA SMITH; LOGAN, RICHARD; APPELBAUM RICHARD; BARRINGER, LEE; and KAYE, MICHAEL

   1970   "Social mobility, maternal practices, and scholastic achievement of Negro and white children." Progress report to Social and Rehabilitation Service and Social Security Administration, HEW Grant no. 371-CZ.

BLAU, ZENA SMITH; OSER, GEORGE T.; and STEPHENS RICHARD C.

   1979   "Aging, social class and ethnicity." *Pacific Sociological Review,* 22 (in press).

BLAU, ZENA SMITH; ROGERS, PAMELA P.; OSER, GEORGE T.; and STEPHENS, RICHARD C.

   1978   "School bells and work whistles: Sounds that echo a better life for women in later years." In *Women in Midlife—Security and Fulfillment* (Part 1). A Compendium of Papers Submitted to the Select Committee on Aging and the Subcommittee on Retirement Income and Employment, U.S. House of Representatives. Washington, D.C.: U.S. Government Printing Office.

BLAUNER, R.
1969 "Internal colonialism and ghetto revolt." *Social Problems,* 16:393–408.

BLOOM, B. S.
1964 *Stability and Change in Human Characteristics.* New York: John Wiley and Sons.

BLUMER, HERBERT
1969 *Symbolic Interactionism: Perspective and Method.* Englewood Cliffs, N.J.: Prentice-Hall.

BORDUA, D. J.
1960 "Educational aspirations and parental stress on college." *Social Forces,* 38:262–269.

BOURDIEU, PIERRE
1973 "Cultural reproduction and social reproduction." In Richard Brown (ed.), *Knowledge, Education, and Cultural Change.* London: Tavistock, pp. 71–112. Also in Jerome Karabel and A. H. Halsey (eds.), *Power and Ideology in Education.* New York: Oxford University Press, 1977, pp. 487–511.

BOURDIEU, PIERRE, and PASSERON, JEAN-CLAUDE
1977 *Reproduction: In Education, Society and Culture.* Beverely Hills, Ca.: Sage. Translation from *La Reproduction: éléments pour une théorie du système d'enseignement.* Paris: Editions de Minuit, 1970.

BOURDIEU, PIERRE, and SAINT-MARTIN, MONIQUE
1974 "The school is a conservative force: Scholastic and cultural inequalities." In John Eggleston (ed.), *Contemporary Research in the Sociology of Education.* New York: Harper and Row, pp. 32–46.

BOWLES, SAMUEL, and GINTIS, HERBERT
1976 *Schooling in Capitalist America.* New York: Basic Books.
1973 "I.Q. in the U.S. class structure." *Social Policy,* 3:65–96.

BURCHINAL, LEE B.; and KENKEL, W. F.
1962 "Religious identification and occupational status of Iowa grooms, 1953–1957." *American Sociological Review,* 27:526–532.

CALDWELL, BETTYE M., and RICCIUTI, HENRY N. (eds.)
1973 *Review of Child Development Research, Vol. 3.* Chicago: University of Chicago Press.

CHARTERS, W. W. Jr.
1963 "Social class and intelligence tests." In W. W. Charters, Jr., and N. L. Gage (eds.), *Readings in the Social Psychology of Education.* Boston: Allyn and Bacon, pp. 12–21.

CHERKAOUI, MOHAMED
1977 "Basil Bernstein and Emile Durkheim: Two theories of change in educational systems." *Harvard Educational Review,* 47:556–564.

COLEMAN, JAMES S.
1968 "The evaluation of equality of educational opportunity." Santa Monica: Rand Corporation (mimeog.).
1961 *The Adolescent Society.* Glencoe, Ill.: Free Press.

COLEMAN, JAMES S.; CAMPBELL, ERNEST Q.; HOBSON, CAROL J.; McPARTLAND, JAMES; MOOD, ALEXANDER M.; WEINFELD, FREDERIC D.; and YORK, ROBERT L.
   1966 *Equality of Educational Opportunity.* Washington, D.C.: U.S. Government Printing Office.

COLLINS, RANDALL
   1977 "Some comparative principles of educational stratification." *Harvard Educational Review,* 47:1–27.
   1976 "*Schooling in Capitalist America* by Samuel Bowles and Herbert Gintis" (book review). *Harvard Educational Review,* 46:246–251.

COOLEY, CHARLES H.
   1909 *Social Organization.* New York: Charles Scribner and Sons.

COOPERSMITH, STANLEY
   1967 *The Antecedents of Self-Esteem.* San Francisco: W. H. Freeman and Company.

CRANDALL, V. J.; DEWEY R.; KATKOWSKY, W.; and PRESTON, A.
   1964 "Parents' attitudes and behaviors and grade school children's academic achievements." *Journal of Genetic Psychology,* 104: 55–56.

CRONBACH, LEE J.
   1975 "Five decades of public controversy over mental testing." *American Psychologist,* 30:1–14.

DAVIS, A.
   1948 *Social Class Influences upon Learning.* Cambridge: Harvard University Press.

DAVIS A., and EELLS, K.
   1953 *Davis-Eells Tests of General Intelligence or Problem-Solving Ability.* Yonkers, N.Y.: World Book Co.

DAVIS, ALLISON, and HAVIGHURST, ROBERT S.
   1946 "Social class and color differences in child rearing." *American Sociological Review,* 11:698–710.

DE PRES, TERRENCE
   1976 *The Survivor: An Anatomy of Life in the Death Camps.* New York: Oxford University Press.

DOUGLAS, J. W. B.
   1964 *The Home and The School: A Study of Ability and Attainment in the Primary School.* London: McGibbon and Kee.

DOUGLAS, J. W. B.; ROSS, J. M.: and SIMPSON, H. R.
   1968 *All Our Future.* London: Peter Davies.

DRAKE, St. CLAIR, and CAYTON, HORACE
   1945 *Black Metropolis: A Study of Negro Life in a Northern City.* New York: Harper and Row.

DROPPLEMAN, L. F.; and SCHAFFER, E. S.
   1963 "Boys' and girls' reports of maternal and paternal behavior." *Journal of Abnormal and Social Psychology,* 67:648–654.

DUNCAN, BEVERLY, and DUNCAN, OTIS DUDLEY
   1968 "Minorities and the process of stratification." *American Sociological Review,* 33:356–364.

DUNCAN, OTIS DUDLEY

1968 "Patterns of occupational mobility among Negro men." *Demography*, 5:11–22.

1967 "Discrimination against Negroes." *The Annals of the American Academy of Political and Social Sciences*, 371:85–103.

1961 "A socioeconomic index for all occupations." In A. J. Reiss, Jr., *Occuaptions and Social Status*. New York: Free Press, pp. 109–138.

DUNCAN, OTIS D.; FEATHERMAN, DAVID L.; and DUNCAN, BEVERLY

1972 *Socioeconomic Background and Achievement*. New York: Seminar Press.

DURKHEIM, EMILE

1964 *Elementary Forms of Religious Life*. Trans. J. W. Swain. Glencoe, Ill.: Free Press.

1951 *Suicide: A Study in Society*. Trans. John O. Spaulding and George Simpson, Glencoe, Ill.: Free Press.

EELLS, K.; DAVIS, A.; HAVIGHURST, R. J.; HERRICK, V. E.; and TYLER, R. W.

1951 *Intelligence and Cultural Differences*. Chicago: University of Chicago Press.

ELARDO, RICHARD; BRADLEY, ROBERT; and CALDWELL, BETTYE

1977 "A longitudinal study of the relation of infant's home environments to language development at age three." *Child Development*, 48:595–603.

ELDER, GLENN H.

1962 "Structural variation in the child-rearing relationship." *Sociometry*, 25:241–262.

ERIKSON, ERIK H.

1959 *Identity and the Life Cycle: Selected Papers*. New York: International Universities Press.

1950 *Childhood and Society*. New York: Norton Press.

FEATHERMAN, DAVID L, and HAUSER, ROBERT M.

1978 *Opportunity and Change*. New York: Academic Press.

FLANAGAN, J. C., et al.

1964 *The American High School Student*. Pittsburgh: University of Pittsburgh.

FREUD, SIGMUND

1960 *The Ego and the Id*. New York: Norton Press.

1949 *A General Introduction to Psychoanalysis*. New York: Perma Giants.

1933 *New Introductory Lectures on Psychoanalysis*. New York: Norton Press.

FRIEDAN, BETTY

1963 *The Feminine Mystique*. New York: Norton.

FRIEDMAN, BARRY L., and HAUSMAN, LEONARD J.

1978 "Is compulsory work for welfare recipients manageable? *Industrial Relations Research Association 31st Annual Proceedings*, pp. 71–78.

FROMM, ERICH

1941 *Escape from Freedom*. New York: Farrar and Rinehart.

FURSTENBERG, FRANK

1971 "The transmission of mobility orientation in the family." *Social Forces*, 49:595–603.

GAUSTAD, EDWIN

1962 *Historical Atlas of Religions in America*. New York: Harper and Row.

GLAZER, NATHAN
1971 "Black and ethnic groups: The difference and the political difference it makes." *Social Problems,* 18:444–461.

GOCKEL, GALEN
1969 "Income and religious affiliation: A regression analysis." *American Sociological Review,* 74:632–647.

GOLDBERG, DAVID, and SHARP, HARRY
1958 "Some characteristics of Detroit area Jewish and non-Jewish adults." In Marshall Sklare (ed.), *The Jews: Social Patterns of an American Group.* Glencoe, Ill.: Free Press, pp. 107–119.

GOLDBERG, SUSAN, and LEWIS, MICHAEL
1969 "Play behavior in the year old infant: Early sex differences." *Child Development,* 40:21–31.

GOLDING, WILLIAM
1964 *Lord of the Flies.* New York: Capricorn.

GOLDSTEIN, SIDNEY
1958 *Patterns of Mobility, 1910–1950: The Norristown Study.* Philadelphia: University of Pennsylvania Press.

GOODE, WILLIAM J.
1963 *World Revolution and Family Patterns.* New York: Free Press.
1956 *After Divorce.* Glencoe, Ill.: Free Press.

GOODMAN, PAUL
1960 *Growing Up Absurd.* New York: Random House.

GORDON, CHAD
1972 "Looking ahead: Self conceptions, race and family as determinants of adolescent orientation to achievement." Arnold M. and Carolyn Rose Monograph Series. American Sociological Association.

GORDON, MARGARET T.
1972 "Mobility and child-rearing: A study of the achievement of black and white metropolitan children." Doctoral dissertation, Northwestern University.

GORDON, ROBERT A.
1968 "Issues in multiple regression." *American Journal of Sociology,* 73:592–616.

GOTTLIEB, D.
1966 "Teaching and students: The views of Negro and white teachers." In S. W. Webster (ed.), *The Disadvantaged Learner.* San Fancisco: Chandler Press.

GREELEY, ANDREW
1974 "Political participation among ethnic groups in the United States: A preliminary reconnaissance." *American Journal of Sociology,* 80:170–204.

GRIER, WILLIAM H., and COBB, PRICE M.
1968 *Black Rage.* New York: Basic Books.

HALSEY, A. H.; FLOUD, JEAN; and ANDERSON, C ARNOLD (eds.)
1961 *Education, Economy and Society.* New York: Free Press.

HAPGOOD, KAREN, and GETZELS, JUDITH
1974 *Planning, Women, and Change.* Chicago: American Society of Planning Officials.

HARTMANN, HEINZ
   1958   *Ego Psychology and the Problem of Adaptation.* New York: International Universities Press.

HARWOOD, JONATHAN
   1977   "The race-intelligence controversy: A sociological approach II—'external' factors." *Social Studies of Science,* 7:1–30.
   1976   "The race-intelligence controversy: A sociological approach I—professional factors." *Social Studies of Science,* 6:369–394.

HAUSER, ROBERT M.
   1970   "Educational stratification in the United States." In Edward O. Laumann (ed.), *Social Stratification: Research and Theory for the 1970's.* Indianapolis: Bobbs-Merrill, pp. 102–129.

HEBB, D. O.
   1949   *The Organization of Behavior.* New York: John Wiley.

HERZOG, ELIZABETH, and SUDIA, CECELIA E.
   1973   "Children in fatherless families." In B. M. Caldwell and H. N. Ricciuti (eds.), *Review of Child Development Research,* Vol. 3. Chicago: University of Chicago Press, pp. 141–232.

HESS, ROBERT D., and SHIPMAN, VIRGINIA C.
   1964   "Early experience and the socialization of cognitive modes in children." *Child Development,* 36:869–886.

HESS, ROBERT; SHIPMAN, VIRGINIA C.; BROPHY, J.; and BAER, ROBERTA
   1968   "The cognitive environments of urban preschool schildren." Graduate School of Education, University of Chicago.

HOFFMAN, LOIS W.; NYE, IVAN F.; BAHR, STEPHEN J.; EMLEN, ARTHUR C.; PERRY, JOSEPH B. Jr.; and SOBOL, MARION GROSS
   1974   *Working Mothers.* San Francisco: Jossey-Bass.

HOFSTADTER, RICHARD
   1963   *Anti-Intellectualism in American Life.* New York: A. A. Knopf.

HOGAN, DENNIS P., and FEATHERMAN, DAVID L.
   1977   "Racial stratification and socioeconomic change in the American north and south." *American Journal of Sociology,* 83:100–126.

HOLLINGSHEAD, AUGUST B.
   1957   *Two Factor Index of Social Position.* New Haven: Yale University Press.
   1950   "Cultural factors in the selection of marriage mates." *American Sociological Review,* 15:619–627.

HOLLISTER, ROBINSON G.
   1978   "Welfare reform and labor markets: What have we learned from the experiments?" *Industrial Relations Research Association 31st Annual Proceedings,* pp. 57–70.

HOMANS, GEORGE
   1962   *Structure and Sentiment.* Chicago: University of Chicago Press.
   1950   *The Human Group.* New York: Harcourt, Brace and World.

HOROWITZ, FRANCES D., and PADEN, LUCILE Y.
   1973   "The effectiveness of environmental intervention programs." In B. M. Caldwell

and H. N. Ricciuti (eds.), *Review of Child Development Research, Vol. 3.* Chicago: University of Chicago Press.

HOVLAND, CARL; LUMSDAINE, A.; and SHEFFIELD, F.
1949   *Experiments on Mass Communication, Vol. III: Studies in Social Psychology.* Princeton: Princeton University Press.

HUNT, J. McV.
1969   *The Challenge of Incompetence and Poverty.* Urbana: University of Illinois.
1961   *Intelligence and Experience.* New York: Ronald Press.

HUSEN, T., et al.
1967   *International Study of Achievement in Mathematics, Vols. I and II.* New York: John Wiley and Sons.

HYMAN, HERBERT H.
1953   "The value systems of different social classes." In Robert Bendix and Seymour M. Lipset (eds.), *Class, Status and Power.* Glencoe, Ill.: Free Press.

INKELES, ALEX, and SMITH, DAVID H.
1974   *Becoming Modern: Individual Change in Six Developing Countries.* Cambridge: Harvard University Press.

JACKSON, B., and MARSDEN, D.
1962   *Education and the Working Class: Some General Themes Raised by a Study of 88 Working Class Children in a Northern Industrial City.* New York: Monthly Review Press.

JACKSON, JACQUELYNE J.
1973   "Family organization and ideology." In Kent S. Miller and Ralph M. Dreger (eds.), *Comparative Studies of Blacks and Whites in the United States.* New York: Seminar Press.

JANOWITZ, BARBARA S.
1976   "The impact of AFDC on illigitimate birth rates." *Journal of Marriage and Family,* 38:485–494.

JENCKS, CHRISTOPHER S.
1979   Who Gets Ahead? The *Determinants of Economic Success in America.* New York: Basic Books.

JENCKS, CHRISTOPHER S.; SMITH, MARSHALL; ACLAND, HENRY; BANE, MARY JO; COHEN, DAVID; GINTIS, HERBERT; HEYNS, BARBARA; and MICHELSON, STEPHAN
1972   *Inequality: A Reassessment of the Effect of Family and Schooling in America.* New York: Basic Books.

JENSEN, ARTHUR R.
1969   "How much can we boost I.Q. and scholastic achievement?" *Harvard Educational Review,* 39:1–123.
1980   *Bias in Mental testing.* New York: Free Press.

JOHNSON, BEVERLY L.
1978   "Women who head families, 1970–77: Their numbers rose, income lagged." *Monthly Labor Review,* 101:32–37.

JOHNSON, NAN E.
1979   "Minority group status and the fertility of black Americans, 1970: A new look." *American Journal of Sociology,* 84:1386–1400.

JOHNSTONE, JOHN W. C.
1978 "Juvenile delinquency and the family: A contextual interpretation." *Youth and Society*, 9:299–313.

KAGAN, JEROME
1972 "The emergence of sex differences." *School Review*, 80:217–228.

KAGAN, JEROME, and MOSS, HOWARD A.
1962 *Birth to Maturity*. New York: John Wiley and Sons.

KAHL, J. A.
1957 *The American Class Structure*. New York: Rinehart Press.
1953 "Educational and occupational aspirations of 'common-man' boys." *Harvard Educational Review*, 23:186–203.

KAMII, C., and RADIN, N.
1974 "Class differences in the socialization practices of Negro mothers." In Robert F. Winch and G. Spanier (eds.), *Selected Studies in Marriage and the Family*. New York: Holt, Rinehart and Winston, pp. 235–247.

KAMIN, LEON J.
1976a "Heredity, intelligence, politics and psychology: II." In N. J. Block and Gerald Dworkin (eds.), *The I.Q. Controversy*. New York: Pantheon, pp. 374–382.
1976b "Heredity, intelligence, politics and psychology: I." In N. J. Block and Gerald Dworkin (eds.), *The I.Q. Controversy*. New York: Pantheon, pp. 242–264.

KANTER, ROSABETH M.
1977 *Work and Family in the United States: A Critical Review and Agenda for Research and Policy*. New York: Russell Sage.

KATKOWSKY, W.; PRESTON, A.; and CRANDALL, V.
1964 "Parents' achievement attitudes and their behavior with their children in achievement situations." *Journal of Genetic Psychology*, 104:105–121.

KELLAM, S. G.; BRANCH J. D.; AGRAMAL, K. A.; and ENSMINGER, M.
1975 *Mental Health and Going to School*. Chicago: University of Chicago Press.

KELLEY, JONATHAN, and KLEIN, HEBERT S.
1977 "Revolution and the rebirth of inequality: A theory of stratification in post-revolutionary society." *American Journal of Sociology*, 83:78–99.

KENNEDY, W. A.; VAN DE RIET, V.; and WHITE, J. C. JR.
1963 "A normative sample of intelligence and achievement of Negro elementary school children in the southeastern United States." *Monographs of the Society for Research in Child Development*, 28:1–112.

KEYFITZ, NATHAN
1968 *Introduction to the Mathematics of Population*. Reading, Mass.: Addison-Wesley.

KLINEBERG, OTTO
1935a *Negro Intelligence and Selective Migration*. New York: Columbia University Press.
1935b *Race Differences*. New York: Harper and Row.

KOHLBERG, LAWRENCE
1966   "Development of moral character and moral ideology." In Lois W. Hoffman and Martin L. Hoffman (eds.), *Review of Child Development Research, Vol. I.* New York: Russell Sage Foundation.

KOHN, MARTIN
1977   *Social Competence, Symptoms and Underachievement in Childhood.* Washington: V. H. Winston and Sons.

KOHN, MELVIN L.
1977   *Class and Conformity: A Study in Values* (2nd ed. with "reassessment"). Chicago: University of Chicago Press.

1969   *Class on Conformity.* Homewood, Ill.: Dorsey Press.

KOHN, MELVIN L., and SCHOOLER, CARMI
1978   "The reciprocal effects of the substantive complexity of work and intellectual flexibility: A longitudinal assessment." *American Journal of Sociology.* 84:24-52.

1973   "Occupational experience and psychological functioning: An assessment of reciprocal effects." *American Sociological Review,* 38:97-118.

LAMB, MICHAEL, and STEVENSON, MARGUERITE B.
1978   "Father-infant relationships: Their nature and importance." *Youth & Society.* 9: 277-298.

LASSWELL, HAROLD D.
1951   *The Political Writings of Harold D. Laswell.* Glencoe, Ill.: Free Press.

LAZAR, IRVING; HUBBELL, VIRGINIA R.; MURRAY, HARRY; ROSCHE, MARILYN; and ROYCE, JACQUELINE
1977   *The Persistence of School Effects: A Long-Term Follow-up of Fourteen Infant and Pre-School Experiments.* Final Report to the Administration on Children, Youth and Families. Office of Human Development Services.

LAZARSFELD, PAUL; BERELSON, B.; and GAUDET, H.
1948   *The People's Choice.* New York: Columbia University Press.

LEFCOURT, HERBERT M.
1966   "Belief in personal control: Research and implication." *Journal of Individual Psychology,* 22:185-195.

LENSKI, GERHART
1961   *The Religious Factor.* Garden City, N.Y.: Doubleday.

LEWONTIN, RICHARD C.
1976   "Race and intelligence." In N. J. Block and Gerald Dworkin (eds.), *The I.Q. Controversy.* New York: Pantheon.

LIEBERSON, STANLEY
1978   "A reconsideration of the income differences found between migrants and northern-born blacks." *American Journal of Sociology,* 83:940-965.

1973   "Generational differences among blacks in the North." *American Journal of Sociology,* 79:550-565.

1963   *Ethnic Patterns in American Cities.* Glencoe, Ill.: Free Press.

LIEBERSON, STANLEY, and WILKINSON, CHRISTY A.
1976 "A comparison between northern and southern blacks residing in the North." *Demography*, 13:199–224.

LIEBOWITZ, ARLENE
1977 "Parental inputs in children's achievement." *Journal of Human Resources*, 12:1242–1251.

LIGHT, RICHARD J., and SMITH, PAUL V.
1971 "Statistical issues in social allocation models of intelligence: A review and a response." *Review of Educational Research*, 41: 351–367.

LINDERT, PETER H.
1978 *Fertility and Scarcity in America*. Princeton: Princeton University Press.

LIPPITT, RONALD, and WHITE, R. K.
1947 "An experimental study of leadership and group life." In T. N. Newcomb and E. L. Hartley (eds.), *Readings in Social Psychology*. New York: Henry Holt.

LIPSET, SEYMOUR M.
1964 "Religion and politics in the American past and present." In R. Lee and M. Marty (eds.), *Religion and Social Conflict*. New York: Oxford University Press.

1960 *Political Man: The Social Bases of Politics*. New York: Doubleday.

1959 "Democracy and working class authoritarianism." *American Sociological Review*, 24:482–501.

LIPSET, SEYMOUR M., and BENDIX R.
1959 *Social Mobility in Industrial Society*. Berkeley: University of California Press.

LOGAN, RICHARD
1970 "Maternal childrearing practices associated with high scholastic achievement in children of eight different class-color-sex groups." Doctoral dissertation, University of Chicago.

LORGE, I.
1953 "Difference or bias in tests of intelligence." *Proceedings of the 1952 Inivitational Conference on Testing Problems*. Princeton: Educational Testing Service, pp. 76–83.

LYNN, D. B.
1974 *The Father: His Role in Child Development*. Belmont, Cal.: Wadsworth Publishing Corp.

MACCOBY, ELEANOR E.
1966 *The Development of Sex Differences*. Stanford: Stanford University Press.

MACCOBY, ELEANOR E., and JACKLIN, CAROL N.
1974 *The Psychology of Sex Differences*. Stanford: Stanford University Press.

MASLOW, ABRAHAM
1943 "The authoritarian character structure." *Journal of Social Psychology*, 18:401–411.

MAYESKE, GEORGE W., and BEATON, ALBERT E. JR.
  1975   *Special Studies of Our Nation's Students.* Washington, D.C.: U.S. Government Printing Office.

MAYESKE, GEORGE W.; OKADA, TETSUO; BEATON, ALBERT E. JR.; COHEN, WALLACE M.; and WISLER, CARLE E.
  1973   *A Study of the Achievement of Our Nation's Students.* Washington, D.C.: U.S. Government Printing Office.

McCLELLAND, DAVID C.
  1961   *The Achieving Society.* New York: Free Press.
  1955   *Studies in Motivation.* New York: Appleton-Century-Crofts.

McEADDY, BEVERLY J.
  1976   "Women who head families: A socioeconomic analysis." *Monthly Labor Review*, 99:3-9.

MEAD, GEORGE HERBERT.
  1934   Mind, Self and Society, Chicago: University of Chicago Press.

MEAD, SIDNEY E.
  1962   "American Protestantism since the Civil War: From denominationalism to Americanism." In A. Eisenstadt (ed.), *American History, Book II: Since 1865.* New York: Thomas Y. Crowell.

MERTON, ROBERT K.
  1968   "The Matthew effect in science." *Science*, 159:56-63.
  1957   *Social Theory and Social Structure.* Glencoe, Ill.: Free Press.
  1948   "The self-fulfilling prophecy." *Antioch Review*, 8:193-210.

MERTON, ROBERT K., and LAZARSFELD, PAUL F. (eds.)
  1950   *Continuities in Social Research.* Glencoe, Ill.: Free Press.

MILLER, DANIEL R., and SWANSON, G. E.
  1958   *The Changing American Parent.* New York: John Wiley and Sons.

MINTON, C.; KAGAN, JEROME; and LEVINE, J. A.
  1971   "Maternal control and obedience in the two-year-old." *Child Development*, 42:1873-1894.

MORGAN, JAMES N.
  1962   *Income and Welfare in the United States.* New York: McGraw-Hill.

MORTIMER, JEYLAN T., and LORENCE, JON
  1979   "Work experience and occupational value socialization: A longitudinal study." *American Journal of Sociology*, 84:1361-1385.

MOSTELLER, F., and MOYNINAN, D. P.
  1972   *On Equality of Educational Opportunity,* New York: Vintage.

MOYNIHAN, DANIEL
  1967   "The Negro family: The case for national action." In Lee Rainwater and William L. Yancey (eds.), *The Moynihan Report and the Politics of Controversy.* Cambridge: MIT Press.

NAKAMURA, C. Y., and ROGERS, M. M.
  1969   "Parents' expectation of autonomous behavior and children's autonomy." *Developmental Psychology*, 1:613-617.

NIEBUHR, H. RICHARD
1929 *The Social Sources of Denominationalism.* New York: Henry Holt.

NYE, IVAN F., and HOFFMAN, LOIS W.
1963 *The Employed Mother in America.* Chicago: Rand McNally.

OPPENHEIMER, VALERIE, K.
1970 *The Female Labor Force in the United States.* Berkeley: Institute of International Studies.

PARSONS, TALCOTT
1964a "Social structure and development of personality: Freud's contribution to the integration of psychology and sociology." In Talcott Parsons (ed.), *Social Structure and Personality.* Glencoe, Ill.: Free Press, pp. 78–111.

1964b *Social Structure and Personality.* Glencoe, Ill.: Free Press.

PARSONS, TALCOTT; BALES, ROBERT; OLDS, JAMES: ZELDITCH, MORRIS JR.; and SLATER, PHILIP E.
1955 *Family: Socialization and Interaction Process.* Glencoe, Ill.: Free Press.

PEARLIN, L. I.
1971 *Class Context and Family Relations: A Cross National Study.* Boston: Little, Brown.

PEARLIN, LEONARD I., and KOHN, MELVIN L.
1966 "Social class, occupations, and parental values: A cross national study." *American Sociological Review,* 31:466–479.

PEDERSON, EIGIL; FAUCHER, THERESE A.; and EATON, WILLIAM W.
1978 "A new perspective on the effects of first-grade teachers on children's subsequent adult status." *Harvard Educational Review,* 48:1–31.

PERSELL, CAROLINE HODGES
1977 *Education and Inequality.* New York: Free Press.

PETTIGREW, THOMAS F.
1964 *A Profile of the Negro American.* New York: Van Nostrand.

PIAGET, JEAN
1952 *The Origins of Intelligence in Children.* New York: International Universities Press.

1948 *The Moral Judgment of the Child.* Trans. Marjorie Gabain. Glencoe, Ill.: Free Press.

PITTMAN, DAVID J., and SNYDER, CHARLES R.
1968 *Society, Culture and Drinking Patterns.* Carbondale: Southern Illinois University Press.

PLOWDEN, B., et al.
1972 *Children and Their Primary Schools, Vols. I and II.* London: Her Majesty's Stationery Office.

RAPPOPORT, DAVID
1950 *Emotions and Memory.* New York: International Universities Press.

RASCH, GEORG
1960 *Probabilistic Models for Some Intelligence and Attainment Tests.* Copenhagen: Nielson and Lydicke.

REISS, ALBERT J.; DUNCAN, OTIS DUDLEY; HATT, PAUL K.; and NORTH, CECIL C.
   1961   *Occupations and Social Status.* New York: Free Press.

RINGER, B., and GLOCK, C.
   1954–55   "The political role of the church as defined by its parishioners." *Public Opinion Quarterly,* 18:337–347.

ROSEN, BERNARD C.
   1964   "Family structure and value transmission." *Merrill-Palmer Quarterly,* 10:57–76.

   1961   "Family structure and achievement motivation." *American Sociological Review,* 26:574–585.

   1959   "Race, ethnicity, and the achievement syndrome." *American Sociological Review,* 24:47–60.

   1956   "The achievement syndrome: A psychocultural dimension of social stratification." *American Sociological Review,* 21:203–211.

ROSENBERG, MORRIS
   1965   *Society and the Adolescent Self-Image.* Princeton: Princeton University Press.

ROSENBERG, MORRIS, and PEARLIN, LEONARD I.
   1978   "Social class and self-esteem among children and adults." *American Journal of Sociology,* 84:53–77.

ROSENBERG, MORRIS, and SIMMONS, ROBERTA G.
   1971   *Black and White Self-Esteem: The Urban School Child.* Washington, D.C.: American Sociological Association.

ROSENTHAL, ROBERT, and JACOBSON, LENORE
   1968   *Pygmalion in the Classroom.* New York: Holt, Rinehart and Winston.

ROTTER, JULIAN B.
   1966   "Generalized expectancies for internal vs. external control of reinforcement." *Psychological Monographs,* 80:609.

ROUSSEAU, JEAN J.
   1968   *Social Contract.* Trans. Maurice Cranston. Blatimore: Penguin Books.

SAMPSON, WILLIAM A., and ROSSI, P. H.
   1975   "Race and family social standing." *American Sociological Review,* 40:201–214.

SCARR-SALAPATEK, SANDRA
   1976   "Unknowns in the I.Q. equation." In N. J. Block and Gerald Dworkin (eds.), *The I.Q. Controversy.* New York: Pantheon, pp. 113–130.

SCHAEFFER, EARL S., and BELL, R.
   1958   "Development of a parental attitude research instrument." *Child Development,* 29:339–361.

SCHULMAN, SAM: GOTTLIEB, D.; and SHEINBERG, SHEILA
   1976   A *Social and Demographic Survey of the Jewish Community of Houston, Texas.* Houston: Jewish Community Council of Metropolitan Houston, Inc.

SCOTT, JOHN FINLEY
   1971   *Internalization of Norms.* Englewood Cliffs, N.J.: Prentice-Hall.

SEARS, ROBERT R.; MACCOBY, ELEANOR; and LEVIN, HARRY
1957 *Patterns of Child Rearing.* Evanston, Ill.: Row, Peterson and Company.

SEARS, R. R.; RAU, L.; and ALPERT, L.
1965 *Identification and Child Rearing.* Stanford: Stanford University Press.

SEEMAN, MELVIN
1967 "Powerlessness and knowledge: A comparative study of alienation and learning." *Sociometry,* 30:105–123.

1959 "On the meaning of alienation." *American Sociological Review,* 24:783–791.

SELIGMAN, BEN B., and ANTONOVSKY, A.
1958 "Some aspects of Jewish demography." In Marshall Sklare (ed.), *The Jews: Social Patterns of an American Group.* Glencoe, Ill.: Free Press, pp. 83–86.

SEWELL, WILLIAM H.; HALLER, A. O.; and OHLENDORF, G. W.
1970 "The educational and early occupational status attainment process: replication and revision." *American Sociological Review,* 35:1014–1027.

SEWELL, WILLIAM H., and HAUSER, ROBERT M.
1975 *Education, Occupation, and Earnings.* New York: Academic Press.

1972 "Causes and consequences of higher education: Models of the status attainment process." *American Journal of Agricultural Economics,* 54:851–861.

SEWELL, WILLIAM H.; HAUSER, ROBERT M.; and FEATHERMAN, DAVID L. (eds.)
1976 *Schooling and Achievement in American Society.* New York: Academic Press.

SEWELL, WILLIAM H., and SHAH, VIMEL P.
1968 "Parents' education and children's educational aspirations and achievements." *American Sociological Review,* 33:191–209.

1967 "Socioeconomic status, intelligence, and the attainment of higher education." *Sociology of Education,* 40:1–23.

SHAYCROFT, M. F.
1967 *The High School Years: Growth in Cognitive Skills.* Pittsburgh: American Institute for Research and School of Education, University of Pittsburgh.

SIEGEL, PAUL M.
1970 "Occupational prestige in the Negro subculture." In Edward O. Laumann (ed.), *Social Stratification: Research and Theory for the 1970's.* Indianapolis: Bobbs-Merril, pp. 156–171.

SILVERSTEIN, BARRY, and KRATE, RONALD
1975 *Children of the Dark Ghetto.* New York: Praeger.

SIMMEL, GEORG
1950 *The Sociology of Georg Simmel.* Glencoe, Ill.: Free Press.

SIMPSON, RICHARD L.
1962 "Parental influence, anticipatory socialization, and social mobility." *American Sociological Review,* 27:517–522.

SOLLENBERGER, RICHARD T.
1968 "Chinese-American child rearing practices and juvenile delinquency." *Journal of Social Psychology,* 74:13–23.

SPOCK, BENJAMIN
  1957 *Baby and Child Care.* New York: Pocket Books.
  1945 *The Common Sense Book of Baby and Child Care.* New York: Duell, Sloan and Pearce.

SROLE, LEO; LANGER, THOMAS S.; MICHAEL, STANLEY T.; OPLER, MARVIN K.; and RENNIE, THOMAS
  1962 *Mental Health in the Metropolis.* New York: McGraw-Hill.

STARK, RODNEY, and GLOCK, CHARLES Y.
  1968 *American Piety: The Nature of Religious Commitment.* Berkeley: University of California Press.

STOLZENBERG, ROSS, and WAITE, LINDA
  1975 "Intended childbearing and labor force participation of young women: Insights from nonrecursive models." Johns Hopkins University: Metro News Center for Metropolitan Planning and Research, Vol. 3, No. 14.
  1977 "Fertility Expectations and Employment Plans." *American Sociological Review,* 42:769–783.

STOUFFER, SAMUEL A.; SUCHMAN, EDWARD A.; DE VINNEY, LELAND C.; STAR, SHIRLEY; and WILLIAMS, ROBIN M. JR.
  1949 *The American Soldier: Adjustment during Army Life, Vol. 1.* Princeton: Princeton University Press.

STRAUSS, ANSELM (ed.)
  1956 *The Social Psychology of George Herbert Mead.* Chicago: University of Chicago Press.

STRODTBECK, FRED L.
  1964 "The hidden curriculum of the middle class home." in C. W. Hunnicutt (ed.), *Urban Education and Cultural Deprivation.* Syracuse: Syracuse University Press, pp. 15–31.

SWARTZ, DAVID
  1977 "Pierre Bourdieu: The cultural transmission of social inequality." *Harvard Educational Review,* 47:545–555.

TONNIES, FERDINAND
  1957 *Community and Society: Gemeinschaft and Gesellschaft.* Trans. C. P. Loomis. Lansing: Michigan State University Press.

TREIMAN, DONALD J., and TERRELL, KERMIT
  1975 "Sex and the process of status attainment: A comparison of women and men." *American Sociological Review,* 40:174–200.

TURNER, RALPH H.
  1964 *The Social Context of Ambition: A Study of High School Seniors in Los Angeles.* San Francisco: Chandler.

U.S. BUREAU OF THE CENSUS
  1977 "Educational attainment in the United States: March 1977 and 1976." *Current Population Reports* (Series P-20, No. 314). Washington, D.C.: Department of Commerce.

VEROFF, J.; FELD, S.; and GURIN, G.
  1962 "Achievement motivation and religious background." *American Sociological Review,* 27:205–218.

WAITE, LINDA J., and MOORE, KRISTIN A.
1978 "The impact of an early birth on young women's educational attainment."
Social Forces, 56:845–865.

WALLSTON, BARBARA
1973 "Effects of maternal employment on children." *Journal of Child Psychology and Psychiatry*, 14:81–95.

WARREN, BRUCE L.
1970 "Socioeconomic achievement and religion: The American case." *Sociological Inquiry*, 40:130–155.

WEBER, C. U.; FOSTER, P. W.; and WEIKART, D. P.
1978 *An Economic Analysis of the Ypsilanti Perry Preschool Project*, Monograph No. 5. Ypsilanti: High/Scope Educational Research Foundation.

WEBER, MAX
1958 *The Protestant Ethic and the Spirit of Capitalism*. New York: Charles Scribner and Sons.

WEIKART, D. P.; BOND, J. T. and McNEIL, J. T.
1978a The Ypsilanti Perry Preschool Project: Preschool Years and Longitudinal Results through Fourth Grade. Monograph no. 3. Ypsilanti: High/Scope Educational Research Foundation.

WEIKART, D. P.; EPSTEIN, A.; SCHWEINHART, L.; and BOND, J. T.
1978b The *Ypslianti Preschool Demonstration Project: Preschool Years and Longitudinal Results*. Monograph No. 4. Ypsilanti High/Scope Educational Research Foundation.

WESTINGHOUSE LEARNING CORPORATION
1969 *The Impact of Head Start: An Evaluation of the Effects of Head Start Experience on Children's Cognitive and Affective Development*. Columbus: Westinghouse Learning Corporation, Ohio University.

WHITE, ROBERT
1963 "Ego and reality in psychoanalytic theory." *Psychological Issues*, 3: Monograph 11.

WILSON, J. Q.
1960 *Negro Politics: The Search for Leadership*. Chicago: University of Chicago Press.

WILSON, WILLIAM J.
1978 *The Declining Significance of Race*. Chicago: University of Chicago Press.

WINCH, ROBERT F., and GORDON, MARGARET
1974 *Familial Structure and Function as Influence*. Lexington, Mass.: Lexington Books.

WINCH, ROBERT F., and GREER, SCOTT A.
1968 "Urbanism, ethnicity and extended familism." *Journal of Marriage and Family*, 30:40–45.

WITHEY, STEPHEN B.; COBLE, J. A.; GURING, G.; ROBINSON, J. P.; STRUMPEL, B.; TAYLOR, E. K.; and WOLFE, A. C.
1971 *A Degree and What Else? Correlates and Consequences of a College Education*. New York: McGraw Hill.

WRIGHT, B. D., and PANCHAPAKESAN, N.

1969   "A procedure for sample free item analyses." *Educational and Psychological Measurement,* 29:23–46.

WRONG, DENNIS H.

1966   "Trends in class fertility in western nations." In Reinhard Bendix and Seymour Martin Lipset (eds.), *Class, Status and Power.* 2nd ed. New York: Free Press, pp. 353–361.

YOUNG, ANNE M.

1973   "Children of working mothers," *Monthly Labor Review,* 96:48–56.

ZAJONC, R. B., and MARCUS, GREGORY, B.

1975   "Birth order and intellectual development." *Psychological Review,* 85: 74–88.

Index